THE
FIGHTER'S
MIND

Also by Sam Sheridan

A Fighter's Heart: One Man's Journey Through the World of Fighting

THE
FIGHTER'S
MIND

INSIDE THE MENTAL GAME

SAM
SHERIDAN

Atlantic Monthly Press
New York

From *Atlas* by Teddy Atlas and Peter Alson
Copyright © 2006 by Teddy Atlas
Reprinted by permission of HarperCollins Publishers

Excerpt from *Blood in the Cage* by L. Jon Wertheim. Copyright © 2009 by
L. Jon Wertheim. Reprinted by permission of Houghton Mifflin Harcourt Publishing
Company. All rights reserved.

Excerpt from *Cut Time: An Education at the Fights* by Carlo Rotella. Copyright ©
2003 by Carlo Rotella. Reprinted by permission of Houghton Mifflin Harcourt Publishing Company. All rights reserved.

Excerpts from *Musashi's Book of Five Rings* copyright © Stephen Kaufman.
Reprinted by permission of Tuttle Publishing, a member of the Periplus
Publishing Group.

From *Zen in the Art of Archery* by Eugen Herrigel. Copyright © 1953 by Pantheon
Books, a division of Random House, Inc. and renewed in 1981 by Random House, Inc.
Used by permission of Pantheon Books, a division of Random House, Inc.

From *Applied Sport Psychology: Personal Growth to Peak Performance* by Jean
Williams. Copyright © 2006. Published by the McGraw-Hill Companies and reproduced
with permission of the McGraw-Hill Companies.

From *The Art of Learning: A Journey in the Pursuit of Excellence* by Josh Waitzkin.
Copyright © 2007 by Josh Waitzkin LLC. All rights reserved. Reprinted with the
permission of The Free Press, a Division of Simon & Schuster, Inc.

From *Zen Mind, Beginner's Mind* by Shunryu Suzuki; protected under the terms of
the International Copyright Union. Reprinted by arrangement with Shambhala Publica-
tions, Inc., Boston, MA. www.shambhala.com.

Excerpt from *Fresh Air Fiend: Travel Writings* by Paul Theroux. Copyright © 2000
Paul Theroux. Reprinted by permission of Houghton Mifflin Harcout Publishing
Company. All rights reserved.

Published simultaneously in Canada
Printed in the United States of America

FIRST EDITION

ISBN-13: 978-0-8021-1935-3

Atlantic Monthly Press
an imprint of Grove/Atlantic, Inc.
841 Broadway
New York, NY 10003

Distributed by Publishers Group West

www.groveatlantic.com

10 11 12 13   10 9 8 7 6 5 4 3 2 1

To Patty, with appreciation; and the wind, sand and stars

PREFACE

Rediscoveries are common among philosophers; the human mind moves in a circle around its eternal problems.

—A. J. Liebling

"Fighting is fifty percent mental." Through the ages, grizzled fighters and veteran trainers have said words of that nature to eager young fighters, to reporters, to anyone who would listen. Tim Sylvia, a former UFC (Ultimate Fighting Championship) Heavyweight champion, said (in the finest Yogi Berra fashion), "Fighting is ninety percent mental, half the time." We've all heard it from a dozen different places.

But what do they mean? Fighting is two guys in a ring or cage, smashing each other, the ultimate physical endeavor. It's meat on meat. How could something so physical be more mental than physical? What do all these professionals intend to convey with the word "mental"? Is it an empty cliché?

This book is an attempt to answer that question, a question that appeared simple but began to unfold into peeling layers of complexity. It started as a purely selfish quest; I was curious. After a few months of interviews and talking to great fighters I began to see the universal nature of the answers. The more you look around, the more you see that everyone is fighting something.

I made it a point to go after great fighters when I could, guys who, in the words of boxing champion Gabriel Ruelas, "swum the deep waters." When Gabe said "deep waters," he was talking about big title fights, championship rounds, the rarefied air where life and death are on the line. Deep waters are the moments when a great fighter is facing a superior athlete, a man who has spent his whole life honing lethal skills, in front of millions of people; when the great fighter is fighting better than he ever has before, better than anyone thought possible, and the opponent is still coming. When a man's only hope is to reach down deep into himself and find a way to snatch victory from the jaws of defeat. The fighters in this book have been tested in ways that few have. They've seen through the vagaries of their human soul.

I had been thinking about these things for years but the concrete book germinated during a conversation with the publisher and writer for Victory Belt: Erich Krauss. His company publishes instructional books such as BJ Penn's *The Book of Knowledge* or Randy Couture's *Wrestling for Fighting*. The books are filled with diagrams and photos, step-by-step walk-throughs of specific techniques. Erich wondered if I was interested in writing one of those books.

I thought about it. Erich was talking to all the great fighters, he had tremendous access, but I wasn't so interested in the specific techniques, like Couture's clinch-trip takedowns, as much as I was his overall game-plan strategy. How come Couture was so much better than his opponents at devising plans and then executing them? Sure, the x-guard is interesting, but how does Marcelo Garcia think about jiu-jitsu? That was the book I wanted to write; these are the kinds of questions I was interested in answering.

There are those who think athletes can't speak intelligently about what they do. They see the postgame interviews, from giant men who sound like simpletons: "I just go out and do what I do" or "I take it one game at a time" or, for fighters, "I just go out to kick his ass." The verbal, conscious part of the brain may be turned off when they're performing—but that doesn't mean it always is.

I knew that when you talk to fighters about their thoughts, their mental state, they can surprise you, they've thought about it more than you might expect. You just have to learn how to listen properly (not that I was always successful) and know what you're listening to. You have to winnow through the chaff to get at the truth. But I thought it could be done, and regardless was worth a shot.

When I first thought of this project I figured this book's readers would be mostly fighters, guys who compete, interested in another aspect of strategy. But I started hearing from people who'd been in accidents, who found my first book inspiring, guys like Mike Tewell, who lost the use of his right arm, and then Matt Peterson, who wrote me from Maine.

> I am 28 years old. 10 years ago I experienced an accident in college that left me paralyzed—a C-5 quad, to be exact . . . Fighting has been in my blood since I can remember.
>
> After sustaining my spinal cord injury fighting took on a new form. Naturally, I don't throw fists in the streets anymore, but the spirit of the fight that you outline in your book is still strong with me . . .
>
> The sport of MMA has helped me get through more than a couple of days where I would have rather stayed in bed. There are times when going to work or class—especially around this time of year here in Maine—seems like an insurmountable task, but then I remember the athletes of this sport and what they go through to get where they're at, I take a deep breath, and then throw the covers off to get the day started.

Renzo Gracie's line, "Everbody is fighting something" is the truth. Maybe this book could be of use to everybody, not just MMA (mixed martial arts) fighters. Matt Peterson has become a friend and was recently elected a state representative in Maine. Yes we can.

This book is mostly about fighting: boxing and mixed martial arts. They are called sports, but in sports the real world is nominally held at bay, locked outside stadium doors for the viewer. No one is starving in football, there is no genocide in baseball, no terrorism coverage on ESPN. We watch a game to escape from the news, from politics. The rules are clear, there's a winner and a loser, and everything is as fair as we can make it. Of course, sports are about everything in life, too, barely beneath the surface. Sports are about race and religion, class and poverty. Outside life squeezes in through the edges of the field and climbs in under the ropes. Terrorism and genocide show up, like smoke drifting in through the cracks.

Prizefighting is something more again. We create a life-and-death struggle on demand. And while watching my football team lose is one thing, it can't compare with the empty lurch in my stomach when I see a friend, or a hero, losing a fight.

A fight, a prizefight, has some elements of that sporting fairness and clarity, there is a winner and a loser. Rules, weight classes, referees and judges; we try to make a fair fight, as fair as human ingenuity can make it. No surprises, no advantages other than what you bring inside your "business suit."

But we invite the real world in—we ask for damage. There is a savage price to be paid. Prizefighting operates in a grey area, on the dark fringes of the sporting world. The fans are a slightly different type, perhaps a little more aware of the darkness and the light, a little more accepting of good and bad. Watching men fight is like watching a bullfight or a dog-fight. On some level you stop judging and thinking and instead feel in your bones, and connect to an older, primordial sense of spectacle. Fighting is much greater than a sum of its parts; it is more than a sport, more than any other form of competition in modern society. It is about truth, and great fighters are more than just athletes. They are the reason I wrote this book, an attempt to plumb the depths, to learn something from those on the far end of experience.

I realized the more dialogue with great fighters I leave in, the better; because I know there are things I don't understand, there are things that I'm missing, but you might listen for them and hear them, even if I don't. You might hear what you need to hear.

This is my gift back to the fighters who gave me so much in the first book. A book for fighters, and we are all fighting something.

SAS
December 16, 2008
Marina del Rey, California

THE
FIGHTER'S
MIND

FIRE AND BRIMSTONE

Dan Gable wrestles the Soviet Union's Rusl Ashuraliev
during the 1972 Olympic games in Munich. (Courtesy: AP)

College wrestling, to its participants and its fans, is not so much a sport as a secret religion, a calling, a fanatical sect that captures you body and soul.

—Kenneth Turan

As I drove through a snowy wasteland to Waterloo, Iowa, I could feel the emptiness stretching away, across Canada, to the North Pole. It was cold, about three degrees without wind chill, and the snow fell dense and light, too cold and windy for it to stick to the windswept road. Thin snakes of curling snow twisted back and forth across the highway. Bodaciously cold. The rental car was cozy, my little cocoon of traveling heaven.

Waterloo is a small industrial town, and my destination was easy to find, right off the highway. The car crunched through the ice in the parking lot, empty save for one other car. I parked near it for warmth.

The Dan Gable International Wrestling Institute and Museum was chilled and clean. It felt deserted, complete with echoing footsteps. And then a thin, serious young man came out, Kyle Klingman, whom I knew only electronically. He helped run the museum (though he's since moved on) and he was my link to the greatest living American wrestler, Dan Gable. Interestingly, Kyle is not a wrestler, but he had the burning intensity of *something,* some kind of athlete. I later found out he was an ultrarunner.

I wandered through the museum, catching up on wrestling, pro wrestling history, and all things Gable. Actually, I was pretending to catch up; in reality I knew very little about collegiate or Olympic wrestling, the wealth of names. Signed pictures of Olympians covered the walls. The museum was bigger than I expected, and well organized, although there wasn't much but photos. The pro wrestling section was small but fascinating, a little-known slice of history. It hadn't always been dominated by fake, theatrical matches. There was a large picture, a black-and-white framed photo of a stadium in the 1930s, packed with 14,000: folks in suit and tie, ladies in hats, all for a wrestling match. Kyle informed me that into the '50s some pro wrestlers would actually wrestle for real, in private, to decide who was better, and then they would "work" (fake) the public event, with the real winner prevailing in "the work." Otherwise, an overly technical match might be boring for the crowd.

I sat in Frank Gotch's favorite chair. Gotch was the "greatest American wrestler ever," competing at the turn of the century when professional wrestling was primarily real. Wrestlers traveled the world and competed in bullfight rings in Spain and stadiums in Russia; Gotch was considered an icon in the early days of the twentieth century and wrestled in front of a crowd of 30,000 at Comiskey Park.

Gotch had studied under Farmer Burns, another great American catch-wrestler. These guys were doing submission wrestling with key locks and chokes before the Gracies learned jiu-jitsu. Burns wrote things that sound suspiciously like Eastern philosophy; he advocated the practice of deep, studied breathing, flowing like a river—meditation by another name.

I realized long ago that modern MMA had been deeply shaped by American wrestlers, who had found a professional avenue for their refined and savage arts. I was here at the beating heart of American wrestling to explore the wrestler mentality, with the hands down greatest living American wrestler. Many of the fighters I was interested in, Pat Miletich and Randy Couture, had set out to emulate Dan Gable. So here I was.

Gotch's leather chair was comfortable, with excellent lower back support. If I'm ever a millionaire I'll have a furniture maker copy that chair for me. A burly older man came out to say hello. His name was Mike Chapman and he'd read my book. He was an interesting guy, a professional journalist who'd written sixteen books, a combat sport enthusiast who'd practiced wrestling, judo, and sambo, and a historian—he'd just written a book about Achilles.

Mike and Kyle were excited I was interviewing Gable the next day. They had set the whole thing up, as I could never get Gable to respond to a phone call. Kyle and Mike wondered if I was nervous about meeting Gable. I hadn't been before but now I was getting there.

Dan Gable is nothing less than a living legend. He seemed unbeatable as a young wrestler. He went 183–1 in high school and college, pinning twenty-five consecutive opponents. He won gold at the 1972 Olympics *without getting a single point scored on him.* If you don't know wrestling it's very hard to appreciate the surreal quality to that achievement. It's one thing to win a gold medal; it's something entirely different to dominate a sport as completely as that. It demonstrates not only greatness but a kind of monstrous determination, a drive to a killer instinct on a completely different level.

As a coach, he won twenty-one consecutive Big Ten titles and nine consecutive NCAA titles (with a total of fifteen) from 1978–1986, in what is known as the "Gable Era." Gable wasn't just great—he was *dominating,* not only as a wrestler, but as a coach, too. And that domination was very famously and publicly born of insanely hard work. Dan Gable trained much, much, much

SAM SHERIDAN

harder than everyone else. He worked out five or six times a day; he ran from class to class with ankle weights strapped on. He's the definition of driven. For Dan "more is more." His drive, his fanatical devotion to the blue-collar philosophy that "harder work means better results," coupled with his unprecedented success has made him a mythical figure in his own time. Hard men gush like teenage girls when they talk about him.

At its heart, wrestling is about intensity and pure conditioning. There is always a body on you, continuously in contact. The whole point is to dominate physically, and there aren't a lot of ways to rest in a match—basically you're going the whole time, all six or nine minutes. Wrestling is more tiring than fighting because it's *pure,* and it's more exhausting than grappling because it's so positional. It's a battle of will, and nothing destroys will like fatigue. Mike Van Arsdale, an Olympic wrestler who fought extensively in MMA, told me how much harder wrestling is, cardiovascularly, than fighting. In wrestling, you're not going to get punched, you'll just be dominated. Of course technique and strategy figure in but they are distant stars to strength and conditioning.

What Gable brought to the table—what made him different—was his fanatical drive. It allowed him to push a dominating, tireless, relentless pace in practice and in matches. "Fanatical" is a clichéd concept in sports, but for Gable it seems like one of the only appropriate descriptions. He pushed so hard no one could keep up. He brought a whole new level of conditioning to the sport. He improved constantly, he studied diligently, he refined his game. Through example, Gable brought all that intensity along with him into his coaching career, and it paid off: his teams dominated and annihilated the competition for most of his career.

I drove back down to Iowa City the next morning for my interview with the great man, through a complete white-out blizzard. Seven inches fell in a couple of hours. My friends and family would

6

have been scared if they could have seen it. Only three or four *really* close calls. Who needs coffee when you've got adrenaline? But I wasn't going to miss my interview, not now. Gable would have driven through the snow.

The Gable homestead is a beautiful place, twenty-odd acres in the country. Most of Iowa is flat but where Gable lives there are rolling hills, timber, a sense of wilderness. I parked and walked across the snow to his office, a cabin he had built out back of the house. He had a fire glowing in the iron-and-glass woodstove. I was jealous—it would make a great writing studio, with a big full bathroom, a sauna, and a small gym.

By now I *was* a little intimidated to meet the man. For wrestlers, Dan Gable is Jesus and Buddha. Douglas Looney, in *Sports Illustrated,* had called him "America's Ultimate Winner." Wrestlers will say he's the Greatest American Athlete in History and they will be fighting serious—wild-eyed—when they say it. Wrestlers carry Dan Gable in their hearts. I didn't know what to expect, and I wondered if he'd be annoyed by some snot-nosed nonwrestler asking questions.

The man himself is just that, just a man dealing with his legend. Dan is of medium size and build, still thick in the shoulders and hands, his hair gone thinning and nearly bald, big glasses, light Irish complexion. He's in his fifties and has had to pay the price for his unrelenting workout routines and wrestling schedules, with dozens of minor and major surgeries, hip replacements.

He shook my hand and launched into a quick, decisive interrogation. Who was I, where was I from, what was I doing, where did I live now? I had the sense that Gable was holding me up to the light like a jeweler, examining me carefully with those big eyes behind his thick glasses. He needed information to assess me, and he got it quickly and without stopping—he was intense and it was no act. In fact, there was almost an air of apology to it, as if he was aware that some consider him too intense, but he couldn't do anything about it.

He gave me a tour of his house, showed me some things he'd won, the Gold Medal. We ambled back to his office, woodstove ticking warmly, and sat down. Dan launched into the interview, without me asking a question. In fact, I think I managed one question during the whole interview. He told me what was what, and I hoped my tape recorder was working.

Dan wanted to be clear. "Here's where I come from," he said with no prelude. "I'm a little fanatical. I'm on the extreme. If we had a thousand athletes and ranked them, and number one is the most disciplined and extreme, well, I'd be ranked right up there. I never changed my career, and my whole life was preparation for my profession."

Dan started in at the YMCA at four years old and mentions that he was already a little fanatical. He swam as a kid and won local meets; he played every sport that little kids play and then he found wrestling. "I had a mom and dad who were intent on making this kid special, on giving him good advice. I heard good things from everyone around me." It was "do as I say, not as I do," but "their credibility stayed high because it was a blue-collar town, everything was pretty routine—smoking and drinking and family fights." Frank Gifford wrote a book in 1976 about courage, in which he profiled Dan Gable. Gifford recounts how Dan's mother, when she found out that Dan was nervous about an upcoming wrestling match (at age twelve), said loudly to him that she would take away his wrestling shoes and get him some ballet slippers. She was apparently famous for comments like that.

In junior high, Dan went from the Y into school athletics. He had great success in other sports—he was the quarterback on an undefeated football team—but "wrestling was an unbelievable commodity in Waterloo at that particular time, so I was closest to that." There were some big name coaches in town, and kids were winning state championships. Dan fondly recounts how his eighth-grade math teacher (who was also a wrestling coach) got him on the right track with his academics. "But my academics was my wrestling—my other academics were an education for me, sure, but I wasn't going to have to use any of that. Not like I was going to use my wrestling. I had my major going from the beginning."

We sat companionably in front of the fire but I rarely got a word in. Dan has a terrible earnestness, a ferocity of concentration that swells into an almost frightening intensity and then fades back to normal. It warms my heart to realize that his interview is like his wrestling: it's relentless. His voice is rough, coughing and growling.

As a kid he was something of a terror, with dozens of tales of "Dennis the Menace"–type shenanigans—chasing cats up trees and over the roof, feuding and battling with his parents and the world around him. In an interview with ESPN, Dan laconically said to the interviewer, "When I was a little kid, if I came in here I'd be looking to tear the place apart." Gifford wrote, in his purple prose, "When Dan was a boy he was well on his way to becoming a Class A monster . . . his language was blue and his misdeeds violent."

In high school, during his sophomore summer, while Dan and his parents were away on a fishing trip, Dan's older and only sister, Diane, was raped and murdered at the family home. A lot is made out of this tragedy, how it drove Dan, but I suspect that Dan's character was already firmly in place. The terrible, unthinkable horror simply revealed a little more of his iron nature. Dan took it personally. He kept his parents from selling the house and moved into Diane's room. He'd already lost his sister, and he decided he wouldn't lose his house. He fed the event to the hunger inside him.

Between his tenth-grade year and all the way through college, Dan won 181 wrestling matches. He was considered unbeatable. And then, in 1970, for his last match ever in college, for his third NCAA title, the unthinkable: Dan lost to Larry Owings, a good, tough sophomore from the University of Washington. Gable went on to a pinnacle of greatness, but thirty-eight years later he is still thinking about Owings.

9

"No matter what you do, you never forget certain things. People think that loss is over and done with?" He snorts derisively. "That's never over, that goes to my grave with me . . ." he trails off, then continues, mellower, wiser. "Even though I have kind of figured it out, I know how I should have won that match. But that's not the most important factor. The most important thing is: Could I have won that match and gone on to the levels I reached in the Olympics and coaching?" Here Dan is haunted, his thoughts far away. "I should have been able to do that, but I haven't convinced myself I could have."

These things plague him even now. He has a further, secret confession to make. "Here's something I realized in the last two months: I've been disappointed in my athletic career by a few things. Beyond losing that Owings match, I was always somewhat disappointed in the way I won the world championships and the Olympic games. Even though I was unscored on, in the last two minutes of that match I coasted."

Dan is incredulous, having a hard time believing it himself. *Yes, it's true.* The shame of it, coasting.

"I have been trying to figure out why I coasted to victory, because as a coach I don't preach that. I always say when you get up, build-build-build on your lead." He sighs, disturbed deeply by his own allegations.

"It goes back to this Owings match, when I didn't wrestle a good match. I was distracted, hearing things around me in the stands. I fought my way back into the match, came from behind, and pulled ahead. I was ahead by two points with thirty seconds left. But me, winning by two points? C'mon, I win by fifteen points or a pin!" The disgust rises in his voice. "I pin people! It wasn't good enough to win, I had to pin him. So I went for the pin again. However"—and Dan grows wise again —"I didn't *read* the match. I didn't read the history of it. Twice before I'd tried to pin him and he'd escaped both times. I'd use arm bars and he had real loose shoulders and he could gumby out of there. It was just natural for me to try to dominate." He growls, exasperated, "Yeah, coaching was involved but it was just my way. I went for the fall. He had the opportunity to score and he did by escaping. There was the referee's call but I lost that match. What did that match do for me? CHOOM!" He makes his arm take off like a rocket. "It shot me up. I improved in the year following that loss as much as I had in the previous seven years.

"But now, here's the point. In the finals of the World, in '71, the last period, I'm up by five points, and the athlete I'm competing against stops wrestling. Now it could have been a false thing, trying to lull me, but I had been really working on my mentality since the Owings match. When you're beating somebody, you keep adding on. But now, when he shut down, I shut down, too. I coasted to victory. The only way he could win was if I gave him the opportunity to pin me. So I didn't give it to him. At the time I couldn't say why. When I wondered at it afterward, and analyzed it, me being overly aggressive was the only way I could lose. That Owings match taught me to do what I had to do to ENSURE victory."

Dan is not sure if he's happy with this version of history. He shakes his head and talks about "taking a knee" in football—taking the safe way out, to protect a victory—and he gets very angry with himself, with the world. "Taking a knee is NOT MY WAY! *It's not my way!* That's what I preach, that's what I demand, that aggressiveness."

There's part of the price Gable pays for being such an intense perfectionist—he's somewhat dissatisfied with one of the most perfect performances in the history of sports.

When Dan started coaching at the University of Iowa he was introduced to a whole new slew of problems. He was just the assistant coach, and although it was competitive, the University of Iowa was not a wrestling powerhouse. Iowa State (where Dan had gone), Oklahoma State, those were the big dogs.

"I had athletes with the same talent I'd been around my whole life, and I figured they'd be as good. In the competitions we started with the easier teams, and I saw tremendous performances. So I told the head coach to raise his expectations, because his were much lower than mine. I told him he wasn't seeing it. He said, 'Just wait and see,' and when we finally got into competition with someone who was rated higher than us, I think it was Michigan, the athletes didn't represent themselves. They didn't wrestle well. Now, for me, when you go against higher competition you get MORE out of yourself. In the quarterfinals of the Olympics you got to be a little better, and then even better in the semis, and so on. You step it up as the season progresses. Now this team wasn't representing itself. And it wasn't a fluke—it happened again against the higher competition. I started to think about mentality. I'd always had it, but we didn't have a good example in the room." He could see these kids thought they were working hard, thought they trained tough, but there were depths unplumbed.

Gable used himself as that example—because part of it, that extremism, is showing *what is possible*. He said, "I'm just off the Olympics, besides being a coach I'll get out there, and work harder in the room to show it." He needed living proof of what incredibly self-motivated people could do, and as he got older he had to find it in his wrestlers, hone it, and bring it out because a few individuals like that will raise the level of the whole team.

It's like the nuclear bomb in the years before anyone had made one. The secrets of the first atom bomb weren't technical, not really—everyone in the scientific world knew how to make one, more or less; the theory was public. It was just whether the thing itself was possible; that was the secret. Could it work? Would it ignite the atmosphere in a chain reaction, destroying the world? Gable played a similar role with his first teams, even with his Olympic teams. He showed them what they were capable of. Gifford wrote, "Face to face with Gable, they were able to see what had to be done."

To Dan, there is no top end, no limit. You can always add new levels, and the guys who realize this go on to do amazing things. Dan gets fired up about this. He talks about the four-minute mile—how the journalists of the day were convinced the four-minute mile was the limit of human speed. In 1954, Roger Bannister crashed that wall and ran under four minutes because he believed overtraining to be a myth. Bannister said, "The man who can drive himself further once the effort gets painful is the man who will win." The following year, a few dozen athletes broke the barrier, this barrier that had previously been thought of as scientifically impossible. It reminds me of what the monks in Thailand had said, that the longer you meditate the more you realize pain is just an illusion.

Gable is a true believer and, more to the point, he's *proven* it. Gifford writes, "Dan talks in 'odd' phrases. Odd in that they are sometimes clichés. Only, when Dan says them, the moss falls off because they come from the lips of a man who has demonstrated since boyhood that he means every one of them." In a way, that is the point of this whole book.

Dan gets up and walks me over to a picture of a horse race. It's Secretariat at the Belmont Stakes in 1973. Secretariat is so far ahead of the other horses, thirty-one lengths, that they don't even appear to be running in the same race. When you watch the race, you see Secretariat way out in front, pulling away. And then he keeps on pulling away, pulling away. This is what Dan is all about, confounding experts, performing at levels that no one dared yet imagine. There's always another level. People may not understand it, may not be able to grasp it, but there's always another level.

As a coach at the University of Iowa, Gable built a wrestling powerhouse and led the team to fifteen NCAA victories. I spoke with Tom Brands, one of his standout wrestlers who is now the head wrestling coach at Iowa. Tom (and his brother Terry) were outstanding wrestlers in the Gable era. Tom was a four-time all-American, a three-time NCAA champ, and won the gold medal at the 1996 Olympics. He won basically every award there is to win.

Tom said of Gable, "It's complicated but it's simple. He steered you as you needed it. He says this all the time, 'I can make pumpkin pie out of cow manure.'" What becomes clear in talking to Tom is that Gable studied his wrestlers the way he'd once studied opponents. "He would push the right buttons, eventually," said Tom. "It wasn't innate, I think it was trial and error, hard work, study, he'd eventually figure a guy out, what he really needed."

Tom tells a story about Gable and apples. Tom was a redshirt freshman, and in a gruesomely hard practice. Gable was toward the end of his coaching career, perched high on the bleachers and eating apples from a box. He was really pushing his varsity wrestlers, with two-on-ones and other killers, and he kept saying, "This is the last one of *these*," but the torture never seemed to end. One of his wrestlers started breaking, pushed past his mental endurance by Gable and what he was asking for; he started wanting to quit. The wrestler began screaming at Dan, "You're a liar, you said that was the last one, I thought you were a man of your word!" Dan didn't say anything, but he started throwing apples at him. Tom recalls wrestling with apples everywhere, apples underfoot and under bodies—because practice didn't end—with this one wrestler screaming and crying, "going off the deep end." The wrestler having the meltdown didn't get it. Dan just kept pelting him with apples. Gable wasn't insulted. "He wasn't in your face, 'that's not how you talk to me,' but you could see that if you were talking like that, you're out of line. You're not as tough as you need to be. This was the test and *you can't handle it*. You're failing, right now, and you don't even realize it."

As head coach, Tom Brands has won the NCAA championship and word is that all the other sports at Iowa are doing better—inspired by the example of intensity.

Gable knew he couldn't expect everyone to wrestle and train as he had. "A lot of people make that mistake. They've been successful so they try to apply it straight on to everybody else. A lot of great athletes don't make great coaches, because they're already fixed on what they were doing to be great, as individuals. Because I've been a fanatic and an extremist, I know it works well and for me. But I've made adjustments for a whole range of people."

Tom gets a little frustrated by some of my questions. He thinks I'm looking for that one moment when Gable took him and said the key words that changed his life. Those words aren't there (and I'm not expecting them). Tom conjectured for me, "He created an energy through mystery. He's a serious guy, but these things are mysterious. What makes the real tough guys tick? We don't know, except they're badass sunofaguns. They're fanatics. It's not simple, it's complicated." Tom thinks about it.

"You learn the number one thing—it's about making guys feel good about their future and the direction that they're going. One time at a tournament, as a real freshman, my brother and I both lost both our matches—I got pinned—and Gable put us in the corner and pointed his finger at us and scolded us. But it was so positive, because we were just freshman and he let us know we were valuable to what he was doing, that he counted on us. It was so gratifying. He expected more from us."

Gable expects more from you, and he convinces wrestlers to expect more from themselves. His standard is set to the highest level. It reminds me of the old expression "to make a man trustworthy you must trust him."

Tom goes on to say, "A lot of coaches will tell their guys, 'you gotta believe in me, trust my system and believe in it,' but the bottom line is, it's about the damn coaches *believing in the athletes.* Gable believed in me, in my brother, in all these other guys."

It's how Dan made pumpkin pie.

In his tenth year as head coach at the University of Iowa, Dan was going to break all the records. It was being dubbed "Season X" and T-shirts were printed, the proverbial champagne was iced. In a shocking turn his team came in second in the country.

15

"We crumbled on the edge of that championship, we went from first to second, but we were losers. Sure, we were second out of a hundred and ten teams, but if you're on top, then anything coming down feels like a loss. I got hate mail the next day, saying I'd lost my touch, that the team will never be good again."

He ruminated, "I went back and really tried to figure out what happened. I think the downfall of the X season lies much earlier, five years earlier, in '83. We had the top-recruited class in the nation, for the first time ever." Dan means that his team had gone out and found the best high school wrestlers in the country. That's what having a legendary coach will do—it will bring the best young wrestlers, who will sacrifice a lot just to be in the room with Dan Gable.

"Well, those guys, they could carry us through with talent. And the work level fell off. And I fell for that. I was scared of doing something wrong. And the next year, we didn't have quite the same class, but it was still very good. Now, up until '87 we were still winning, but they weren't the extremists. Now, they worked hard, but not to the level that raises everyone up. Not to the level that affects the people below them.

"It comes back to dealing with adversity. Too much adversity, too much losing, and it becomes the 'same old same old.' It becomes a habit— it's not devastating. But if you only lose once in a while, at rare CRUCIAL times, you can build to a much higher level. You can use that as fuel." Dan was forced to relearn what his harsh mistress, greatness, demanded.

"My best wrestlers, most of them, were winning before they came here. They might not know any holds, or have a lot of skill, but they'd go all out, beat somebody up and run them into the ground. They knew how to win before they knew how to wrestle. That's the critical thing. And then we take them and mold them and teach them, and in a few years they're amazing. It's easier to teach the skills than the mentality."

I asked Dan if there was any way to teach the mentality—it's part of the mystery that Tom Brands was alluding to. Dan nods, *that's the point.* "I don't give up on kids that don't have it, but I have them surrounded by kids who DO have it. Without examples, it won't happen. And there's not many out there who have it. A lot of them have the science, but only a few have the mentality. I would count five or six kids in all my years coaching that really fall into that mentality or character. But they influence others. They win matches before they get on the mat. And what's really good is when the whole team gets labeled that way." They start to see where the standard is, and those below rise to meet it and are vastly improved even if they don't get all the way there.

"We've had that as a team, when we'd win the meet before the meet. I can't ever tell you that all ten athletes were all that. Of the ten maybe four or five would really have that mentality. And that's unusual. Usually it's one or two that can really bring that extreme-level influence. These guys who just know how to win."

"Would you call that the killer instinct?" I ask. He nods.

"Killer instinct, a little bit. You can't make up for time lost. If you miss a practice it's gone. But I do think—one of these guys that I'm talking about—CAN, because of the LEVEL OF EFFORT AND INTENSITY THAT THEY CAN ACTUALLY PUT INTO A SINGLE PRACTICE!" his voice has grown again, almost to shouting. Then he subsides and continues in a normal voice.

"They can get so much out of themselves in a practice, they'll make up that lost time. The effort that's coming out of their body is so great, they're at such a level. I had a kid who could make up a week in one practice. He could make it up, very few can do it, and that's that mentality that I'm talking about."

Dan goes thoughtful again, musing out loud. "Is it just the body? But I look at those guys that I'm talking about, and not all of them had that incredible physical gift. At least two that I can think of are doing what I'm talking about, weren't physical specimens—which takes it down to one area—between the ears."

That's what I'm after, and I pursue it. But Dan won't or can't elaborate. You just have to keep your eyes open and look for it. "Because I'm like that, maybe I can pick it out easier. But it's not an easy thing to recognize. In our sport, for somebody just to make it through a difficult practice is pretty extreme for other people to imagine. But then you have those few guys who are really unique this way. It's impossible for people to understand them. People think that they're working hard, and they are, but there are other levels. You've got to have all the support, and the environment, and you have to have an imagination that's unreal."

I was reminded of the stories of Dan's childhood, where he would pretend to be a famous ballplayer and talk about how "real" it felt to him. Imagination is a crucial component, oft overlooked. If you can't imagine running a four-minute mile, how can you ever run it? Gandhi said, "Men often become what they believe themselves to be. If I believe I cannot do something, it makes me incapable of doing it. But when I believe I can, then I acquire the ability."

Dan continued, "People don't want to work hard. They want to get to the top without really paying the price. I just read a story where they interviewed these people who wanted to be great, and the question was: If you could go to the Olympics, be guaranteed a gold medal and then die two years later, would you do it? And fifty percent answered yes!"

Dan is disgusted, and incredulous. For so many reasons. He goes into a hypothetical, which takes on the air of a farce.

"If I was going to wrestle in the finals of the Olympics against a Russian, which I did, and if I knew he had been trained specifically to beat me, which he had—but then if I knew the guy was on steroids, that would HELP me. Whereas some might think 'oh, he's cheating' or he's got an unfair advantage, for me you didn't pay the price. You're not as committed as I am. It'll tear him apart.

He may be strong, but all I have to do during that nine minutes of wrestling is loosen one single wire in his brain, make him do something that isn't perfect, and he'll fall apart. That's what I feel.

"Breaking somebody is the goal. You get him to quit trying to win, he tries to survive. It's there a lot, but often people don't see it. You have to have done it quite a few times or you'll miss the key point, because he can come back," Dan warns me. "Once he shows signs of breaking, if you don't take advantage, there's a chance of him coming back. So keep pressure on at all times."

Then Dan laughs a little. "But there's a catch-22. It's not as black and white as black and white. Sometimes you shouldn't attack to win, and it's hard to have both instincts. For the Owings match, I couldn't have understood it without going through it. But then I had the instinct in the Olympics. And I used it to eliminate the chance of losing, pretty much."

The Gable museum had a viewing room where an ESPN special on Gable was shown. It was a basic overview. His triumphs were documented, his tragedies more so. There was a fascinating blurb by some talking head, saying, "As Dan got more famous, as he became known to more and more people, his focus was all the time becoming narrower, more purely about wrestling." Gable had won gold at the '72 Olympics in Munich, without a single point scored against him, one of the dominant performances in sporting history. Three days later, Munich descended into tragedy, with terrorist attacks, the hostage crisis, and the eventual deaths of the Israeli athletes. When Gable got off the plane back in the United States, a reporter shoved a camera in his face and asked him about the atmosphere in Munich. Dan responded lightly, that the weather was about the same as it was here. He was embarrassed when he realized his mistake, but Dan Gable's world had shrunk to himself and wrestling, to the head of pin.

THE CHOIRBOY

Freddie Roach. © Miguel Salazar

What usually wins fights is not so much style as content.
                                        —A. J. Liebling

Wild Card Gym is on the corner of Vine and Santa Monica, in a part of Hollywood that has resisted gentrification; it's still a rough neighborhood, at least at night. Although Freddie Roach, the owner, recently expanded, the gym is small for its massive reputation. During midday it's crowded to the point where you're actually stepping on people's toes. Freddie is there almost every day, unless called away to help some world-famous fighter figure out his next opponent.

Freddie Roach is a boxing trainer, a Hall of Famer, and Trainer of the Year in 2003, 2006, 2007, and 2008. He's coached a "who's who" of boxers in his career, from Manny Pacquiao and James Toney to Mike Tyson. Oscar de la Hoya hired him to train for Floyd Mayweather Jr. in the hardest-hyped "superfight" in the past ten years. Freddie's considered one of the two or three best trainers in boxing and is frequently called in to troubleshoot career-defining fights for big-name fighters. He's a superstar. The walls of Wild Card Gym are covered with old fight posters and pictures of Freddie and his brother with champions, ex-champions, and celebrities. The timer dings and holds sway, marching through the day, like a flashing red-eyed idol.

A boxing trainer's link to his fighter is more intense, more mutually dependent, than any other coaching relationship in sports. It is private, one-on-one, the trainer focused with his whole being on the fighter. It's a long relationship, built over years, thousands of hours in the gym, day in and day out. Trainer and fighter are closer than family, and there are many father-son teams out there. The fighter is something of an extension of the trainer; often trainers will use the royal "we" as in "when *we* had to fight so-and-so," but only the fighter is in the ring. This is a relationship under dire stress. The consequences are severe, money is short. This is a hurt business.

Freddie Roach isn't a big guy, only five-foot-five with short, Irish red hair, myopic-thick glasses, and pale, freckled skin. His face is familiar from the TV, in the corner for all kinds of fighters. He had the fighting nickname the "Choirboy" for his boyish look (as well as "La Cucaracha," for the obvious reason). He's one of the most unassuming men you've ever met, although his physical presence has an awareness to it that palpably extends outward. That awareness he has makes you pay attention—quiet and powerful. You get the feeling he sees everything in the gym, even when his back is turned. Even if you didn't know who he was, you'd know he was somebody.

Freddie was featured heavily on HBO's dramatic series 24/7 for the buildup to Mayweather/de la Hoya fight, and on the show he admitted publicly to having Parkinson's brought on by boxing. Sometimes he stands with his hands stuffed under his armpits to keep them from shaking. But when he climbs into the ring to work mitts with a fighter all weakness falls away. He moves like a young man, crisp and sure. And he can catch. When he hit mitts with Mike Tyson, somebody asked, "Is that Bruce Lee in there with Mike?"

Freddie has been to the wars, without a doubt. As a fighter, he was known for his reckless style—he would take a few hits to give one. He was good enough to make it to the top, where he lost big fights to world champions; he was a very good fighter but not a great one. Perhaps Freddie mumbles more than he might otherwise, but he's not punchy. His mind and his intellect are deep, his eyes quiet and shielded behind his glasses. You get the feeling Freddie knows all kinds of things. Like any good boxing trainer—anybody who is good at making a living building fighters—he can look right through your exterior and see what's happening inside.

Freddie sits at the front desk and watches his domain with a wary eye, but he's eminently approachable, with the usual coterie of fighters and friends lounging, soaking up the presence of one of boxing's greats. He enjoys himself, enjoys his day, and chats with all kinds, from this Russian trainer with his eastern bloc protégé to that crusty old boxing writer. For a while I lived ten minutes from Wild Card and I would hit mitts with his brother, Pepper, and then sometimes catch Freddie for a few minutes to talk. I gave him a copy of my first book and told him about this project. I had boxed under Tommy Rawson at Harvard, and Tommy had refereed a lot of Freddie's fights. We had the Massachusetts connection and I milked it. Massholes recognize each other, something about those grim New England winters, the endless slush of spring.

Pepper is Freddie gone awry. The brothers grew up in Lowell, Massachusetts, and were boxing from childhood. Freddie says Pepper was the really talented one—people thought he was going to be the next Willie Pep. Willie was one of the greatest pure boxers ever—he famously won a round without throwing a punch, just with his grace of movement and skill. Pushed hard by their father (himself a seasoned pro), they both boxed from six years old, and they fought and won Golden Gloves and amateur competitions. But then the older brother, Pepper, fell into drugs and crime and his career derailed.

Pepper himself snorts at Freddie's "Willie Pep" comparison, and says, "I was just older than Freddie, so he looked up to me. Freddie was always the one."

Freddie is a firm believer in the old saw, "Fighters are born not made," because as a former fighter he knows the multitude of variables that go into making a world champion. They are infinite. If you start trying to make a world champion from scratch, you're doomed to failure. First of all, you need the right athlete. He's gotta be tough, strong, fast. You need a guy who's showing promise, who has come far down the path of commitment, and you help him proceed. Nobody makes a world champion from nothing; he creates himself under the trainer's shaping eye—over the long years, staying with the plan, and fighting through the pain and uncertainty. He has to maintain the dream. "They're special people," Freddie would say again and again, often with a rueful, sideways grin, his secret smile of amusement. "If I didn't get talented guys, I wouldn't be a good trainer." It's not *just* the athleticism, the speed and the power, but that has to be a part of it. Nobody becomes a world champion who isn't naturally stronger and faster than other men. But then there comes the dedication, the ability to learn and listen, the fire to get in the ring and work and get up and run every morning. And it's not six months, or even a year; anyone can do that. It's five years, it's eight years, ten years. That's some serious fuel. The monastic lifestyle, "clean living" has to be a choice.

Freddie's an adult; he's not a father to his fighters. He's not going to make someone do all these things, but he'll help someone who's come this far. He trains men, not boys. He'll allow prima donnas and bear with craziness, because that's part and parcel of being a "special person." Big-time fighters are usually a little nuts, their place in society somewhat unknowable, and Freddie knows they have to be, to survive in this brutal business.

Freddie's not going to try and change most fighters from the ground up; he's just another fighter, primarily. He's going to help you see some things you might not have seen, to fine tune some things that will work. With the notable exception of Manny Pacquiao, a tough explosive fighter whom Freddie took and nurtured for a long time and turned into a world-beating technician.

Freddie and Teddy Atlas had a philosophical difference over the training of Michael Moorer. Moorer, who features prominently in *Atlas,* Teddy's autobiography, is a fascinating example of an extremely talented fighter, who won two world championships but at times seemed to hate boxing. Moorer came up under the intense tutelage of another legend, Emanuel Steward, with whom he had a father-son bond. At light-heavy, 175 pounds, Moorer went on a run that has never been duplicated—22–0 with twenty-two knockouts. With nothing to prove at light-heavy, and sick of starving himself, Moorer went after the bigger money, at heavyweight. Moorer grew out of his familial relationship with Steward, and then Teddy Atlas was a good fit. Still, Moorer would have days when he didn't want to train. He would sulk and make life hard for everybody around him. "I was an asshole, straight up," Moorer said when I asked him about it. And he laughed. "I was doing things in order to keep my toughness. That's not me, that's the game I was in."

When I met Michael he was working with Freddie as a trainer and teacher, around Wild Card, still touching the game that defined him. To me, he seemed like a big black boulder, slope shouldered, powerful, melancholy perhaps, reserved, almost baby-faced. His presence, his handshake, made me think of Mike Tyson's challenge to a reporter who was pestering him, "You wouldn't last two minutes in my world." I wouldn't last two minutes in Moorer's world. He felt like a survivor from another time, a harsher world, with his iron grip and scarred hands, arms, face. He was quiet, polite, with the mildness of a man who has done what he set out to do.

Atlas describes in great detail the intricate head games that he played with Moorer to get him to train and fight the right way, and they won a world title together—an impressive achievement, and something Freddie speaks of very respectfully. The heavyweight strap is a serious thing. But later, Michael Moorer left Teddy and went over to Freddie Roach. Freddie was quoted as saying, "I let Michael be Michael," and Teddy responds in his book that, "The whole point was not to let Michael be Michael." It reflects their stylistic differences, their backgrounds. Atlas used to train kids, build fighters, shape young men. Moorer even says that Teddy taught him a lot about being a man. Freddie treats his fighters like professionals.

I asked Freddie to describe how he sees the job of the trainer, in terms of the mental side of things, and he answered simply, in his Boston accent. "My job is to get inside their head. I want to get to where I know what they're thinking, and they know what I'm thinking. Trust in me. When they have complete trust in you, then they'll listen to you in the corner, better than some stranger. Make the connection." That's all Freddie is going to try to do—connect with his fighter. It's something he saw the legendary Eddie Futch do, both as a fighter under his tutelage and, later, as an assistant. "Eddie could communicate. He got his point across. He got fighters to trust him."

It's probably why world champions consistently seek Freddie out. They know he isn't going to give them a lot of grief, that he's going to get them ready in a professional manner and let them run their own mental show. He wants to get in their head but not to change anything, just to help them see some things that he sees. He's learned from his own mistakes.

"I skipped the fear because I started so young," Freddie muttered to me one afternoon, his voice just barely audible, sometimes hoarse, but clear. "I never had fear in a fight until after the first time I got knocked out. Because I had a hundred and fifty amateur fights and twenty-seven pro fights before I got knocked out.

I was never even hurt by anybody—I was invincible. Then one day I never saw the punch coming, and I woke up on the floor." Freddie laughs, smiles, and eyes me sideways through his thick glasses. "I got up, the guy rushed me and put me down again, and *fuck,* and then the ref stopped the fight." He shook his head, deeply amused by his younger self's chagrin. "From that point on, I knew I could be knocked out and that changed my whole game. My attitude. Before that, I would go in reckless. I would take a couple to get mine off, too. But then I knew what could happen, and it made a huge dent in my fighting career. I wasn't fearless anymore. It put a question mark in my head." Freddie maintains that was the beginning of the end, the start of the downhill slide of his fighting career. He also broke his hand and had a long layoff, which led to his living a less pure lifestyle, furthering the decline.

Freddie contrasts this with the example of Manny Pacquiao. Manny is one of Freddie's most famous charges, a Filipino lightweight with a dynamic style. Manny is the most popular person in the Philippines by far, bigger than any celebrity or politician. He's considered a national treasure. In an interview, the Philippines' secretary of the environment said, "Manny Pacquiao is our greatest national resource."

Manny's amazing, an "action" fighter: explosive, strong, ripping fast. His body is a piece of Filipino iron, taut, whiplike. He came to Freddie years ago with a lot of ability, but raw, and Freddie polished him into a gleaming gem, the pound-for-pound king. The bewildering technical display he put on against Oscar de la Hoya showcased all his tools, a master in his prime. And Manny has been stopped, earlier in his career.

Freddie said, "Manny, he's been KO'd and he just says 'There's always a winner and a loser, tonight just wasn't my night,' and that's a pretty good attitude to have. It didn't hurt Manny. It made him better. He learned from it, he knows it could happen, and most guys don't think it could ever happen."

Freddie was talking about himself. I asked him more about it, trying to get at the root of it. Why did a loss for Manny become a positive thing and a loss for Freddie become a negative one?

Freddie said, "Well, first thing is my defense was my offense. When I'm punching you, you can't punch me. I was a hundred percent attack. When I got knocked down and hurt, when I lost that fight, I just couldn't accept it. For me, losing is unacceptable. I won't even do sit-ups in the ring because you're never supposed to be on your back in there. I had a fighter who once wrote 'Oh Shit' on the bottoms of his shoes—so if he got knocked out you'd see it on TV—but I could never do that." It was the beginning of the end for Freddie. He went about fifty-fifty for the rest of his professional career as a fighter. Stylistically, defense wasn't part of his game.

"Manny, he's more accessible, he can accept when things don't go his way," Freddie said.

"I think maybe it's about the Philippines, the lifestyle there. They're pretty passive in a way. I mean, the traffic is bad and the street is filled with horns, but nobody gets road rage. I was watching basketball and I'd see fouls that would lead to a fistfight in the United States, and they would laugh it off. Manny knows that every fight has a winner and a loser, and sometimes it's not his night. But for me it was unacceptable. For me, there was only a winner." There's something very durable about that fatalistic acceptance of third world survivors. Manny's father abandoned the family when he was twelve, and he grew up dirt poor in the Philippines. Even today, when they go to Vegas for a big fight, Freddie stays in his hotel room alone and Manny has ten people living with him in his suite. It creates strength, a buffer of home and country. You can watch him relaxed and at ease with the distractions of his extended family around him.

"Manny took that stoppage, he dealt with it, and he learned from it. It just wasn't his night. Now, he works his abs religiously

30

so he never gets knocked out by a body shot again. They found a weakness in him, so he works to take it away."

Freddie discussed how Ray "Boom Boom" Bautista, another fighter of his, was dealing with the same issue: coming back after being knocked out. Freddie peers at me through the long tunnel of his thick glasses and drawls, "Is he going to come back as a better fighter or is his career over?"

"So how are you going to help him?" I asked.

Freddie says, "You give him a lot of positive reinforcement, tell him it could happen to anybody, 'You've knocked out a lot of guys.' Fighters are hardheaded, and when they're stubborn and doing something wrong but keep winning, they can always fall back on that 'winning formula' thing. But now, with one loss, I got some clout. When you lose I got some ammo." Freddie will use the loss to work on some fundamental things that he had been trying to get Boom Boom to do. He'll work on the little things, but the little things add up.

A tall, good-looking older man with long blond hair, wearing a casual, tropical suit came in the door and Freddie's eyes lit up. It was Donny Lalonde, a former world champion who'd knocked down Sugar Ray Leonard in the fourth round (although he'd lost in the ninth). Donny was into real estate in Costa Rica. That was the thing about Wild Card—it was chock-a-block with celebrities, and anybody could wander in. Donny shook hands and leaped into the conversation. I told him I was looking into the mental aspect of fighting, and Donny chuckled and said, "You've got to have already done the thinking in the gym. In the fight, you can't have your mind wrapped up. You can't be thinking instead of fighting. It's about reacting."

Freddie told us a funny story about the purely mental side of things, about Steve Collins fighting Chris Eubank for the middleweight title in 1995. Collins had very publicly gone to a hypnotist to make him stick to Freddie's game plan. Whether or not that made a difference was sort of besides the point, because his opponent, Eubank, thought Collins was inhuman now, just a fighting machine. Freddie laughed, "So the bullshit worked and the hypnotist took thirty-three and a third for the next three fights!" He means that the hypnotist took that much of Collins's purse, which is a lot more than a trainer gets.

This topic led us to the "Rumble in the Jungle," when Muhammad Ali fought George Foreman in Zaire. Ali, one of the great psychological warfare practitioners in boxing, had local witch doctors "hex" Foreman, and Foreman, somewhere in his heart, believed it had worked. Which means it had. Just the shadow of doubt can spell doom.

Freddie weighed in on an eternal boxing debate: "Everyone always asks, 'Ali or Tyson?' Well, Ali would have fucked with his head and made Mike a mess going into the fight. Pure power for power, Mike would have knocked him out, but Ali could have gotten to him mentally, and I think he would have, because Mike was so weak mentally."

Josh Waitzkin, a chess prodigy and martial artist (and whom I'll write more about later), wrote a book called *The Art of Learning,* and in it he describes the different types of chess kids he was teaching. He discusses at length "entity" versus "incremental" forms of learning, so classified by developmental psychologists. "Entity" kids think their chess skill is born of natural and innate ability, a pure talent, while "incremental" kids think they learned chess incrementally, step-by-step, and that hard work pays off.

Josh would give his students impossible problems, well beyond their level, that no one in the class could solve. So all the kids would fail that problem. But then, when he gave them other, manageable problems afterward, the entity kids would struggle; they had broken mentally, and were unsure of themselves. The incremental kids would just go back to work, slogging away. Entity kids were brittle; when they lost, their faith in their talent was shaken. The incremental kids, who believed in the power of labor, would keep digging in the trenches, even if faced with insurmountable problems.

It reminded me of Gable talking about a wrestler on steroids: make him do something that wasn't perfect and he'd crumble. Maybe that was the steroid trap—it would make you physically stronger but mentally weaker, prone to breaking.

When Freddie Roach lost, his world was shaken and he never fully recovered. He knew his skill had come from hard work, but he was convinced his invincibility was a pure thing, a part of the universe, and when that was revealed to be untrue it had hurt his game.

One of the old boxing truisms is "Frustrate a puncher and he'll fall apart." A "puncher" is a fighter who hits hard, with a big punch. It's a natural gift that coaching can help, but you can't teach power. The puncher relies on his big punching. He hits guys and they go down. As he works his way up through the boxing ranks, this is the law of the land—he hits them and they disappear. Now, he gets to his first title fight, his first big fight, and he hits his opponent— *boom*—and the guy is still there. The guy can handle the punch and keeps coming. So the puncher hits him again, but the other guy is still there. Now comes the crucible for the puncher. Does he go to pieces? Or does he buckle down and keep fighting? Can he find another way to win? Mike Tyson, one of the greatest punchers of all time, rarely fought past six rounds. If he hit you and you were still there, he'd mentally break. He'd bite your ear off, to foul himself out of the fight, or not answer the bell.

Successful fighters have things that work for them, and work incredibly well, but the great champions are those who can accept, internalize, and understand defeat. Waitzkin's tai chi teacher, the renowned William C. C. Chen (whom I studied with briefly), called this "investing in loss," and it means study your defeat without ego, let defeats happen in practice without reverting to your old habits, and then grow from it. It's an essential skill, for even during a fight the fighter needs to be able to understand—and accept—when he is losing, and change his game plan. In order to win.

THE TENTH WEAPON
OF MUAY THAI

Mark DellaGrotte making weight in Thailand.
(Courtesy: Mark DellaGrotte)

I dutifully followed my annoying, oblivious GPS through the ice-black back streets of Cambridge, Massachusetts, into Somerville. Somehow that little box knew what it was doing and I ended up where I was supposed to be, on the broad street of Broadway. The gym nestled underneath a lawyer's office, on a street littered with dive bars, dry cleaners, and lawyers. I walked to the small, nearly hidden side door, and as I pulled it open a wave of humidity roiled out into the cold winter air.

I had been to Sityodtong Academy before, to shoot an interview for the *Boston Globe,* but the place had been empty. Now it was packed. Sityodtong Boston (the other is in Pattaya, Thailand) is a tiny gym with astoundingly low ceilings—just when you think they couldn't get lower there's a beam that is even closer to your head. There are several places where if I bounced too hard I might ding the top of my skull. There was a dense crush of humanity—all men, almost all young, nearly all Massholes, and the air was swampy with their breath. There were three different levels of muay Thai going, and there were probably a hundred guys training in a gym that was crowded when it had thirty guys in it. It felt like a slave-ship hold, or a submarine. If there was a fire about five people would make it out and the rest would burn or suffocate, bodies stacking up, jamming the door . . .

Mark DellaGrotte came out and shook my hand, and he was warm and welcoming in that Boston way. He laughed and said with his heavy accent, "I feel like we know each other although we never met," which was true because I had seen him fight and watched him coach on TV, and he'd read my book.

Mark is a young, pleasant-looking guy with dark hair and an easy smile, an obvious Italian background. His eyes are bright and watchful, often underneath a Kangol cap, a little old-school Boston street. Mark's been extremely successful with adapting muay Thai for MMA; he's become known as one of the best pure striking coaches in the game and a great tactician. The fighters he coaches were on a vicious winning streak in the UFC, something like 9–0 when I showed up. He's doing something right.

He set me up with one of his coaches, a guy who was smaller than me and "with great control," just to mess around, and we had a good time, just playing. I thought of how things had changed since MFS, when Pat had thrown me in with Tim Sylvia. Of course, every now and then someone might land a clean leg kick, which would garner a harder kick in return, but we kept it pretty civil. Mark wanted me to have fun and be happy—but he also wanted me to be out of the way, not to get mashed by his top guys or spazz out and hurt someone with fights coming. He was everywhere at once, listening to complaints, hollering advice, keeping time. I was a little amazed about how extended he was, doing everything himself, but he seemed to thrive on it.

Over the next couple of weeks I hung around and talked to Mark when I could, and I got to know him a little. His gym is in the basement of his father's law office, and he grew up right in the area. He talks about his youth with a little reservation. "I grew up with a bunch of rough kids. A lot of them are either dead or in jail, and I was on both sides of the fence. I had friends who were troubled, but we weren't broke and we were raised well. Every time one of my friends got into trouble, I'd go hide in the gym."

Mark credits traditional martial arts with keeping him straight, "on the right path." Mark met guru Guy Chase and studied the "Inosanto curriculum." Dan Inosanto was Bruce Lee's greatest student, and his curriculum is a combination of many arts: jeet kune do (Bruce Lee's hybrid fighting style, which combines a dozen traditional arts with Western boxing), pencak silat (an Indonesian hybrid martial art with a lot of weapon aspects), shoot wrestling (ground fighting, a precursor to modern MMA), and kali eskrima (Filipino stick fighting). Mark's initial exposure to martial arts, with a broad background and the philosophical tradition of "borrowing what works best" from different places, would prepare him well for MMA.

Mark originally opened a Multicultural Martial Arts center in the same place where the muay Thai gym is now. This was in 1992, a year before the UFC started and *vale tudo* was still a relatively unknown Brazilian tradition.

Mark still wanted to fight, and he discovered and fell in love with muay Thai, spending time and fighting at the famous Sityodtong Camp in Pattaya, Thailand (for a long time, Sityodtong and Fairtex were the only camps that took on foreigners). It turns out we may have overlapped in Thailand, although we never met.

Mark had been bit by the Thailand bug. "I went back to Boston, and two months later I was homesick for Thailand." He trained hard, and fought well, and earned a place in the camp. Eventually, he was welcomed into the Sityodtong family by Kru (teacher) Yotong.

In 1998 he turned his martial arts center into a Sityodtong muay Thai academy. Kru Toy, Kru Yotong's son, would come and visit for a month at time.

But Mark found another trainer who would have far more impact. He heard rumors of a Thai boxer who was working on some shady visa in a Vietnamese kitchen on Newbury Street. This was Ajarn Thong, with the fighting name Satsit Seebree, who had been a successful Thai boxer and whose family owned and ran a small camp in northern Thailand. Mark brought the Thai boxer into his home to live, and he laughs about it.

"I had Thailand right here. I lived it in this little basement apartment in Somerville. Ajarn moved in with me and Marie [Mark's long-suffering girlfriend and now wife]. I learned the language, he held pads for me every day, and I lived Thai style. The sink would get clogged and I'd find chicken feet in it, so I'd yell at Ajarn, 'You can't throw food down here, we're below the street,' but he'd swear he didn't do it."

Mark is laughing hard now. "What, I don't eat this, Marie don't eat this, how'd it get in here?" It almost sounds like a sitcom setup.

Mark continued to go back and forth to Thailand regularly. He fought in the world famous Rajadamnern stadium in April 2003 and won with a second-round TKO, on a low kick. "That was a high point for me, and Kru Yotong urged me to semiretire. I wasn't going to go that much further, and I was more important as a teacher now, for preserving the art. I'm a conservator of muay Thai traditions and techniques."

A few years later, though, when Mark was back at Sityodtong, training and relaxing, something odd happened. "I'd been at the beach all day. I had a belly full of rice and a sunburn, and when I got back to camp I noticed all this commotion—and I knew somebody was fighting that day." Turned out the somebody was Mark, fighting a Thai in an "exhibition" bout for Songkran, the water festival. He hadn't been training to fight but he was assured repeatedly that it was only an exhibition.

"So I called a friend of mine, Peter Hoovers, a Dutch guy who lives in Thailand—he knows everybody—and I asked him about it. He laughed and asked me, 'Have you ever heard of a white guy fighting a Thai in an exhibition match? No such thing, you're gonna fight the kid.'"

Mark had actually been slated to fight this same fighter some years earlier. "He was an ex-military guy, had something like four hundred fights. I had nothing to bank on but being totally relaxed."

Mark jumped in the back of the truck with his trainer and went to the fight. "Right before the first exchange I knew it was on. You could feel the energy." It was a real fight, no holding back. But Mark smiles.

"It was probably my best fight ever. I kept chipping away at him, and in the third round I finished him with a series of head kicks. I was in the worst shape of my life, I was overweight. But some guys are like that. I was a nervous fighter, my business was based on my reputation. For some guys, it's better if they don't even know. They're just training hard and sleeping well, and then you tell 'em: 'the fight's today.' I didn't have time to think about it, to scenario the fight to death. When a fighter has too much time to think about it, he actually clutters his thoughts."

Mark recounts seeing this with the older Thai trainers, something I'd seen as well. "The retired champions, I'd see them drinking and smoking and not training. But they could take fights and stay so relaxed because they had so much experience. I saw one retired champ who was horribly out of shape take a big fight, and by the fifth round he was putting on an old-school clinic—spinning elbows, climbing up on the guy. I could relate to that now. If you got no pressure, nothing to lose, and you're mentally content, you can fight and not get tired, stay within your parameters.

"I learned a lot about the mental game from the Thais. I think the biggest thing about what they do is they're very proud of the art, of their camp. They have the utmost respect for muay Thai. It's really the one thing they claim as theirs. The only reason Thailand has always been free is that muay Thai has always been around to protect it. When you have something you hold dear, you consider sacred, it's harder to take it from you. For the kids who fight, it becomes about business much later on, but they always have that base pride to rely on."

*   *   *

On the other side of the country, at the Fairtex muay Thai gym in San Francisco, I spoke to an old-school Thai fighter named Jongsanan, the "Wooden Man." He'd earned that nickname because he took so much damage and never seemed hurt; when opponents kicked him he seemed made of wood. Jongsanan is a decent-sized Thai but still short, with a big round head, battered doughy face, and heavy scars over his eyes. He was smiling, enjoying himself, his mind sharp and his grasp of English good, even though his accent is thick, and he speaks in a soft Thai burble. His real name is Anucha Chaiyasen, "Noom" to his friends, but to me he was Jongsanan. He was a little bored with me, but still happy and pleasant with that natural Thai goodness and warmth that is so refreshing. He had been a two-time Lumpini champion and an ISKA welterweight champion, among other things. He was a Fairtex lifer, brought to San Francisco to help anchor the gym in America. He spoke quickly and laughed all the time at himself.

"I'm really quiet. I'm not mean or an asshole. I listen to my trainer. That's it. My trainer tells me one thing, I do one thing. If he tells me two things, I do two things." He grinned and shook his head. That's it. In Thailand, that's the mental game. It's not complicated.

"I am slow. In the gym they call me big head, balloon head. Twenty years ago in the camp they call me balloon, at Bang Pli." Bang Pli Fairtex was the same camp I had spent six months at, back in 2000.

"My first trainer, Molit, was the big trainer for me. He brought me up and took care of me. When I was at the top it was different. 'Jongsanan' becomes my style. 'Forward, don't show pain.'

"It all comes down to my trainer. If you don't listen to them you out. Because of gambling. They control you, to be wooden man. I don't want to be wooden man, I want to be a smart guy." Here he makes the arm gestures of a muay Thai fighter with a shifty, smooth style. "But my trainer control me, and Philip [the owner of the camp] behind me, too. He wants strong fighters, good fighters that are aggressive and strong. Every trainer has a different technique of looking at the body, to teach him how to be a forward fighter, or a technical fighter. Or fast fighter, or heavy punch, or leg kick, it depends on body style. I'm tall and lean, and I have 'big lung' *bod dee*—good stamina. They just see big lung. I can run with the top fighters, when I am young. I follow them in everything."

He's talking about the camp system in Thailand, a whole different universe. The fighters there are essentially chattel, property. They have no options, owned by the camp. If they want to leave and fight elsewhere, the new trainer or camp has to buy their contract. So you do what your corner says, what the boss says. It's what happens in the third world when you're poor—you do what you have to do to eat.

"Sometimes when they try to teach me smart things, I can't get it. I can only do one thing, keep coming forward. They try and teach me fake here, step back." He is laughing, short and quick, shaking his head. "I can't do it. That's why my trainer teach me the style of knee knee knee, come forward. I have to train very hard for that style, but I am healthy, lucky with that, fighting all the time. I come very fast, and I win first eight fights at Lumpini stadium. Then I lose one, then I win for another seven times or so, and always the same. First three rounds I get beat up, because I start slow. Techniques are not good, but I have good heart and I can take it. And now I am glad to beat them up, after they beat me first. After that punishment. So they call me 'Wooden Man.'

"I hate the balloon head nickname, so I don't say it when the newspaper ask," he said gleefully. But Jongsanan turns thoughtful about what having a nickname and public identity can do for a fighter.

"For me it was the same thing as 'Golden Boy.'" He was talking about Oscar de la Hoya, and Golden Boy Promotions.

SAM SHERIDAN

"It was his promotion name, and he has to represent it. It is a real thing for him. He has to be the Golden Boy. Rampage is the same, Quentin Jackson. The nickname and the personality in the ring have to mesh up. Even if you are a nice guy, in the ring you have to mesh with your promotional personality. They call me that way, I have to be that way, that's how I feel."

It goes back to what fighting is all about: honesty and identity. You have to know who you are. There is no dissembling about your character in the ring. There is *deception*—fighting involves faking one thing and doing another. As Randy Couture said, "No lies get told when you're in there." You can't lie about being in shape, about knowing the techniques, about being faster than him, about being stronger or tougher. The truth will out.

"You have to listen to the corner. Think of nothing, listen to my trainer and Philip. They control you to be that way, and the Thai fighter has to be like a robot. I fight you eye to eye, I see you. The cornerman, the third eye, he see everything, he see me and you. The corner change the game."

The reason for such strict controls over fighters? Jongsanan smiles at the innocence of my question, the naivete.

"Gambling. Ninety-five percent of fans are there for betting, to make money. The fan can make you fight different way. In the U.S. the fan come to support you, to see your skill, to see a show. Over there it's for betting, and it makes me upset. If muay Thai fighters in Thailand could get respect like here, it would be so good for the Thai boy. But in Thailand they can't afford the ticket unless for gambling to make the money back.

"If you love muay Thai here, you can be a good fighter. Here they respect you, and nobody will beat you up if you lose. You won't lose your home, your living, like in Thailand. Here they admire you even if you lose. Seventy-five percent of American fighters survive by themselves. They fire you if you aren't a good corner. Totally different in Thailand. In Thailand you have to do what corner say, you can't fight anywhere else.

44

If somebody else wants to train you he has to buy your contract out from me."

When you watch a muay Thai fight, you become aware of how important composure is. The Thais fight with epic, steely composure, never showing pain or emotion—unless it's to try and sway the judges. They act with their faces about how they feel the fight is going. It's almost like soccer players when teams try and draw a foul, or the B-movie acting in the NBA. I asked Jongsanan about it.

"Use face, it comes to the judge—you kick me hard, but I show it's okay, *maybelai* [the ubiquitous Thai word for "never mind"]. The judge say oh, he's okay. For the judge, for the system, for the crowd, for you, for the gambling guy."

"John" Wayne Parr is an Australian muay Thai legend, and he provided more insight into the Thai appreciation for composure. Wayne lived and fought in Thailand from 1996 to 2000, and has since continued his professional muay Thai career. He's been fighting the best in the world for nine years in Japanese megaevents such as the K-1 Dynamite show. In 1999 he was a rising star, featured in the first kickboxing magazine I ever saw, "on the beach" in Darwin, Australia. I remember the Thai publicity shots of him posing with six-guns, like a cowboy. That same magazine had the advertisement for the Fairtex muay Thai camp, which looked pretty good to me after sailing across the Pacific. He and I discovered each other on Myspace as I was finishing this book, and I asked him about the mental game he'd learned in Thailand.

"The first lesson I learned is never show any emotion while fighting," he wrote me from Australia. "And if you want respect from the Thai fans, you never give up until the final bell. I've seen some Thai boys fight their heart out, for four and a half rounds, getting a sound beating. Then, for last half of the the last round, they stopped fighting and waited till the clock ran out. When we got back to the camp the boys would cop an ear full from the trainers, till the point where they would start to cry. They would be ordered, even though they were busted up, to run and train the next day—because they didn't deserve a day off until they learned to fight till the end."

He continued, "If you fight with all your heart, take punishment, get cut yet still manage to wipe the blood out of your eye and keep walking forward, the Thais will accept you as a warrior. It might sound strange, but to have the respect of the Thais is just as important as a win, because they have a very high standard. If they give you the thumbs up you're halfway there to becoming a champion."

Wayne told stories of seeing other Westerners come in to Thailand to fight but quail at the first sight of their own blood. Muay Thai utilizes the elbows to attack, and the tip of the elbow can cut like a knife. Many foreigners would fold up their tents when they got cut, but not Wayne.

"I would rather go out with half my face missing, losing the fight, but still getting a pat on the back from the Thais. They would say, *Jai Dee,* or good heart. If you can prove yourself in Thailand, then once you come back home fighting other Westerners feels easy; you have already faced the scariest of scary. There is nothing that they can do that the Thais haven't done. I fought an English guy in 1998, he cut me five times in five rounds, I ended up with fifty-four stitches after the fight. Not once did I think about giving up; I kept walking forward, applying pressure. I lost the fight but even now I have people coming up to me, saying how they love to play that fight in front of their friends who have never seen muay Thai, to show them what being a warrior is all about."

Back in Boston, Mark and I talked about Thailand. Years ago, I spent six months training in Thailand, and by the end I felt the disconnect between Thai trainers and Western ones. It goes deeper than just language, although that's a big part of it. The foreigner coming in has a hard time understanding the system, who's in charge, what it all means. The Thai trainer can't easily communicate the more complex ideas of timing, breathing, or composure—

and they might not anyway. They train together in the ring but watch each other across a cultural chasm. I thought Mark would probably understand this as well as anyone. He speaks fluent Thai and has spent a good portion of his adult life in Thailand.

Mark muses aloud. "It was hard for me, figuring out what makes them tick. I watch Kru Yotong raise everybody, and he's watching to see who wants to be there. When two little kids argue, they get the gloves put on and go fight five rounds in the ring, with all the adults cheering like crazy. I realized what it's all about—it's ranking." Mark's face lights up with the remembered revelation.

"When the fighters eat, they eat in order—like a wolf pack. The alpha eats first, the omega eats last. The whole camp is like that. The champs go first, and the little kid who lost, he gets fed last and gets picked on for a few days. The fed stay fed. It's survival. A lot of those little kids, their parents couldn't afford them."

Mark develops this theme, and he's got a destination in sight. "Kru Yotong takes them in, they don't have anything else to fall back on. When you have nothing, and then you have a father figure or mentor, and food and training, you become connected to that person. I do the same thing here. After training we hang out, we eat together, our families know each other, they've all been to my house and I've been to theirs. *Camp means camp*—food, shelter, and fire."

Mark smiles when he says this, for he's revealed the secret.

"That sense of pride that comes from *camp,* that is really important. There are other factors that are important, too, that are tied to that, like honoring your traditions. Then comes the modern world, which is the business aspect, making money. If my students don't pay I can't run this camp. And finally, of course, there's the primal source in every fighter, gameness. Being cut out to do what you do. But the camp has room for everyone, guys who don't fight hold pads or find another way to fit in.

"I keep everyone so close to me, that's what makes me successful. They're part of a family. A lot of my students here have grown with me. It becomes a passion and makes them stronger. At the end of a hard training session, I have them all walk around with their hand up, because they're all winners and they're all MY winners."

He pauses, thinking long and hard.

"That's most of it, for a trainer. It's about building that trust. You don't marry someone you just met, right? The guys who are around long enough, they trust me because they see what I'm about, for the top guys and the amateurs. A trainer you don't respect and trust you can't learn from, so I have to maintain my integrity, you know?"

I asked Mark to elaborate on his game plans, on all the success he was having in the UFC. How was he going about it?

"That trust is crucial if you're going to have success with a game plan in a fight. Of course, the first thing you got to think about is: Can my fighter listen to a game plan? Can he execute? Or will he be too emotional? Emotional fighters are useless to give game plans to. So are amateurs, someone too inexperienced. They can't hear you, anyway. So with a guy like that, you don't even tell him what the game plan is. You just train him so that what he's doing is the game plan and he doesn't know it."

I think it was Cus D'Amato, the legendary boxing trainer, who said, "I get them to where they can't do it wrong even if they tried," meaning he would train his fighters to do the right thing until it was instinctual.

"But if a fighter can listen and stay composed, the first step is understanding the opponent. I don't watch tape over and over, I watch just enough to know what's happening. You have to go with your gut reaction, the first time you see the fight. Because the more you watch, the more you can convince yourself of something else. You clutter your mind. When I was a fighter, the more tape I watched, the more I'd be surprised by stuff." Mark breaks into a surprised voice, playing the confused fighter. "He didn't look like he had power but he hits hard! I never saw him throw a left lead kick but he's been doing it all night!" He laughs. "So I watch enough tape to get an understanding, then I shut it down.

"With MMA these days, everyone's traveling. So I find out where he's preparing, who's in his camp. Is he in Thailand? Or is he at Team Quest? If everyone at whatever camp he's at has a great single-leg takedown, we'll work on defending that.

"Always, there is the individual you've got. Like Kenny Florian, he doesn't do well if you overbuild his confidence. His brother helped me understand that. He relaxes too much. Jorge Rivera is similar, but he's also nervous, so I keep him relaxed, telling him 'you'll kill this guy' through training so he'll sleep well and train hard. But then right at the fight I'll start making him nervous, 'You better watch out for this guy he's really tough,' because Jorge needs that edge.

"I definitely watch the opponent and his trainer on their way into the cage. How smooth are they operating, how relaxed are they? Are they nervous? Where's the ice? Where's the mouth guard? Are they fumbling around? Well, if the captain of the ship is a nervous wreck, there's a problem on board. And the reverse is important. When I come in, it's like clockwork, everyone has a job, everything is on schedule. I keep it perfectly organized, like feng shui I know where everything is and everything is right. The fighter gets water the second he thinks of it, he gets his mouth guard the second the referee asks for it. He turns to me, and boom, I slide it in. If a trainer doesn't know something, or is nervous, it's the beginning of the end, because it will carry over into the fighter. When you see chaos in the locker room that's a bad sign.

"I still go to a lot of amateur muay Thai fights, and for a guy's first fight I just make sure he knows it's a sport. There are people here, this is a controlled environment, he's not gonna kill you with a knife! In fact, when it's over, you guys are going to be best friends for about a month." He laughs. "I've just seen it so many times. I tell my first timers, 'You may hate it or you may love it, but you'll learn something. It'll be a great experience.'"

That night we drove through the frozen streets in a caravan to Legal Seafood. I sat between Kenny, Mark, Patrick Cote (a top 185-pounder), and assorted guests. We all listened rapt to Marcus Davis, another UFC professional with a battered friendly face, tell truly terrifying ghost stories. As we ate I felt the warmth of camp all around me.

THE KING
OF SCRAMBLES

Marcelo Garcia (Courtesy: Marcelo Garcia)

If you continue this simple practice every day, you will obtain some wonderful power. Before you attain it, it is something wonderful, but after you attain it, it is nothing special.
　　　　　　　　　　　　　　　　　　　—Shunryu Suzuki

Mixed martial arts, the modern-day proving ground for hand-to-hand combat systems, introduced ground fighting into the collective conscious. Royce Gracie proved, beyond the shadow of a doubt, that fighters who couldn't fight on the ground were easy pickings for those who could. He used a family variant of the Japanese martial art *jujutsu,* called Brazilian (or Gracie) Jiu-Jitsu. What the world didn't know was that MMA fights had been taking place in front of massive crowds in Brazil for fifty years or more, under the catch-all name *vale tudo,* "anything goes." The Brazilians knew the value of ground fighting, and the Gracie family knew how to take a good striker out of his element. The philosophy has always been a part of fighting—take your enemy from where he wants to be, make him fight your fight.

　　　Simply put, jiu-jitsu is at the heart of MMA. The art today is essentially interchangeable with submission wrestling, or grappling. At this point it's semantics, although jiu-jitsu usually includes practice in the *gi*. The *gi* is the white judo kimono and is how jiu-jitsu was originally taught, but in MMA the rules have been changed so the *gi* is not allowed. Fighters learn a style they (inventively) call "no-*gi*."

No-*gi* is quite different than *gi*. The *gi* training utilizes the fabric—sleeves, collars, pant legs—to control the opponent, while no-*gi* is submission wrestling, with no fabric grabbing allowed. I personally don't like training in the *gi* because it negates all my natural advantages, strength and slipperiness and conditioning. And my first day in it, in Brazil, I tore my rotator cuff.

I am focused almost entirely on no-*gi*, and that's what I will primarily be referring to from now on. Modern MMA mixes the no-*gi* game with punching, kicking, elbows, and knees; grappling for MMA is quite different than grappling for no-*gi* competition, where there are a lot of slick moves that won't work if someone can punch you in the face.

A simple rule change to the sport-fight world—allowing fights to continue on the ground—opened up infinite possibilities. Ground fighting is part of the open-ended nature of MMA, a huge part of what makes the sport so exciting.

At its core, jiu-jitsu is about applying leverage, creating mismatches, through superior position. I find a way to isolate my opponent's arm and attack the elbow with my whole body. Maneuvers range from wrenching arms out of sockets to cutting off blood flow to the brain ("blood" chokes are allowed, while attacking the trachea is not—temporary versus permanent damage). Viable targets are almost any large joint, from ankles, elbows, and knees to shoulders and neck. The experienced ground fighter has thousands of ways to wrestle his way around an opponent (or to cause his opponent to fall into these positional "mismatches"). He doesn't match strength for strength, which is what collegiate or Greco-Roman wrestling is, and why wrestling is so exhausting. Though there's a deep technical game in wrestling, the end goal is physical domination through powering the shoulders to the mat (though there is a lot of wrestling in jiu-jitsu, and strength and size count for a lot). Jiu-jitsu's goal is harm, and it makes for a completely different game because there are ways to avoid harm without expending lots of energy.

A submission wrestler tries to choke or threaten such grievous injury that the opponent is forced to "tap" and concede victory (or accept the injury). This is the submission, and the beauty of it is that no real permanent damage is done as long as you submit. It's by far the most benign way to win an MMA fight. Orthodox wrestling has only a few ways to win—points or a pin—while jiu-jitsu has thousands and thousands of submissions and positions.

One of the fascinating things about jiu-jitsu or submission wrestling —or catch wrestling (for Josh Barnett, a modern MMA fighter who maintains that his submission wrestling is "catch-as-catch-can" dating back to Burns and Gotch)—is that it is almost wholly about knowledge. It is one of the few pure arts where a more knowledgeable small man can destroy bigger, stronger, faster men, as Royce Gracie has shown. Renzo Gracie (a younger cousin), one of the great practitioners in still fighting, said, "The beauty of the art is that it is so efficient. It molds itself to whomever is practicing. As long as you stick with it, you can be a good fighter. It's not only certain body types or athleticism. I've seen guys that couldn't run or jump for shit, with no coordination at all, become unbelievable champions because they dedicated themselves. The other fighting arts, even judo, wrestling, boxing, they all depend on athleticism. I train judo my whole life but the moment I get out of shape I lose everything. Boxing you need speed, even when you have a lot of experience. Jiu-jitsu is about dedication and knowledge."

Here's a basic primer on ground fighting (if you train, please skip ahead):

When two men are fighting they often fall to the ground. The Gracie theory is that 80 percent of fights end up on the ground;

certainly there is a very good chance it's going to happen, particularly if a fight goes past a few punches.

When you and I fight, you rush me and we tumble to the ground. There's an initial "scramble" for position, where nothing is set. The first basic truth of ground fighting is that if you can manage it you want to be on top. The guy on top is "winning"; he can punch harder (in MMA—not grappling) and his weight is working for him. The guy on the bottom is at a disadvantage if all other things are equal. However, rarely is everything else equal. Some fighters are extremely skilled at fighting from the bottom position. It all starts with the "guard." The guard's development as an offensive position—a place to attack *from*—revolutionized fighting.

The guard is basically the missionary position. If I'm on the bottom, I have my legs wrapped around your waist. This is the best position for me on the bottom, because it contains the other basic truth of ground fighting: it's all about the hips. Your hips (literally, and as an indicator of your body) need to be free to attack me, and you attack with your hips as much as anything. When you're watching two jiu-jitsu players fight, it's not what their hands are doing that matters. The real battle is in their legs and hips. So I'm underneath you, but you're "in my guard," that is, my legs are wrapped around your waist. If my legs are locked it's a "closed" guard. By controlling your hips I can greatly limit the damage you can do from the top, and I can set up all kinds of submission attempts from the bottom, as well as sweeps in which I reverse the position, "sweep" you over, and end up on top. I have all four of my limbs against your two. Animals do it—watch the bears fight in the Werner Herzog documentary *Grizzly Man*; it's an MMA clinic (with biting).

Jiu-jitsu has a progression of positions. The top guy, you, works to improve his position to facilitate his attacks. When you're in my closed guard, there are not a lot of submissions you can attempt on me, and I can control your posture so you can't punch me too much or too hard. So you work to "pass" my guard—to get your legs around mine, to get your hips free so you can set up the leverage mismatches. If you pass one leg you're in my "half-guard." Now, I still have both my legs wrapped around one of yours, and partial control of your hips, but it's generally not as safe for me. You have a lot more submissions, and it's easier for you to punch me. In strict submission wrestling, half-guard is very effective for the bottom man, but in MMA, where the guy on the bottom can be eating punches, it's more dangerous. You throw some punches, drop an elbow in my face—but that's not the point. The point is you freeing that leg; the real battle is you getting your hips free. Now you pass to "side control." You free your remaining trapped leg.

You've got your hips and legs free and off to the side of me, at 90 degrees, often chest on chest. Now I'm really starting to be in trouble. Side control is a very dominant position for you. I'm desperate to get back to guard or half-guard, to get my legs back around your hips, to get some control back.

From side control there are a lot of submissions and attacking options for you and basically none for me. This is also a stable spot; it's hard to get you off. From here, you might go to "mount," which is basically guard in reverse. This time you have your legs on top of my hips, and usually you're sitting on my chest with your knees up under my armpits and raining down punches—think "bully in grade school" position. This is obviously a very dominant position for you, although it's a little less stable. I have a better chance of sweeping you and reversing things from here than I did from side control.

The final step is if I turn over to avoid damage and you "take my back." You climb onto my back, your chest on my back, and attack me from there. There are hundreds of other ways to take my back, from all kinds of other positions. The back is perhaps the most dominant position in MMA, but only if you get your "hooks" in, meaning you get your legs wrapped around my waist from the back so you can cling to me and control my hips and match my movements to stay on my back. Otherwise, I'll turn and get you off, then you'll be on your back and I'll end up in *your* guard. So as you take my back it's critical to get your hooks in, and from there you usually start working the choke. Fighters have gotten a lot better at defending their backs, so whereas it used to be the end now it's not always such a sure thing.

That's basically the progression of position in jiu-jitsu and ground fighting in MMA (with apologies to all those who know the game; I know there's a lot I left out, but I'm trying to keep this basic). Guard to half-guard to side control to mount to the back. Of course, there are hundreds of variations and hundreds of ways to get to any of these positions, and there are ways to skip steps and go right from guard to mount, for example. There are many different styles of guard, with names such as "butter-fly" and "rubber" and "x-guard." There are countless positions for the hands and arms, underhooks and overhooks, and arm drags and so forth. It is this immense variety that gives jiu-jitsu and ground fighting artistic depth. It's a dialogue between minds, bodies meshed and communicating in a subtle, endless game— a game fueled by a desperate life-and-death urgency, where joints get smashed and fighters choked unconscious.

The ground game jiu-jitsu still seems more mysterious to me than stand-up fighting (punching and kicking, range and footwork). I understand what I don't understand in stand-up fighting, whereas watching high-level jiu-jitsu I often don't even know what questions to ask. I'm getting better, although my training is still interrupted by my ribs popping out with mind-numbing regularity (a recurring injury).

When I first started studying jiu-jitsu, the first thought in my mind was, *wow this is just like chess*. And it is, in a sense, because chess also has a strong positional component. In chess, you understand the board, take a strong position, and good things happen. You don't necessarily see the way you're going to win, but with a dominant position you start to force your opponent to do things like take bad positions until you capture material. In the beginning you do good things, such as occupying the center of the board, and you position your pieces where they have open files to attack. You *develop* with *tempo,* you improve your position and force him to retreat, which builds in a time advantage for you that will show up later, in chances to take pieces.

Jiu-jitsu (and fighting in general) has this element; you may not be sure what submission you'll get, but getting into a dominant position is a major step toward winning. And in MMA position is its own reward, because the better your position, the more effectively you can punch and elbow and soften up your opponent.

What I've realized since then is that jiu-jitsu differs from chess in major ways. There is a huge physical component, where strength and speed and conditioning matter, but muscle memory (not a part of chess) plays a titanic role. Moving through positions happens too fast to think. Your body has to have learned what to do, how to protect your arms, how to shift weight to avoid a sweep. In order to be good, you need to log in the mat time, thousands and thousands of hours of just getting beat on by better guys. As Pat Miletich says, "You gotta take a lot of beatings."

Still, there are some practitioners who are so good, so dominant, that it seems they must be doing something different. One of the most recent examples is Marcelo Garcia.

The image that springs to mind is the grainy footage of the Abu Dhabi Combat Club (ADCC) Submission Wrestling World Championship in '03, the biggest submission grappling tournament in the world. The tourney, usually just called Abu Dhabi, was created by Sheikh Tahnoon bin Zayed Al Nayan, son of a former UAE president. He was a combat enthusiast and friend of the Gracies. With a love of grappling and some money he started a championship in Abu Dhabi, and to this day it is the one contest where pure grapplers can make some money.

Abu Dhabi happens every two years. Now, due to its size, popularity, and visa issues, it usually takes place in the United States or Brazil. In terms of submission wrestling, it's the cream of the crop, extremely rarefied air.

In '03 Marcelo Garcia appeared out of nowhere to blitz his weight class (66–76 kg). He was awarded Most Technical Fighter and made it to the second round in the Absolute, where fighters from all weight classes can compete. Marcelo's a small guy with a friendly face, an ordinary physique, and a serious look in his eye. At Abu Dhabi, he was like a killer spider monkey, swarming all over these guys, making the best submission wrestlers in the world look helpless. In 2005 and 2007, he not only won his division but placed second and third, respectively, in the Absolute division. He was competing with the best heavyweights, guys fifty or seventy pounds heavier than himself. Go YouTube Marcelo Garcia right now and come back.

Mike Ciesnolevicz, a 205-pound fighter at Pat Miletich's gym in Iowa and one of the better grapplers at the camp, remembers the first time he rolled with Marcelo. He'd seen the Abu Dhabi footage and tracked Marcelo down to a seminar. This was back in 2004, just as Marcelo was appearing on everyone's radar. Mike recalls with a deep and offended sense of shock how quickly Marcelo forced him to tap out. Mike C is a stud on the ground; he's a high-level grappler who rolls with the toughest guys and rarely gets tapped. Marcelo tapped him in fifteen seconds. Then he did it again, a minute later, *with the same move*. It's the kind of thing that Mike does to me, a smaller guy with about a year of on-and-off grappling experience. Nobody, but nobody, does that to Mike. He laughs about it. "I didn't know there was someone out there who was that good at jiu-jitsu. I told Charles McCarthy, Rory Singer, all these UFC guys about him and they were skeptical. But now they've all trained with him and they all agree that he's amazing." Mike laughed some more.

"First thing they all said, 'I've never been treated like that on the mat.' He's not a normal black belt. I can hold my own with most normal black belts. He's on a different level." It was Mike C who made me look harder at Marcelo.

Marcelo isn't using some secret ninjutsu technique—he's just doing things so quickly, so well, and so far in advance of his opponents that he makes them look stupid. He just seems to have more options, as if everybody else has learned only a limited form of what he does.

So I went down to Florida to pick Marcelo's brain. How does Marcelo Garcia think about jiu-jitsu? He'd recently moved there and was training at American Top Team, under the watchful eye of Ricardo Liborio.

American Top Team (ATT) is probably the biggest MMA gym in the United States at the moment, with the most top-level pros. It's the brainchild of Ricardo Liborio, who was a member of the mythic Carlson Gracie Team and a founding partner of the groundbreaking Brazilian Top Team. Liborio is also a name in the world of jiu-jitsu; some people say that he has the best game in the world, but his days of competing are long behind him. Now he's the spark plug and linchpin for ATT.

I'd met Liborio briefly in Brazil. He'd understood what I was doing instantly (more so than most of the Brazilians), and he gave me his number and invited me down to ATT. He's an extremely pleasant and warm guy. He'd be the perfect foil to my understanding of high-level jiu-jitsu and Marcelo.

I flew into Fort Lauderdale, Florida, and rented a car. ATT was in Coconut Creek, a little north of Lauderdale, lost down into the flatlands. I drove through the press of humidity, the flat swelter of the tropics, and the sense of some vast inland mangrove swamp somewhere outside the strip malls. You can't see much landscape in this part of Florida, it's so flat; there's not much except the stormy clouds, epic and tortured mother-of-pearl cumulus over a blazing pastel blue and red sky.

When I walked into American Top Team a vast, cavernous twenty-thousand-square-foot MMA dream gym, the first person I met was "Chainsaw" Charles McCarthy.

Charles was a fighter who'd been on the Spike TV reality show *The Ultimate Fighter* (a guarantee of some celebrity) and who fought in the UFC. He was a friend of Mike C, and he had liked my first book, which was cool. If Mike C vouched for him I knew he must be okay and Charles felt the same way about me.

Charles is a square-jawed, black-haired young guy who seems a little short to fight at 185 but he actually has a big cut to get there—he's a very dense dude, a brown belt in jiu-jitsu and a smooth ground fighter.

Jiu-jitsu players don't get belts for free. You have to earn them in a very strict sense and be able to do a lot of things to advance, including compete. A black belt may take ten years of study.

And *who* you get your belt from matters—lineage is very important in jiu-jitsu. So teachers are stingy, especially with black belts, because they will be judged by the caliber of their students. A brown belt is a very high level of jiu-jitsu. Charles runs his own school and manages fighters, already at twenty-eight on the backside of things, thinking more about the future.

I told him about the new book and what I was here to do. I asked him to describe Liborio's game to me. He chuckled. "Rolling with Liborio? You just get flattened. He's so strong, he's unstoppable. It's a methodical flattening. You know it's coming but you can't stop it, because he's more technical *and* much stronger than you." He laughed again, "It's like being pancaked by a steamroller. The pavement thinks it's pretty tough, but as soon as the steamroller comes through it gets flattened. It's like rolling with your dad when you're eight years old. He's a total nightmare, and he's not even going full speed. It must be kind of awful to be Liborio, because no one can compete with him." Charles grew wistful. "It has to lose a little something, it has to get pretty boring."

Ricardo Liborio is a burly, powerful man, with no neck and massive rounded shoulders, the classic build for jiu-jitsu. With a distinguished full head of gray hair and a cherubic face with bright eyes, Liborio is always smiling. He's gleefully welcoming, almost childlike, and he grabs me with a firm hug.

Over the next week we repeatedly went out to lunch or dinner, and he had no qualms about meeting me every day and chatting for hours, even though the demands on his time were immense.

He is sure of his "recipe," his method of building an MMA team. "You have to be open-minded," he said, "and understand that everybody is different. But there is a recipe, at the same time. You gotta train hard, bring the right people in and do what it takes to move to the next level. It's about understanding the game. You can get your ass kicked in one fight, and maybe he's better or maybe it's just his day, he's got the right game on the right day, and he matches up with you. But you can improve your game, take it further and jump to the next level."

He'd smile at me with tired eyes over his food late at night, or over lunch, and answer the phone and talk to his nanny. He was juggling a gym full of egos, running a business, and caring for a sick infant daughter, and he was wearing a little thin around the edges. But his enthusiasm never flagged, not for a moment.

Liborio told me stories of when he started jiu-jitsu, back in the early 1980s, when he was fifteen. He was a part of the formative years of the sport, when all the icons of today were young and just finding the gym: Murilo Bustamente was a purple belt, Wallid Ismail, Bebel, Zé Mario Sperry, Amáury Bitteti was just a kid. Liborio was incredulous when he said, "Everybody was so young at the time."

"I had a gift for it, I liked it and I got my blue belt in two months. As I progressed I quickly started teaching, too, and I realized that not everything I do is best for my students. The game varies body to body, and you got to understand that."

Liborio spoke about Carlson Gracie and his MMA team, probably the most important MMA team of all time. Carlson passed away in 2006, but I had met him in Rio and even gone to cockfights with him. Scotty Nelson, owner of OntheMat.com and a lifelong jiu-jitsu enthusiast, had allowed me tag along when he went to private parties with Carlson. "Carlson really was the original fighter who adapted jiu-jitsu for MMA. He had his power game, and he's said many times 'never train jiu-jitsu that doesn't work no-*gi*, make sure it works both ways,'" Scotty said. This is something that Marcelo also does, as when he tore through his first Abu Dhabi he'd been training mostly *gi*.

Scotty, Carlson, and I had been watching a UFC (with a whole family of old-time jiu-jitsu players around us) and Carlson was critical of Pe De Pano's game, because he was doing things that were *gi*-related, in the UFC, and getting stuffed, while BJ Penn's game was working beautifully. Carlson felt strongly that training instincts to work only in a sport setting was a mistake; you had to train all the time for the fight, for self-defense. Carlson's legendary team had split up long ago, scattered to the winds, and Liborio was part of that diaspora.

Liborio talks about the cultural differences. In Brazil, there is a lot of training but less instruction. What he means by "training" is synonymous with "rolling" or "sparring," when the guys just roll hard with each other, looking for a submission. This is a huge part of learning jiu-jitsu, developing those instincts through struggle. Training against real resistance is essential to learning about the intensity and pace of a real fight. This idea, called *randori* in traditional Japanese martial arts and promulgated by Jigoro Kano (the founder of modern judo), is the beating heart of jiu-jitsu. You need to develop a feel for what a fight is like, the intensity of the moves, how desperation fuels the struggle.

For the same reasons it is beneficial, just rolling can be limiting; sometimes you end up in survival mode, doing the same things over and over, sticking to your few bread-and-butter techniques. This trap can be even worse with the pro fighters, who often think they've had enough instruction and just want to train. Jiu-jitsu players, probably because of the Brazilian-to-English transition, use "train" like boxers use the word "work"—they use it for everything.

Liborio makes sure that his pro fighters get instruction as well as training every day. "For the good guys, the black belts, it's just as important—they need the resources."

We talked at length about "Minotauro," Rodrigo Nogueira, the Brazilian Top Team fighter with whom I'd gone to Japan for the Pride Fighting Championship four years ago. Rodrigo had just captured the UFC interim heavyweight belt from Tim Sylvia and was the first fighter ever to have had both the UFC and Pride heavyweight belts. Liborio knew him well, had trained him for fights, and had interesting insight into Rodrigo.

"He was born with some kind of slow nerves, man," Liborio said with his Cheshire cat grin. "He doesn't get frustrated when he gets beat up. Frustration can take your stamina, your appetite for winning. You get angry at yourself, not the guy beating you. Not Rodrigo. He often gets his ass kicked in the first round and most people would think, 'What do I have to do different?' but he just waits calmly for his chances. People say he starts slow, but he starts at the same speed he's going to run all through the fight. He keeps going at the same level, and by the end he's going faster than the other guy, who gets tired."

Liborio develops his point emphatically, jabbing at me with a thick finger. "You have to unnerstan' you *can* lose. Somebody can beat your ass; but you can overcome, don't get frustrated. You can't be a quitter, you have to understand loss, that you *can* lose—it's not your time, it's not your day. Just because you lose doesn't make you a loser. It's not the same fight every time. One day the guy was so powerful, but maybe he's not doing everything right and he gives you a chance to be better than him. But you can't take it, for whatever reason. But next time? Be humble enough to understand it's not the same fight every time. Most guys will give you a chance if you don't gas out or emotionally break."

He paused and looked around and thought about how he was going to convince me of the importance of this idea.

"Everyone is the same for the first two minutes, everyone has a chance to win, but after that you start to separate physically and technically."

He ponders the point, methodically. "You have to have the fire to develop, to find other ways to win. You can really change your game if you improve in certain ways. You have to keep working hard, withstand the *presion,* unnerstan'? The pressure. If you can resist it, and not get frustrated, you'll step up eventually. One day you'll just start beating other guys, some move you could never do, one day you'll be able to do it."

Sean Williams, a Renzo Gracie black belt (you see the lineage qualifier? He's not just a black belt, he's a *Renzo Gracie* black belt; he trained extensively with the great man) who teaches in Hollywood, California, once told me a story of how when he was a purple belt he'd broken his jaw. It had forced him to the sidelines for two months. "As I was recovering I watched a lot of tape, and when I came back the other purple belts who'd been giving me problems were suddenly easy for me." It seems to be the consensus—if you keep at it, one day you make a breakthrough.

I asked Liborio what he thought of Marcelo's game. The "game" in jiu-jitsu is someone's style, and it's a reflection of their environment, their teachers, their body type, and their personality. It's as much an artistic expression as an athletic one.

Marcelo had recently moved down from New York, and Liborio had been watching him train. "Marcelo understands balance well," Liborio said. "He can get you off balance very easily.

He gets you to shift your weight around. The way he moves his hips, I'm telling you, you can put a three-hundred-pound guy on him and he'll find a way to move his hips. He's got speed, but it's not 'Oh wow' speed, it's just the way he moves, and he has a lot of knowledge. He researches the position and there's no wall for him—that I can't get there." Liborio is talking about mental barriers, that Marcelo doesn't think of certain positions as static, or unwinnable. He has the creativity to look for new ways to "get to" good positions from the bad.

"How does that process happen? How do you get to where you can think three or four moves ahead of everyone?" I asked him. I remembered something Chainsaw Charles had said about rolling with Liborio: he knows what you're going to do next before YOU even know what you're going to do next.

Liborio spread his arms wide and smiled. "It's just knowledge man. It's the same for everyone. You go over the basics and pretty soon you're dreaming about it like everyone else. Be honest and humble enough to learn from everybody."

He thought about it for a while. "With jiu-jitsu, you really don't know what he's thinking, but you feel how he's reacting. I can feel when he wants to change the game and I stop it and change it another way. It's one of the few fighting sports you can do with your eyes closed, because it's about feel.

"You have to stop and understand, to listen to the position or you'll miss an opportunity. Guys don't listen to teachers they don't like, or don't respect, but you gotta be open if you want to be the best. As soon as you close yourself off you start to lose." That sentiment would be repeated, almost word for word, by every serious jiu-jitsu practitioner I talked to.

Liborio handles all aspects of running American Top Team, and he's constantly revising his theories on the team and leadership.

"The leader has to be open, too," he said. "He has to be searching, too, he can't say 'Oh, I know what everything is already.' You have to be honest and humble enough to ask how different things go, and learn from everybody, because if you keep your eyes screwed shut and if you think you know everything you'll start losing. I believe in hard training, in the recipe. You have to respect your limits but unnerstan' you're an athlete and push on them. You WILL get your ass kicked. You WILL get tired, but eventually you'll be kicking ass.

"I don't think I was the best fighter, but I can be the best teacher. Because I really care about the guys, all my guys. I care what happens."

Just watching Liborio around the gym you can see that nearly everyone feels they have a special relationship with him (me included). He takes the time to have a few private words with everybody, in particular with every single little kid in there. Liborio spends time down on their level, in their private world.

I know from being a student, and the son of educators, that when a teacher is genuinely invested in you—when a teacher actually cares—you can tell, and it makes a big difference. My mother in particular had taught at a variety of institutions, from New England colleges to Indian reservations in New Mexico, and she had come to the conclusion that basically the best thing you can do is love and show unconditional interest—it was the only real way to connect to students. As a student, you can feel it even if you never put a name to it.

"I've been on different teams. I can remember the struggle to get attention on Carlson Gracie's team—it's impossible for one man, with so many good guys, to pay attention to everyone. So now I am just trying to bring in more coaches. You have to put the money back into the team, and the team has to keep growing or they'll leave.

"You need someone in charge, though, because that's the big problem with pro fighters, the egos. When they reach a certain level, with the money and the spotlight, they need a leader. And they need to respect the leader and understand the program."

*   *   *

The question of ego was one that I had discussed at length with Eddie Bravo, a jiu-jitsu instructor in Hollywood who developed an innovative guard style and was a commentator at the UFC. Eddie is uniquely positioned in the sport; because of his commentating he was always rubbing elbows with the best fighters in the business. And watching them, carefully.

"Ego is a big reason that guys stop advancing in the sport," Eddie said. "Because in jiu-jitsu it feels so bad when you tap. You got killed. Jiu-jitsu is great because it filters out the assholes who can't control their egos, the douche bags who can't handle showing physical inferiority. But for these fighters, once they get famous, they can't just roll, everyone wants to tap them. The famous guys start limiting their training. It's very hard to take risks to get tapped when you get famous. So they stop progressing.

"Everybody has ego. I have it, too. But you have to be the black belt and the ego has to be the blue belt—you have to be controlling it. I don't like tapping. I'm teaching my students how to beat me and they are dying to do it, even though they respect me. But I'll roll with everybody, and I get tapped by my students. I got some vicious dogs in here. But you can't be one of those instructors who thinks it's bad business to show weakness so they stop rolling. I'm selling evolution. You grow or you die."

Eddie's been criticized for his style, which he touts as the future of no-gi, as having ways to be beaten. Eddie just laughs about it. "Of course, nothing's a hundred percent. Every style has a counter. But it's good to have options. Rubber guard [Eddie's style] doesn't work every time. It's like a punch combination that doesn't work—you don't abandon it. Go back to it. Set it up differently."

The only reliable indicator of future success in MMA has always been the quality of training partners. You needed good guys around you to perform at a high level. You need killers "in the room," as Gable would have it. The best fighters in MMA nearly always come from the best camps, drawn together to push each other. Liborio was well aware of it.

"The victory is never yours, it's the teams, it's everybody. The boxing coach, the training partners, the guy who sets up the training schedules and buys the tickets. It helps to have a big gym, with a lot of big name fighters, because you can get them fights on many cards. I can say to promoters if you want Jeff Monson you need this guy on the undercard."

On our last day together, Liborio said something that really stuck with me.

"Maturity is a big part of success in fighting, because it means you understand the game—that losing is part of the game. It doesn't mean to let yourself get conquered, but to know that you can win again, at the right time you can be great. The key to doing well in competition is to *accept*." Liborio holds the word reverentially in his mouth, emphasizing with his face and body. "*Accept* you can lose, you can not perform. Take this big bag of rocks out of your backpack, take the pressure off, and you'll do better. Once you understand that, man, you can do well."

At the ATT gym I rolled with Chainsaw Charles and had the familiar feeling of helplessness. You can feel when the guy you're rolling with is too good for you to threaten, and vice versa. I held my own for a while, but when he wanted to he took me out of my depth, into places where my knowledge was surfeit. Do I grab that ankle? Do I make space with my shoulder? He tapped me pretty quickly. And then I watch him with Liborio, and Liborio is moving at maybe half speed and he's dominating and frustrating Charles. I'm used to the feeling, but for good grapplers to run into great ones is particularly frustrating and hard on the ego. Charles has a bread-and-butter move that works on everyone but, when he tries it on Liborio, Liborio takes his back, time and again. The deeper knowledge leads to far deeper anticipation. Liborio knows where Charles is going and lets him go there, but he makes it much worse for him when he gets there. Charles's sense of his ability is a little offended, but he just shakes his head and asks Liborio about it at length.

Liborio discusses the problems with favorite moves. "Often you have a guy, and he does something that's very consistent. He has one great takedown that he always does and he gets every-body with it. In his gym. In a different environment, a new, bigger gym, where he can't take guys down with it, he breaks mentally. In a fight it's just like that."

Liborio went on to the flip side of the problem. "You can be in a fight and you get a chance for an armbar. Now, the guys you train with are all good black belts and they never give you the armbar, you never get it, but you can't skip drilling the armbar because you might get it in a fight. It has to be in the arsenal."

Marcelo Garcia is the latest incarnation of the iconic martial art-ist, the smaller, unassuming, nondescript man who comes out of nowhere to defeat his opponents with ease. I watched him roll with a former judo Olympian who's built like a bodybuilder and must weigh more than two hundred pounds. The judo guy spent the whole five minutes running for his life, standing up and leaping out of reach, backing off, playing like he was going to engage but never engaging. It's the only way to survive with Marcelo.

As with the movie *Ali,* about the greatest boxer of all time, Muhammad Ali, there's something lacking in writing about Marcelo Garcia. The fictional film with Will Smith playing Ali was good, until the fights start—then it falls apart. Because the whole point of Ali was the way he fought, the way he moved. That a big man could be so graceful, so fluid—it's entrancing to watch. It's beau-tiful to watch him fight. I could watch Ali shadowbox for an hour. I often thought they should have just cut to real fight footage in the movie, because Ali as a myth and a man doesn't really make any sense unless you watch him move, unless you see him fight.

Marcelo is something like that. You have to watch him roll to appreciate him. I'm not saying he's some mysterious Jedi knight who does magical things—although at times it appears that way. Like all great jiu-jitsu players, Marcelo does the basic things extremely well, nearly unstoppably. He does the basic things to the best guys in the world. He took Renzo Gracie's back for ten minutes in Abu Dhabi—something you wouldn't have thought possible.

I remembered what Mike C had said about Marcelo, the excited look in his eyes when I pressed him about it.

"He's all he's cracked up to be. I never had a chance. It was embarrassing because a lot of people at the seminar were watching, and they knew I fought in the IFL. Then I watched him do the same thing to everyone else. You couldn't tell who was a white belt and who was a black belt—he made everybody look like a beginner."

I asked Mike to analyze Marcelo's game as best he could. Mike thought about it, and then he slowly answered, "He's so dedicated. He can think so far ahead and he never settles into a position. He's always moving on you, forcing you into transitions. People don't realize you have to be in great shape to keep up with him on the mat, and he'll run you out of gas in a minute. People are used to getting into a position and sort of thinking, like closed guard or half-guard. But Marcelo is gone, he's attacking, and by the time you get there it's too late. He's under you sweeping, he's arm dragging, he's x-guard sweeping you. He never stops. I was waiting for my chance to try something. He's a nightmare—you have to keep up his pace to even have a chance."

One of the few things I had learned for my no-gi game was that conditioning could make up for a lot. Most of the guys I roll with are much better than me, but sometimes I can just keep moving, squirming and scrambling, and make things difficult for good guys. Especially in a bad position you have to become a perpetual motion machine.

"He started out in '03 with arm drags and x-guard sweeps, and he put them on the map, he dominated with those. Now people start figuring that out, he comes along and he's hitting crazy guillotines from every position. He has a whole series of back attacks. I've been following his DVD series. I've got all four sets."

Mike is talking about the common practice of famous guys putting together instructional DVDs as a way of making money. It's the old-school way to learn MMA, to buy DVDs and study your heroes, to go to seminars.

"While you're learning what he's BEEN doing, the old stuff, he's pulling out new stuff. Stuff people haven't seen, now he's got so many ways to get an omoplata and a guillotine and a crucifix, they are the big things his latest set focused on. There were three or four DVDs on the omoplata alone, I didn't realize there were so many variations. He's revolutionized different positions. While you're trying to figure out what he did, he's moved on to two and three more positions. He had everything mapped out in his head already.

"Last time I rolled with him, it was all new crazy shit I'd never seen. He tapped me three times with the same move, and I can't even figure out what it was. I thought it was a fluke at first. Then I saw some pictures, and he taught it the next day at the seminar: an omoplata with one leg to finish, the monoplata. I knew what it was and thought, Oh he's not getting me with this, so I countered but he shifted to a variation of the triangle armbar, and it was crazy. I had nowhere to go. Now I do it at our gym and blow people's minds. They make me show them what it was, because it's a wild thing. And I'd watched all his DVDs and his matches and never seen it.

"He's not strong or superfast—he's got solid athleticism in all areas. His mind is better. He causes scrambles, but it's all calculated, his mind moves so fast he KNOWS what you're going to try and do. He knows your options. He's a solid athlete, but its not that. He causes scrambles and causes you to think when he already knows what's going on. You're moving so fast without thinking that you walk right into stuff. He caught me with something three times and I should have figured it out. But he makes everything happen so fast, from different angles and different positions. You don't figure it's the same move. You think you're doing good and then you're tapping. There were times when he had me in stuff and I was still fighting—I didn't even realize he had me. I didn't know I was in a submission. He was just holding me."

It all makes Mike laugh.

"I wouldn't have thought anybody his size could tap me the way he taps me. The highlight of me rolling with him was I almost got hold of his leg and put his back on the ground." Mike laughed again. "I almost got to half-guard. He's like a ball, when you try to put him on his back, he never settles for a position. He's always got his legs in, elevating, working under you. I've never seen him in closed guard looking for something. He's always moving, causing scrambles. He's the king of scrambles."

Marcelo is also known as not only the nicest guy in the game, but he is jokingly referred to as maybe the nicest guy on earth. So many fighters and jiu-jitsu guys I talked to confided in me that Marcelo was their best friend that it became comical. Everybody is his best friend. From the first time I met him he lived up to that billing, smiling, gracious, warm, and sincerely interested in what I was trying to do. He's got a round face, wreathed in smiles, and narrow eyes.

I am a little in awe of Marcelo, and some of that admittedly comes from my inexperience. I'm a low-level grappler and when I see what he does to the high-level guys I find it a little incredible.

So here I was, finally sitting down to lunch with Marcelo, and as we started talking he wanted to make one thing very clear in his thick Brazilian accent: he's not so special.

"Why do I beat a lot of people? Because I love it so much, that's why. Everything about jiu-jitsu, I love it—the school, the mat, the ring. I always believe that. Maybe I am not better than my opponent, but I know for sure I love my training more." He smiled at me. It was all so simple. The birds chirping, the sun shining down around us in suburban Florida, Marcelo beaming at me.

Thanks a lot, Marcelo, I thought. That's a big help in trying to understand your thought process. It was funny how hard it was to get these guys to talk about how they *think.* While many will admit that the great jiu-jitsu players do think about jiu-jitsu differently, they get resistant when you try to quantify that.

I'd asked Scotty Nelson about it; Scotty had been a white belt with BJ Penn back at Ralph Gracie's gym. "Do some guys think about jiu-jitsu differently than you and me?"

"Absolutely," he'd replied. "All the top guys think about it differently. I was hanging out with Nino Schembri. He was the guy, back in the day, submitting everybody. I asked Nino, 'How did you get good at submissions from all these different positions?' He said he looked at all the bad positions, all the spots where he wasn't strong, and tried to figure out a submission from there. He doesn't fight to get into the right position—he learns and practices submissions from positions he's uncomfortable in. Nino said, 'I'll never be the best wrestler, I don't want to be, but I figured out all the takedowns and have a way to flow into a submission. Off a double leg, I look for the triangle. Off the single leg, omoplata. If he goes for a high crotch, I dive over for a crucifix. I take what they give me and make a strong position out of a weak one.'"

Maybe more revealing is the level of dedication that Nino showed, the clinical, thoughtful way of thinking about jiu-jitsu, the depth of his study. It's that level of commitment that is distinct.

I found that pattern repeated. Many good jiu-jitsu players will just train and because they know enough to beat most people they stop studying and learning. The great ones, though, are fanatical students, analyzing positions and all the tiny adjustments that make a position or a sweep work. The difference between a regular student of jiu-jitsu and the great players is the dedication to studying the game. Sean Williams, who got his black belt in four years from Renzo despite being sidelined for months with injuries, would fill notebooks after every training session, writing down everything he could think of. BJ Penn, the so called prodigy, who some think of as a mysterious genius, is the same way. The stories about him from his early days at Ralph Gracie's Academy are all about his fanatical drilling of small positional changes. BJ would laugh about those days and talk about how jiu-jitsu invaded his dreams and daydreams, in the shower, biking home, lying in bed. All the great players talk about it, how it becomes an obsession.

I pressed on with Marcelo. We started talking about where he came from, Minas Gerais, a big inland state in Brazil. Marcelo was from a remote town and, like many in Brazil, he started young in judo. Then he saw his first videotapes of the UFC. "I thought, I wanna do this," he said. Marcelo found his first school and it was an hour and a half by bus away from his home. He was fourteen and could make it only two or three times a week. "You can always train jiu-jitsu if you want to bad enough," he said. Where he lived there was only a small university and a few options—his father was a retired banker, his mother worked at home. He didn't have the money to go elsewhere to study. But Marcelo realized he could make jiu-jitsu his profession. "I just enjoy it so much. I hope I can make enough to live off it someday. But I decide to make it my life."

In his off days, he would just wait and think about the next time he'd get to go train. "I loved the energy, of matching with each other. I loved the way I felt after training, that I'd done my job today. And after a few weeks I realized I could do this forever. I started with four friends, and I was the biggest one—I grew up early—but I was the worst one. The worst one of my friends. I wasn't a natural, but even then I enjoyed it so much, and I kept making the long journey. After two months one friend dropped out, and I just kept improving. There was one guy who was a man, and he used to beat me up, but then he stopped for five months, and when he came back I could control him. I had proof that I was getting better. I wasn't a good student, and even now I never say I am better than anybody, but I know I love jiu-jitsu more than anybody. I love the energy and that it gets deeper the more you study."

Inwardly, I sigh. No silver bullet. "Is it just that you know more?" I asked him. "Sweeps, holds, counters . . . ?"

Marcelo's eyes lit up at "counters." He liked that one. "I think I have a lot of counters, unnerstan'? I try to make him go into the position I want. I study a lot. I try not to make any mistakes, I try to be perfect, and I have a little more knowledge than most. It's something I think about, how to get him to put his hand there or his leg where I need it.

"Guys who face me, when they believe they can win, and when they are strong and come hard, that's tougher. When they are tentative, or have too many strategies, when they try to beat me in my game . . ." Here he grins and his face lights up. "That's not gonna work, guys. Of course I get caught sometimes, but most of the time I can handle it.

"I'm always thinking when I'm rolling, and sometimes the guy can't follow my pace and lets me get too far. When it goes too fast, then it's just reaction. You have to train hard for that, train all the time."

When Marcelo was sixteen, his training wasn't hard enough to satisfy him. He felt stifled by the future in his small town, the long commute limiting his training to three times a week. At a competition a teacher named Paulo Cezar invited him to move to a nearby city and train at his school. "I asked my mom, and she was shocked but she let me move if I finished school there. So two months later I moved and started studying there."

Marcelo's jiu-jitsu training began in earnest. He loved the gym and the teacher, even though the teacher was just a brown belt. There were a lot of people around to train with and Marcelo trained three or four times a day for three years straight. When he started with Cezar, he was living on the mats, sleeping in the gym at night—a common enough occurrence in Brazil for the young, poor, and dedicated. Eventually he was given a small room off the gym, which he shared with a roommate. Over the next few years Marcelo met his wife, got his brown belt, and moved to São Paulo, where he started training with Fabio Gurgel, an elite-level coach. He was constantly competing in Brazil. Then came the Abu Dhabi in '03. Marcelo had been a black belt for only five months.

Marcelo actually lost the final of the qualifiers by one point. He'd pulled guard and lost a point and his opponent ran for twenty minutes. So he wasn't expecting even to compete and was training in the gi for more gi tourneys. Fabio, the old hand, knew there would be last-minute cancellations, and visa problems, so he had Marcelo make weight and, sure enough, Marcelo got his chance. He had been waiting a long time for it.

"I was really prepared. I felt nobody could take this from me. I had a hard bracket, but I knew that people didn't know me, didn't expect much from me, and wouldn't have a strategy for me. I could play my best game. Everyone else is a big name, he's a Gracie, whatever. I didn't want to respect anybody too much. I thought to myself, I can win this thing. And then I started to make it real. I started to win, and I got stronger after each match." Marcelo not only won his bracket, he submitted Mike Van Arsdale in the Absolute division. Van Arsdale is a former NCAA champion and superstar wrestler who outweighed Marcelo by two weight classes. Marcelo swarmed him, slipped up on his back, and choked him out in a minute or two. In the footage of the match, you can see Van Arsdale's utter surprise and disgust that anyone could do that to him.

Marcelo embodied what Carlson Gracie had told me and Scotty—all his gi training would work no-gi, too. He showed how the x-guard, a new type of guard that gets under an opponent and destabilizes him, could be adapted very well to no-gi. And Marcelo was always aware of what techniques would work on guys no matter the size. He had played a lot of triangle games (the triangle is a kind of choke from the bottom, catching your opponent's head and arm between your legs) in his early days, until he realized he couldn't triangle really big guys. But he could arm-drag and take the back and choke someone any size. As Eddie Bravo said, "Don't be fooled. Marcelo is deceptively strong, his legs are powerful." Mike C had agreed, saying, "Marcelo's legs are as big as mine. And he's got bowling balls for calves." More to the point, Eddie talked about Marcelo's squeeze: "Marcelo has an incredible squeeze. He developed a squeeze and took it to levels that no one knew existed."

When Marcelo puts the choke on, he has developed his *squeeze* to a high level, where it instantly constricts and fighters are helpless against it. In '03, when Marcelo rolled against Shaolin, an awesome, athletic jiu-jitsu fighter, Shaolin and Marcelo spun into a lightning-quick war and suddenly Shaolin was unconscious—he hadn't even had time to tap. Marcelo can apply it from odd places, and fighters think they're safe when they're not.

When I apply a squeeze in the rear-naked choke, it isn't instantaneous—people fight it for a while. I haven't developed my squeeze enough. In the rear-naked choke, you apply pressure to the carotid arteries, but finding the right angle and the right kind of pressure is the trick. Practice can make the choke nearly instantaneous as opposed to painful and slow. Another interesting thing about jiu-jitsu is that it's a game of centimeters. It's made up of tiny adjustments, little things that can mean the difference between success and failure in a move. If I'm sweeping someone I may be doing everything right, yet missing one small but essential step—my foot is an inch off or I forget to put a little push, just a pound of pressure, on the knee—and the position won't work. It's about getting all the little things right.

One thing Marcelo does do, when he rolls with blue belts or white belts, is try for perfection. "The reason I like to train with lower belts is to practice for myself, and look for the perfect positions, to get to places with more facility. To really try and make a perfect position." Marcelo cherishes the notion of perfection. "I can really improve my holds, and practice new things. You can train exactly the position you want to train."

There is an Abu Dhabi championship every two years, and in '05 Marcelo still felt he had a lot to prove. No one thought he could repeat his success. He had to prove it wasn't a fluke. And he did, winning his division again and placing third in the Absolute.

Then in '07, Marcelo said he started to feel the pressure, that he had to win, and he was very focused on winning the Absolute. He won his weight division again, one of the toughest brackets in the tournament. He even won through the Absolute, where he lost the final to Robert Drysdale (99 kg), by submission. Even though Drysdale outweighed Marcelo by forty pounds, that win made him a superstar.

Marcelo was grinning when he talked about it, though. "I improved my game. In my other matches I submitted everyone, which I had never done before. So I had eight submissions, including mine, which was good," and then we both started laughing. His amusement was deep and genuine.

After that, Marcelo decided to make the switch to MMA. He was having trouble staying motivated in his training, and he had something to prove. "It makes me mad. I feel bad, people think I can't do it. I want to prove I can."

Marcelo reminds me a little of Rulon Gardner, the Olympic heavyweight wrestler who fought one MMA fight in Pride. Rulon, a huge man, three hundred pounds of muscle and quickness, had wondered if he could defend himself, feeling a bit slighted by people who punch. I had an odd experience talking to wrestlers on Tom Brands's University of Iowa team. They would say, "Oh MMA, that's serious stuff." I would think, *Everybody here would do fine in MMA.*

There is a fear of the unknown, and imagined disdain. I know the Brazilians, brimming with machismo, often will say after they lose a grappling match, "You wouldn't beat me in MMA." I'm sure Marcelo has heard that one a few times.

Marcelo is adamant. "I want to show I can fight, equally. I have proved it before, but they still say I can't do it." Incongruously, his favorite fighter is Wanderlei Silva, the "Ax Murderer." Silva was a dominant champion in Japan, an intimidating monster, overwhelming in his ferocity—without showing much of a ground game (although he has a black belt). He was a little like Mike Tyson in his prime; he projected an aura of savage invincibility. He's a polar opposite of Marcelo in terms of intimidation. Silva had a staredown that was psychotic and terrifying on the TV screen. He really looks like an ax murderer. Marcelo said, "I never bother getting angry. I don't need it. I don't confuse angry with intense. I think being angry makes you tired. I perform at a high level without it."

Reflecting on what Liborio and Marcelo talked about, I'm struck again by how humble these guys are. How *nice*. How pleasant to be around. I used to think it was a product of being great—that the truly great fighters learned humility in the process of becoming great. But suddenly I am struck with a "chicken or the egg" question—which came first? Listening at length to Marcelo, Liborio, Eddie Bravo, and Sean Williams talk about jiu-jitsu, I start to think that maybe it's the other way around, that you can't be great without humility. The most humble guys, who are the most open and willing to learn, are the ones who become the best. Maybe you can't be great at jiu-jitsu without it.

Don't get me wrong—you need a certain type of arrogance to fight. You have to have the secret in your heart, that you will beat his ass. That you are too tough, too technical, too strong for this guy. You have to believe in yourself more than anything.

But it needs to be tempered with humility outside the ring or the cage. You have to learn from everyone; if you aren't growing you're dying. BJ Penn, the "Prodigy," will sometimes roll with white belts and analyze the awkward, new positions they end up in—not that they're necessarily good ones but there might be something in it. All of the best grapplers have become eternal students, even the *mestre*. Perhaps it is this need that makes great fighters humble: they've been forced to learn it, from the very start, to become great.

Marcelo, when he said "I just love it more," was giving me the secret that there is no secret. His strength was in his joy in the game.

FRIENDS IN IOWA

Rory Markham and Pat Miletich prepare for Rory's fight
against Brett Cooper. (Courtesy: Zach Lynch)

It's easy to do anything in victory. It's in defeat that a man reveals himself.

—Floyd Patterson

My introduction to MMA was a rude one, chronicled in *A Fighter's Heart*. I went out to Pat Miletich's gym in Bettendorf, Iowa, to train and fight an amateur MMA fight and write an article for *Men's Journal*. I ended up getting the snot kicked out of me on dozens of occasions.

The choice of gym was an easy one. I chose Miletich because of his reputation. Pat is the prototype for the modern MMA fighter, one of the first champions who could do everything. Most fighters of his day (the early, below-the-radar days of MMA in the United States in the mid to late 1990s) were one thing or another—either they were strikers or they were grapplers. Pat was the first guy who could do it all; he had submissions, great takedowns, he moved like a pro boxer, and he knocked guys out with head kicks. He was balanced and this led him, eventually, to the top. He was a five-time UFC champion at 170 pounds, but this was during the "dark days" of the UFC, when the promotion nearly slipped into oblivion. He had many of his early fights in the days before weight classes.

Pat made his bones as a coach. He is on the short list of best MMA trainers in the world. His camp, called Team MFS (Miletich Fighting Systems), was the dominant camp in the sport over the past ten years, with at times three UFC belt holders on the mats. It became a self-fulfilling prophecy—all the best guys were training with Pat, so everybody wanted to come train with Pat. Even in the modern MMA world, with the explosion of huge, stacked fight camps, Team MFS is still in the top tier.

In the early days of MMA the fight camps were filled with tough guys and infamous for the beatings and hazings. The Lion's Den, Ken Shamrock's gym, was well known for it, as was Chute Boxe in Brazil; guys who wanted to train had to survive vicious beatings and absurd workouts. MFS in Bettendorf was always the real deal, a place where anybody who showed up would get the living shit kicked out of him for weeks and months on end, but it wasn't hazing. That was just life at MFS. A great part of the success of the camp has to be attributed to that intensity, the highly charged atmosphere that Pat created by combining all the insanity of wrestling workouts with the damage and viciousness of hard boxing sparring.

I've written a lot about Pat, and we've gotten to be friends, which makes me feel like A) I've said it all before and B) I don't see him so clearly. Pat's a good guy and a good friend. He's funny, friendly, maybe a little burned out after so many years and so many champions, but he's still scheming. He's a fighter, and a freakishly tough human being. I'm plagued by a recurring rib injury, but when I cry off a sparring session Pat never believes me—he thinks I'm being a big baby and he suspects malingering. In his whole career, street fights included, he's never been put down from a punch to the head.

I remember Freddie Roach saying that great fighters are "special people," by way of an excuse for any silliness, any diva behavior or eccentricities. Freddie was talking about James Toney. But it's true with a lot of great fighters—you can hem and haw, say this and that, but they're just stronger, denser, tougher, and faster. People talk about Rodrigo Nogueira's otherworldly grip strength, or how Fedor Emelianenko's bones seem to be much heavier and thicker than normal, or how Randy Couture's lactic acid levels drop when he's exerting himself during a choke. Pat's like that, he's special. As Jon Wertheim documented so well in *Blood in the Cage,* there really is a "cult of Pat" in the gym: he's charismatic, funny, and maybe a little crazy.

When I arrived at MFS in '04, another young fighter had made the move out from Chicago to give professional MMA a shot, a twenty-one-year-old kid named Rory Markham. Rory was powerful, with all-American GI Joe looks and an explosive boxing style. He had the same sense of humor as I did, and we got to be friends.

Rory's clean-cut looks were marred only by his hands, which were stubby and white with scars. He'd been a very serious street fighter in high school on the South Side of Chicago. He told me he dutifully went out and got in a fight every Friday and Saturday night for about two years straight. He'd been obsessed with fighting from an early age, and he had his share of demons hidden under a layer of gregarious ease.

Over the years we kept in touch, and sometimes I went to see his fights. He was a big 170-pounder, having to cut from 195 or more, and the first few cuts were tough on him. Rory started as a striker, pure and simple, a banger who nearly always had to eat a few to give a few—but Rory had a good chin that he trusted. He loved to fight, to get in there and mix it up. Still, the more we talked, the further his career went, the more he started to think about the rest of the game. He took a loss here and there, which gave him pause. When he looked at the top of the division, the monsters up there, he knew his physical gifts and striking weren't enough, because those guys could do everything. Rory was a talented, tough fighter but right on the edge in terms of natural gifts. He was fast, strong, and tough enough to blow through most guys in the bottom or middle tier, but he was well aware (from sparring at Pat's over the years) that he wasn't going to be able to do that with the best guys in the world. He had trouble with head movement; he would do it religiously during shadow boxing but almost never during a fight, nearly always getting tagged a few times. Still, even though he knew better, his evolution as a fighter continued mostly in one direction, striking. It was what he loved.

The New England winter afternoon was already growing dark as I boarded the bus to Mohegan Sun. It was the now defunct International Fight League's (IFL) Grand Prix, the end-of-the-year event. I was there for a few reasons—it was close by (I was wintering in Massachusetts), Pat was there, and Rory was fighting on the undercard.

I got on the bus with Pat, Rory, his assistant coach Steve Rusk, and L. C. Davis, his fighter at featherweight who would be competing later for the title. The bus rolled away into the darkness and I was struck by how much MMA history was on board—along with Pat, Zé Mario Sperry, Randy Couture, Carlos Newton, Frank Shamrock, Matt Lindland (Bas Rutten and Renzo Gracie would show up later)—all giants of MMA, all disowned or persona non grata with the UFC, which was having a competing event that night, to which we stood a distant second. Pat, in particular, was feeling the sting as Matt Hughes, his former protégé, was fighting for his career in the main event at the UFC. Both Matt and Robbie Lawler had left Pat for lucrative offers to start up their own gym, and Robbie had been like a son to Pat.

Rory claimed to be feeling good; he was ready and anxious to get this over with. He was fighting second, which was early for him. His opponent, Brett Cooper, was an unknown. Nobody knew anything about him. That happened frequently in MMA, though less so at this level, but it always made me uneasy. Rory had made weight. He'd done an hour and a half workout the day before, the morning of weigh-ins, which sounded funny. Wasn't that a little long? I thought the whole point was to sauna and sweat it out, that last seven pounds of water, without exercising and burning into your reserves. But these guys were professionals and I was sure they knew what they were doing.

Mohegan Sun is a good venue, with steep walls that pack the crowd in around the ring, and it was a full house. Brett Cooper looked small—he'd weigh in at 168, whereas Rory made 170 but put at least ten pounds on overnight—yet he was determined; he had his game face on and long shaggy hair. Pat wanted Rory to jump all over him. To start fast.

When the bell rang Rory went right to him, and Brett, being a little longer, caught him right off the bat. That is standard for his fights—Rory always gets hit. He dug down and started banging. Rory has real power and quickly he had Brett hurt. He even caught him with a head kick. The crowd yelled and it looked all over. Rory tried to finish, but he "fell in" on top of his punches, he got too close, fell into a clinch, and Brett managed to take Rory to the ground. Brett was buying himself valuable recovery time. Rory slipped on a triangle from the bottom, a basic choke (catching the opponent and choking him in a triangle between your legs and one of his arms). He nearly had it—they fought in that triangle for what felt like ten minutes. It looked like it was over, the triangle was on so tight. But Brett didn't tap. Finally, Rory gave it up. He thought about a transition to an armbar, but he didn't believe in it himself. It was half-assed, and Brett pulled out easily. The fight went back and forth briefly before the round ended. Rory, in the corner, was bleeding from several small cuts—but then he always is.

In the second round, Brett was still pretty game and he caught Rory a couple of shots, a grazing knee, and then Rory covered up and ate an uppercut and went down, stunned. Brett leaped in to finish. That was it. The ref waved it off. Rory was TKO'd.

* * *

Contrary to popular belief, the first thing, the very first thing a fighter sometimes feels upon losing is relief. It's over. The stress, the hatred, the desperate battle for survival—it's finished. "When you're knocked down with a good shot you don't feel pain," Floyd Patterson, the "Gentleman of Boxing," once told the *Guardian* journalist Frank Keating. Floyd had been the heavyweight champion after Rocky Marciano retired (he'd beat Archie Moore for the interim title) in 1956, and was almost too nice a guy for it.

"Maybe it's like taking dope. It's like floating. You feel you love everybody, like a hippie I guess," said Floyd.

I remember seeing Anderson Silva lose to Ryo Chonan, and seeing the smile of relief on Anderson's face backstage. I've seen that relief gradually giving way to grief, as the fighter comes to grips with months of life feeling wasted, of the career and financial implications. "The fighter loses more than his pride in the fight; he loses part of his future. He's a step closer to the slum he came from," Patterson also said. Floyd lost a few of his biggest fights under intense national scrutiny, and once he even wore a disguise—a wig and fake beard—in order to get out of the stadium unseen after a loss.

The fighter has lost a part of himself, the part that believed in his own power and invincibility—because what a fight is about more than anything else is will. When you're knocked out, I can do whatever I want to your unconscious body. Your ability to make decisions, to master your own fate is destroyed when you lose a fight. You've been dominated, and to a male of the species there is nothing worse. It violates every genetic principle in your body.

Kelli Whitlock Burton and Hillary R. Rodman wrote an essay entitled "It's Whether You Win," for a book called *Your Brain on Cubs*, about the psychological underpinnings of baseball and fandom. They discuss experiments with lab rats that showed a male being defeated by another male actually has permanent changes in his brain. "Evidently, social defeat is highly effective in producing a state analogous to psychological pain," they wrote. "Social defeat sets in motion a number of brain processes that lead to increased sensitivity to subsequent stressful experiences . . . the hippocampus actually changes after repeated defeat experiences . . . the hippocampus is well known to be crucial for the formation of memories of specific experiences . . . in addition, the hippocampus is one of the few structures that make new nerve cells in adulthood." The research shows that repeated social defeats not only can affect the hippocampus's ability to make new cells, it affects serotonin levels and is probably linked to depression.

What could be a worse social defeat than losing a fight in front of thousands or millions of people? It's so bad it can permanently change your brain. Those same tests also showed that it was worse if the rats were caged alone—if they had companionship they sometimes didn't show any effects. "Subsequent social support is crucial to the defeated rat in returning to a normal state of mind."

The team can save you.

I stood behind Rory and had a hand on his shoulder as the outcome was announced. I could feel all the emotions; the animal still wanted to do something, vainly wanted to affect the outcome somehow, to not give up.

Rory was shocked, and then disappointed—he'd lost before; he knew what it was. He started grieving, mostly for the lost time and missed meals. He'd been cutting weight hard all through Christmas and the very first thing he said was, "I'll never fight this near the holidays again." He was grimly embarrassed. Here was a nobody, a guy he was supposed to blow right through, and he almost had, but that nobody had come back to knock him out. I wasn't so dismissive of Brett Cooper. He'd shown a granite chin, and good striking, and excellent submission defense. He'd impressed me. Rory had clobbered him with a head kick and he'd shaken it off—the kid was obviously tough. But we should have known that. It wasn't that Rory was arrogant but he went in unprepared. Brett had the advantage of having seen plenty of tape on Rory, and knowing that it was his first fight against a name guy and taking it as the biggest fight of his career. Rory tried but subconsciously he didn't see Brett as a threat. In prefight interviews, Rory had maintained he was training hard because he thought he deserved a shot at the welterweight title and that, of the two fighting for it, one might get hurt, drop out, and Rory could step in and fight for the title. That hadn't happened —neither got hurt—and Rory definitely had been looking past the immediate task.

A pet peeve of mine is when fans start griping about a fighter who lost making excuses. Of course he's making excuses. This is his profession, he's going to get back in there, and for his sanity and mental strength he needs to have a reason he can point to for his loss. If he didn't make excuses, if he didn't have a *reason* to think he can win next time, how could he ever fight again? And this is a guy who's dedicated five, ten years of his life to this. When fighters don't make excuses they're pandering to the crowd, because in their heart, and in private discussions with their trainers, they have reasons they lost and reasons they can win the next time. The public line may be, "It just wasn't my night," but there are reasons to hope your night will come.

I have my own experience with loss. I lost my first (and only) MMA fight. I have tons of excuses, believe me, and the worst part was that it was stopped from cuts. It leaves you with questions in your mind. Being a thin-skinned white boy, I bleed easily. (I once heard a trainer discussing an opponent say "he bleeds during the national anthem"—that could be me.) The loss wasn't so bad but the days and weeks after, and getting stuck with a bloody postfight picture as the cover of your book, try living with that. Yeah, I have excuses.

The defining moment for a fighter isn't victory, but the way he deals with defeat. George Foreman suffered one of the most momentous defeats in fighting history, when, as the heavy favorite, he lost to Muhammad Ali in Zaire. It was a crushing, mind-numbing loss. If you haven't seen the documentary *When We Were Kings,* you should.

After Zaire, Foreman wouldn't fight for a year. He fought a couple times, and then he had another tough loss and a terrific attack of heatstroke and exhaustion in the late rounds—he felt he nearly died. George had seen his own mortality and had had enough. He retired from boxing and became a preacher. Then, ten years later, in 1988, Foreman started his comeback, fighting in small shows as an old man at the age of thirty-eight. He was grotesquely overweight, a blimp at 270 pounds, and boxing writers looked the other way in embarrassment. George was humiliating himself. But George kept fighting, five, eight times a year, against mostly unknown guys, gradually losing the weight. When he'd won the title as a young man, Foreman was a physical specimen and a devastating puncher, but he would almost always gas in the late rounds. Now, as a washed-up old man, he was doing better. He said it was because he was fighting without the nervous tension that had exhausted him.

George took it all the way to the heavyweight championship and Michael Moorer, who'd just won the title. Teddy Atlas was training Moorer at the time, and he wrote about the fight in his book *Atlas.* Moorer was the heavy favorite to win, but Teddy remembers feeling pangs of misgivings—he even threw up. "[Foreman] wasn't running from his ghosts . . . A guy who was able to face the truth that way was a dangerous guy. That was why I had thrown up on the day of the press conference. I had recognized that about Foreman," Teddy later wrote. When Foreman came jogging down to the ring, Teddy saw he was wearing the *same shorts* he'd worn in Zaire as a young lion—and now he was a battle-scarred old bull. To wear those same shorts, the ones that had been worn when he suffered the biggest defeat in boxing history—meant that George *couldn't* be stopped. His mind was too strong now. This was his night.

Moorer, the smaller, faster man, took it to George for nine rounds. But he was making small mistakes, standing in front of Foreman for a little too long. Teddy recounted afterward the ploy, "I'm an old man, don't worry about this, don't worry about this slow jab . . ." Moorer maintains that George got lucky. There is no doubt that George was working on something all night, laying a trap, or more like manufacturing a slim opportunity. Moorer maybe got a little cocky. He was putting on a boxing clinic at George's expense, and then he got caught with a one-two in the tenth, a left jab followed by a right straight. It got through, and you can see on George's face just the gleam of understanding, and he instantly dropped another one-two through Moorer's guard. Not big huge punches, but Foreman was a big huge man and a born puncher, and then the second right hand was "on the button" and Moorer was knocked out. Teddy Atlas would later say, "I got angry afterward at people who said Michael quit. They didn't understand. Neither did the people who said Foreman got lucky. He didn't get lucky. He spent twenty years preparing to throw that punch, learning what he needed to get to that precise moment in time."

Foreman won the heavyweight title at the record-breaking age of forty-five, the oldest ever to win it. He knocked out the twenty-six-year-old Moorer. He turned the tables on Zaire—he had made himself the hero of the story, the bigger hero of history.

With Rory bleeding from some tiny cuts and an eye swelling shut, we headed back into the locker room. Rory was swinging from acceptance into despair and back again, a sort of common, obvious thing. He wanted to talk about what went wrong, what he needed. Pat said very frankly, "Wrestling, dude . . ." and it was true. Rory needed to be able to defend those takedowns with his life. When he had his man hurt, he had a window of opportunity that he needed to keep exploiting. Brett's takedowns had bought time to recover.

In the dressing room Zé Mario Sperry, a jiu-jitsu expert and a cofounder of Brazilian Top Team, asked Rory incredulously, "What happened, man? That triangle looked very tight." He was commiserating but curious, professional. Rory shrugged. He wasn't sure why he hadn't finished Brett with the triangle, but he blamed that long struggle in part for his loss—when he finally gave up squeezing, he'd burned his legs out. He'd squeezed and squeezed and felt totally gassed afterward. I think that the manner in which he'd dried out, the one-and-a-half-hour workout from the day before, probably made him susceptible to this, but it is a danger—go for a submission too early in a fight, when your opponent is still strong and he defends well, and you burn yourself out (muscularly) squeezing. Submissions have a much higher success rate later in the fight, when your opponent's already tired. They're rarely perfect in a real fight, but imperfect submission can still work. Now it's about squeezing everything, making his life horrible and depressing until he taps just as a way out, just to get it to stop. If he's already a little exhausted then he might be more prone to look for a way out. (The downside is that when a guy is slippery with sweat he has a better chance of pulling out of submissions.) When he's fresh as a daisy and full of beans he won't quit or believe he has to.

I later looked up Brett Cooper's history and saw he'd fought and won a decision against Conor Heun, who I knew was a good wrestler and a favorite student of Eddie Bravo's, a "rubber guard" practitioner. I never saw that fight, but I could draw some conclusions—that Conor had either taken Brett down or got taken down at some point and worked the rubber guard with skill and confidence. Conor was pretty good on the ground, so I could safely assume that Brett had some decent submission defense or he'd have been submitted. Maybe I would have told Rory not to burn out looking for submissions. Of course, no one had done his homework and looked up Brett Cooper.

Zé talked to Rory for a second and then demonstrated a little thing—a refinement of the squeeze—that Rory could have used to finish. Getting someone to submit is a question of convincing him that he has no options other than tapping. A part of getting a submission is mental; convincing the guy that he's caught, it's over. You make everything tight, squeeze everything down, and it's so horrible that he taps. Rory had the triangle sunk but had squeezed on only one axis, giving Brett a little room to keep breathing. And Brett had known enough to wait in that space, that he could wait Rory out from there. He didn't panic. Zé showed Rory the other axis he'd had to squeeze on, scissor his thighs together as well as pull everything down and tight. Rory, face bloody and swelling, leaped down on the mat to try it. "Jeez, Mario, I wish we'd rolled beforehand," he said with a glimpse of his old humor returning.

I went out to lunch with Pat a while later and set out to pick his brain.

"Careers go through cycles," he said. "Rory had great results from blasting people, he had so much power. But as he moves up a level, he runs into some hard things, learns some lessons, and he's realized he needs to adjust his game. Now he has to concentrate on his grappling and wrestling and I'll bet you he gets pretty good on the ground."

The example that shines is George St. Pierre. GSP was the UFC titleholder at 170 pounds and a spectacular fighter. He's a perfect physical specimen, poised to be a dominant champ, a pound-for-pound great. But GSP never wrestled in high school or college. MMA is rife with spectacular NCAA champion wrestlers, and the conventional wisdom is that if you didn't have it by now you wouldn't get it.

Wrestlers are born and bred in programs in the United States, and they wrestle fanatically in junior high, high school, and college, going to summer camps in Iowa or Oklahoma, a near religious fervor running through the acolytes. If you didn't get in on the ground floor—if you didn't wrestle year-round starting in about sixth grade—you could never come near those top guys.

GSP, though, took to wrestling like a fish to water. He applied himself as an adult, picked it up, and used his newly learned skills to *outwrestle* some of the top 170-pound fighters who had absolutely stellar wrestling backgrounds. George outwrestled Josh Koschek and Matt Hughes, both former Division 1 all-Americans (Koschek had been number one in the nation). John Fitch was captain of his Purdue wrestling team, and GSP was too much for him. This from a guy who never wrestled in high school or college? Conventional wisdom held that this was impossible.

Pat continued, "Jens Pulver used to outwrestle people. He'd take them down and outwork them and scrap—but then he used a low back injury as an excuse to just stand and trade with people. He became a crowd pleaser but, to me, that's bullshit. It's about winning fights. Jens is eating punches and kicks, getting knocked out. Then he beats Cub Swanson with a guillotine and he's back on track."

Pat was talking about a creeping, insidious problem in fight sports, in MMA in particular. Fighting in the UFC is entertainment—it's "asses in seats." That's the bottom line for promoters. People want knockouts, vicious exchanges, and bloody wars and not necessarily the best fighters in the world. Especially the casual fans; they just want to hear that they're watching the best in the world. So do you fight exciting or fight to win?

"Win win win is from boxing and wrestling," said Pat, "but that whole mentality is starting to leave the MMA thing now. Pride [the Japanese promotion] understood that and guaranteed flat fees, so go out and be exciting, you'll get paid anyway. You could lose three and get another three-fight deal."

The more I start to think about the problem, the bigger it gets for me. Do you want to see the most exciting fighters on TV, or the best? Aren't the best boxers more fun to watch? Would you rather watch Floyd Mayweather (the best) or Arturo Gatti (the more exciting)? When Floyd and Arturo finally fought, Floyd demolished Gatti in six rounds without getting hit. Is it pro wrestling, all about the spectacle, or is it fighting?

Pat finished his coffee and said, "In this sport, nobody wins a world title undefeated. You have to lose fights to get better, honestly. Rory likes to bang and put on a show. He had the guy hurt, the guy put a takedown on him, survived him, and turned it around. It was a good experience for Rory."

Pat thought a minute, then continued, "A loss is sometimes just the thing to bring a guy back to earth. Some guys will be on a roll and turn into complete assholes." He smiled. He'd seen that scenario, having had so many champions, so many ups and downs.

Pat is a wrestler at heart, that's where his sympathies lie and where his philosophies about training are grounded.

"In my MMA career, I tried to follow Dan Gable step by step. Gable was a workhorse. His ethic and aggressiveness made everyone he wrestled with better. He made everyone around him better through his tenacity. As a coach he beat the shit out of everyone on his teams well into his forties. Having great training partners kick the shit out of you makes you better, that's how Gable did it; he kicked the shit out of everyone. The ones that toughed it out got great. Those guys toughened up the new guys, and it creates a team of killers." Pat grew up here in Iowa and wrestled, firmly in the grip of the cult of Gable.

Pat ruminates on the MFS slip from the preeminent position in the MMA world. Whereas MFS used to have three UFC title-holders and a half dozen contenders, now there are only contenders; his champions have aged and fallen from the number one spots. Some of it's Father Time, and some of it is the growth of the sport; the field of competition is exponentially deeper than it was even five years ago. But to Pat the reasons are personal.

"I think the problem is that I trained as if I was going to die if I didn't win. We've lost some of that desperation in training right now. It's my fault. I can't train like I used to, with my bad neck, and you have to lead by example." Pat has a neck injury from training that needs surgery, but he resists it, fighting the idea that he's getting older.

He laughed. "I can't scream at guys the way I used to. I used to be screaming all the time. The mind follows the body, so torture the body and the mind gets used to it. The body learns to accept being miserable, and it's no big deal. When you get to a certain level of conditioning you feel like you can walk through a wall.

"As guys get in better shape, they get mentally stronger, and as they get mentally stronger their bodies gets tougher. It's a leap-frog effect."

Pat's style has always been hard-nosed. In high school he'd been an all-state nose guard weighing only 165 pounds (which is tiny for that position). "Uniformly, the coaches described him as both the toughest and meanest player they'd ever seen," Jon Wertheim wrote in *Blood in the Cage*. Being hard-nosed necessitates outworking an opponent.

"I fought this big Cherokee Indian who was a highly ranked cruiserweight boxer at the time, Jason Fickle, and he had a good wrestling background. I planned on taking him down and submitting him, but he kept getting back up. I couldn't hold him down. But I couldn't really change my game plan because he was a good striker who hit hard, so I just kept running my head into the wall. I kept taking him down.

"I was hardheaded like that. If something wasn't working I'd keep trying it until it worked. I was well rounded but I didn't switch that easy. You gotta think that you're gonna win no matter what, that the other guy will start looking for a way out. You're the predator not the prey. You don't give a flying fuck what he's doing, you're just setting him up for the finish."

He laughed, a short bark. "But there's nothing worse than when you think you're setting a guy up for the finish and the whole time he's ahead of you. That's the cool thing about fighting. That's the final stage, when you can lure a guy in. Like when you start being offensive to counterpunch, you throw the one-two and he thinks he's countering and you counter him. That's the end level, when things get really cool."

I asked him how you get there, and he smiled at me.

"There's only one way there—a lot of ass whuppings." He chuckled nastily, but he meant it.

"When you first start fighting, it's tunnel vision, you're freaking out. But as you gain experience things slow down. The combos start to come at you in slow motion. A big part of it is being relaxed. The studies show when police officers' and soldiers' heart rates hit certain levels, they lose motor skills except push and pull, they fall into tunnel vision. They lose decision making. It happens to young fighters, certainly, until they take enough beatings to relax."

That resonated with something else I'd heard when I spoke briefly to Mike Lerario, the site manager at the Army Center for Enhanced Performance at Fort Bragg, in North Carolina. ACEP was doing sports psychology work with Special Forces guys—but not what you'd think, not fear management or kill related but language learning and self-awareness and recovery. They were actively using biofeedback, something called an "M-wave monitor."

"There's a little sensor that attaches to the ear," Mike said. "With infrared it measures the distances between heartbeats. We're looking at variability. If the heartbeat is regular, then the subject has a high coherent state with brainwave activity, which is conducive to being in the zone. If it's irregular, then it's low coherence. There's little lights, so green means high coherence, blue means moderate, and red means low. But we don't train for color, because sometimes excitement is important. We don't want a guy thinking he has to be green before he breaches a doorway. But afterward, for recovery, for planning, then it's important."

Certainly, what Pat was talking about—taking a lot of beatings, being able to be relaxed, coherent—that was key.

I sighed with the knowledge that there's no easy way. You gotta take a lot of beatings. Pat smiled at me. We chewed in silence.

"I give guys game plans in practice, and you sometimes see the lightbulb go off in their head. But there's a limit. Game plans matter but mostly it's about the guy you're fighting.

"Most people's logic is, *Okay this guys sucks on the ground, let's take him to the ground.* But he's so ready for that. Sometimes you say to yourself, Okay he's great at standup and weak on the ground so let's destroy him standing and he's through—get the best of him on the feet and he's crushed, and when you do take him down he'll give up. So sometimes, go right after a guy to mess with his head. But you gotta be well rounded to do that. A guy who's a great athlete, who understands the game—you run right into his punches, beat him up, and he thinks *Holy shit I'm in trouble.*

"I think having fighters watch tape can be bad, too. It will give you a false sense of security. If he looks shitty on tape and comes out blasting, you think *Wait minute, this was supposed to be easier,* and then you're in trouble. And guys will change a lot in this sport, between fights. I think it's better to focus on what you're gonna do and make him be good enough to stop it. Know his tendencies, for sure. And I'll get guys to spar different ways to emulate an opponent, or use certain submission setups. But fundamentals will always wear them down.

"I fought a guy once who had gone down to Brazil and smashed everybody in this *vale tudo* tournament, and I didn't see the tape. So I fought him and beat him, and afterward I watched the tape and I was so glad I hadn't seen it because I would have been petrified—the guy fucked up all the top Brazilians, threw 'em around like rag dolls."

We drank some coffee and the talk moved on to Rory. "Rory's got the physical capabilities to be as good as anybody out there.

But will his mind take him there? He's been very one-dimensional. He didn't perceive himself in any other way. He has to change that perception of himself. He has to understand that he can change his identity. He's young enough. Shit, I went up to Montreal years ago and none of those guys could wrestle, and look at GSP now.

"When guys lose, it's easy to talk about it because of my own experiences. I went fifteen and oh and then lost to Matt Hume, who was the best in the world at the time. But I was disgusted, I was going to retire, I was all through. I thought *Holy shit I'm not that good*. But after a while the fire relit and I went on another run. It's simple: you're going to lose if you're fighting badasses. Randy Couture's been down and out twice. I'll talk about Matt Hughes, who quit to farm full time. I went up and argued with him while he was sitting on his tractor. This is before the Carlos Newton fight, when he won his first belt.

"It's the guys who go to the breaking point again and again and don't give up. It's up to you. Sure, some guys are in it to be a fighter, or to be part of a team, or get girls and be on TV. But there are guys who honestly know that if they don't give up they're going to be world champion. The real guys know if they keep at it they can win a title. I would always mentally convince myself there's no other option."

We started talking about backgrounds, about upbringing and experiences. Pat himself had plenty of fuel, an abusive father who died of cancer young, and a lot of tragedy, brothers dying, going to jail, committing suicide.

"There are some guys out there that are from normal families that are still animals and smash people, but usually it helps if you've had a shitty life. If somebody's starving, then somebody else is getting his ass kicked."

Rory's next fight was in the spring, on the Affliction card in Chicago. The IFL was in the process of folding, its mysterious business plan untenable. Rory was on the verge of being a free agent. There was money to be made.

Rory had decided to address his wrestling head-on. He was sparring less and wrestling more, working out with a local high school coach, Brian Glenn, who had been third in the nation at one point and was about the same weight. We talked on occasion, and he took heart from the success of George St. Pierre. Rory would eventually make his way to Overtime Wrestling and a gym full of Olympians.

I came out a few days before the fight. My first thought had been to get a hotel, stay out of the way. But then you realize that's not what's needed. Fighters, in the last days before a fight, shouldn't be alone. They can't train too much, so their energy level gets high, and the oppressive weight of the oncoming fight looms large. Rory even laughed about it, "Dude, don't leave me alone in my house watching fight tapes and doing push-ups and freaking out."

We went to dinner, we went to the movies, we watched TV. I kept Rory company as he worked out, as he finalized his "cut." There was a big gleaming gym near his house that he liked to use, so his girlfriend dropped us off.

Even before we started Rory was bony and pale, and his natural good humor was long gone. He grew quieter and quieter as hunger and dehydration took their toll—and this for a "catch-weight" (informal) of 180 pounds, a full ten pounds heavier than what he normally had to make.

We sat in the sauna and began to tell stories to pass the time. Rory's background is somewhat typical for a fighter, the estranged father, the single working mother, the tough part of town. Rory has his own demons of rage—he loves to fight. He's capable of getting really crazy. He's looked into the void. He started telling me a story, a story I knew a little of, as we sat dripping onto the bone-dry boards, the heat itching our skins.

"A lot of people said they were his best friend but Ed Bielskus was my best friend. We were inseparable. He lived four houses down from me. He would steal his dad's car to take me to my full-contact karate tournaments. We were hoodlums."

Rory looked over at me, his eyes almost hidden beneath a tight wool hat. He was in a full "sauna suit," made of plastic material like trash bags, and a sweatshirt and sweatpants to keep the sweat sloughing off him. I was sweating like a pig just in a T-shirt and shorts.

"I was fifteen, he was sixteen. We were at the White Hen Pantry, hanging out, corner store . . . trying to whittle smokes off the cashier. Ed wandered off, and about an hour later a cop came by asking, 'Is Rory Markham here?'

"Of course, we got into a lot of trouble, so I dummied up. But listening to his walkie-talkie, I hear him talking about Ed. So I confessed to being Rory and tried to figure out what was going on, and the cop just got me in the car and drove off.

"We came around the block and four stories up, across from the hospital is a parking garage. Ed is standing on one of the pillars, on the northeast corner, up on the pillar. I can see it like a painting.

"There were cops, ambulances, fire trucks . . . and I was thinking to myself, *What a fucking asshole* and I assured the cop, 'Don't worry about a thing.' I thought he was fucking around." Rory's voice was confident, everything a big joke. He paused and shook his head.

"That's something I've had to live with. I was sure I could get him down. Now, Ed had been doing some crazy things, like buying a boat with his dad's credit card, but his dad was wealthy and Ed had never even uttered the word 'suicide' in passing."

The reasons are mysterious. Rory mentioned that Ed was adopted, and that it was troubling him, but it's impossible for Rory to say. You can see that bothers him, the unfathomable nature of it. The unknown horrors of the human heart. If Rory doesn't know this, about his best friend, then can anyone know anything about anyone?

"I said to the cop, 'Don't worry about it.' A counselor was talking to him, but he was shouting for me, 'Get Rory up here!'

"I came through the door, and he said everybody else stay back, and when I got five feet from him he held his hand out and started inching back on the ledge—he told me to stay there.

"I was saying, 'What are you doing? I love you.' I knew he was serious. His eyes were . . . he was not there. I knew shit was fucked up. I remember, with every inch that I came closer, any movement, a hair would blow, and he would inch his heels out over the ledge. His feet were more than fifty percent off the ledge. I tried to talk to him but he just kept shaking his head. He said, 'I just wanted you to be here,' then he threw the keys to his brand-new Ford Explorer—and you know how important a car is for a teenager, it's who you are. And then he went. He jumped like a reverse cannonball—he put his head down so his head would hit first. He flipped into a dive."

The sauna ticked, quietly.

"There was an enormous pool of blood."

Rory paused and spit on the floor. I had nothing to offer him. I thought about this book, and the fighter's mind. The motivations. The heat pressed in around us. Eventually, Rory started talking about the aftershocks, how everyone claimed Ed as a friend, people who barely knew him.

"I'd make weird promises to myself and Ed, and I promised Ed in the bad times that I would become a professional, I'd fight in the UFC. I promised." Rory looked at me and shrugged, and we went out to the chill air.

We went from sauna to the stationary bikes. Rory had a system. He had to keep a sweat going to drop the water weight for the weigh-in. He cut too much, down to 178 at the end of an hour from 185. It came off too easy—but that meant it would go back on easy. He still had plenty of water left in him.

* * *

At the weigh-in Rory's opponent, Jay Ellis, finally showed, a muscular, smaller black man with glasses, a little on edge. Jay had a losing record, and he'd lost several fights in a row, but the worst part is he weighed in shockingly low, 161. Most people didn't catch it but the few fighters who are friends with Rory laughed and a murmur ran around the room. Ellis was a replacement for Taiwon Howard who got hurt, a one-week-notice guy and probably the only opponent the promoter could find. He fights at 155, normally.

Rory can rehydrate and did so with relish; he made 180.6.

In a way, the fight was its own kind of test for Rory—could he maintain his professionalism, could he stay focused without a credible threat?

When the fight happened, Jay Ellis—doing his "crazy" routine —ran at Rory and leaped, basically, completely over him. Rory pounced and started to work, but they were too close to the cage and Jay used his feet to run up the fence and reverse Rory. Then, lo and behold, Rory slipped on the triangle from the bottom and Jay was tapping before it was even closed—because Rory was using the squeeze properly, as Zé had shown him. To Jay, it felt tight, and it felt hopeless. Rory's feet weren't even in the proper position, he hadn't secured the hold. But the squeeze was there.

WITNESS TO THE
EXECUTION

Andre Ward in a virtuoso performance against
Edison Miranda. (Courtesy: Andre Ward)

Unpredictably, the moment of grace breaks upon you, and the question is whether you are ready to receive it.

—Andrew Cooper

Gunpowder was invented in China, maybe as far back as 850, and it traveled to Japan in the form of fireworks. It was never actually weaponized, and when the Portuguese introduced firearms in 1500 the Japanese reacted strongly. The ruling caste saw the social hazards—and an end to their way of life—in the potential equalizer, and so banned it. They continued their endless feudal autumn, wherein most lives had little value, and samurai dueled to the death with the weapons of their grandfathers and great-great-grandfathers—the long and short swords. While the rest of the world plunged into the abyssal arms race, the samurai caste refined their techniques, using the tools they had perfected. These swords were the sharpest-edged weapons ever created by man. Smiths, considered national treasures and guarding their secrets, poured their souls into the blades, folding and pounding the steel thousands of times, over months, years. Horrifically deadly, dueling with those weapons was about as far out on the edge as you could go, walking a hair-thin line between life and death, risking everything to take everything. The modern mind reels at the thought of facing off with three-foot-long razors, where one of us will die. The levels of concentration, stress, and refinement of technique were stratospheric. Miyamoto Musashi, perhaps the greatest swordsman in this era of great swordsmen, wrote a book on fighting and strategy called *Go Rin No Sho* (*The Book of Five Rings*). Musashi was a warrior who rose to prominence by winning all his duels, some sixty of them. He was the culmination of a caste and way of life that devoted the entirety of its energies to study of the sword. He achieved a level of mastery that may never be seen again.

When I started writing this book I was thinking about it as an updated *Book of Five Rings,* which has become a kind of knee-jerk part of any traditional martial arts philosophy; it was even adopted in the 1980s (when the Japanese business model was booming) as a self-help book for businessmen. A lot of people have found inspiration and guidance in the book, for all sorts of reasons, but one must never lose sight of what *Go Rin No Sho* is finally about: *cutting.*

Andre Ward was the only American boxer to win gold in the 2004 Olympics. I have known Andre and his trainer and godfather, Virgil Hunter, since 2003. I wrote extensively about them in my first book, curious about the development of a red-hot boxing prospect in the early stages of a professional career. I had spent several months at King's Boxing Gym, a throwback gym, dank, gritty, and functional. I lived near them in Oakland, in the desert heat, and drove through the dusty streets and sprinted hills and ran the parks. Virgil said to me once, "I knew Andre would win gold at the Olympics because I was influenced in my training by *The Book of Five Rings,* and that's the symbol for the Olympics. Five rings."

Virgil and I have an interesting friendship; he's in his fifties, black, from a militant background—Oakland and Berkeley in the

'60s and the overtones of black power. He'd come up from the streets and I was a white kid from the East Coast who went to Harvard. We were using each other in a classic boxing way: mercenary but mutually beneficial. I was getting good material for my book and Virgil was getting exposure for himself and his fighters. He knew how I saw him, as a wise trainer, and he could play that role, but he also knew it was no bullshit. Virgil really did have a profound understanding of the game. He had the goods and he knew it.

Boxing is about reputations, and Virgil knew that the more I wrote about him the better for him, but only so long as his fighters were winning. Fighting has that beautiful bottom line: win. I don't care how wonderful a human being Muhammad Ali was, without his big wins—if he had lost those marquee title fights—he wouldn't be the sportsman of the century. No one would care if he refused the draft or not. No one would care if he changed his name. So I won't overestimate my importance but I could be a help. Plus we had a genuine liking for each other, a respect because I could understand him; to a certain extent I could pick up what he was putting down.

Virgil met Andre when he was nine years old and saw something in the little boy—the ghost of a killer's punch, some premonition of speed. Andre, his dad, and Virgil had embarked on a career together. Andre's father had been a boxer who loved the sport, and he wanted Andre to learn it properly, how to hit and not be hit.

Andre, or Dre to his friends, trekked to the boxing gym after school and he stuck with it, day in and day out. He was caught in the inevitability of it, like a soldier swept to war, but he was also called by something inside of him. He came to love and hate the gym. The gym is the anvil on which boxers are forged, tempered like a samurai sword with thousands of hammer blows, bending steel into steel. Fighters are born in the dedication to repetition. It's not about who is stronger and faster, although those things can cover for other problems. Nothing can replace natural self-discipline; nothing can replace time in the gym. Andre loved boxing, and you have to love it to be great. To compete at the highest level requires eight or ten years of groundwork, going to the gym and working to get better every day, day in and day out, with no end in sight. You have to love the journey.

Malcolm Gladwell's book *Outliers* is a fascinating look at success. He talks at length about the search for innate talent, and a mind-blowing study he cites is an investigation by psychologists at the elite Berlin Academy of Music. These psychologists looked at the violinists and found a very simple correlation—the more they practiced, the better they were. They checked it with the pianists and found the same thing—everybody had some talent and started playing around age five. "But when the students were around the age of eight, real differences started to emerge. The students who would end up the best in their class began to practice more than everyone else . . . until by the age of twenty they were practicing . . . over thirty hours a week." These were the players who were the virtuosos, the ones who would go on to become famous performers, world-class talents, "geniuses." The lower half, who did only eight hours a week, were destined to be music teachers.

And the incredible thing was there were no "naturals" who were at the top without this commitment. Nobody in the top third didn't practice thirty hours a week since childhood, and there weren't any "grinds," guys who worked that hard but just couldn't make it. There's a magical number: ten thousand hours of diligent, intentional, informed practice. "That's it. And what's more, the people at the very top don't just work harder, or even much harder than everyone else. They work much, *much* harder."

The ten-thousand-hours thing apparently comes up in just about every field and discipline. I had a painting teacher who told me in college, "You just got to push paint around for ten years before you figure it out." Even a prodigy like Mozart got in ten thousand hours; he just started early. Gladwell wasn't the first to notice this. The basic signifier for expertise had been set at ten years of practice by everyone studying these things, but his book is well written and really brought the point home.

With boxers, with fighters, you have to have get your ten thousand hours in before you're too old to fight, which is why you have to start so young. And there is a certain amount of athletic ability and toughness needed. Gladwell makes the point in basketball—if you're five-foot-five, you can practice ten thousand hours with the best coaches in the country and still probably not play in the NBA. But if you're over six-five? If you have the bare minimum of ability? Then it comes down, overwhelmingly, to commitment.

Virgil started sparring Andre at around age eleven, with a kid named Glen Donaire (who's won flyweight, 112-pound titles, as has his brother Nonito, the current IBF flyweight champ). Glen was older, and about the same size, but more advanced and physically mature—he would "put it on" Dre with ease. "I wouldn't let Dre take a real beating, but I'd let him get frustrated. He'd get hit." At this point, Glen so far outclassed Dre that Glen wasn't concerned at all with what Dre would throw back.

Virgil talked at the local coffee shop, Coffee With a Beat, sipping his tea, his eyes hidden behind his glasses. Watchful, his voice was quiet with the sibilance of confidence.

"Dre was running all around the ring, ducking and dodging, turning, grabbing, holding on—not punching but *surviving*. So I encouraged that. 'Don't let him hit you,' I told Dre. I never mentioned fighting back. I wanted to know if he could take it before he started dishing it, to handle the pressure. He can't beat you up if he can't catch you." Virgil as a trainer needs to always evaluate where his fighter is, mentally. Especially at a young age, you need to see what you've got, because otherwise Virgil could waste years of his life training someone who will never be successful.

Virgil smiles. "Sometimes there were tears, but they were *re-taliatory* tears." He laughed.

"I would cheerlead Dre, 'man he missed you by a foot!' and watch Glen. Glen was so confident, he would finally walk Dre down, when Dre got tired, and stand right in front of him and look him over. Glen would stand there and look for an opening to land his punches." This went on for weeks, with Dre learning how to move, to get out of the way, to avoid damage from a better, stronger, more experienced guy.

"So I taught Dre this little hook-jab-type punch, and I told him every time he stops in front of you hit him with this little punch, and then go move again. Lo and behold, the next sparring session, Glen pulls up in front of Dre and pow, Dre pops him and then he goes. Of course, this incited Glen—we've been sparring three weeks and you've never hit me—so he would swarm Dre and try and get that last hard punch in. The next couple of weeks, that was the routine, hit him and move fast. Just as Glen was pouring it on, I'd stop it. I'd let Dre take one good hard shot, and then I'd stop it, middle of the round or whatever. I was looking for one thing."

I can imagine Dre's life—the constancy of the boxing gym after school, the routines and smells of leather and Vaseline, hand wraps and boxing shoes. Ever present was his white father, Frank Ward, who'd been a heavyweight with ten amateur fights, who pushed him and believed in him, and tall Virgil watching and teaching him. Virgil had been an officer at a juvenile delinquent hall his whole working life; one thing he understood was young mens' psyches.

"This went on for a while, and then one day, after Glen hit Dre with a good shot. I said, 'That's it, that's enough,' and Dre said, 'No, no, I'm all right,' and that's what I was looking for, that statement. Now I began to really teach Dre how to hit him with punches.

"I told Dre, you can hit him with anything you want. Number one, he won't believe you can do it, and number two, by the time he does believe it you'll be whupping him. Now Dre already knew *what I been through it can't get any worse, that's all he can do to me* and he knew how to get away from Glen. He started working jabs and hooks and within three weeks he was dominating Glen, and they stopped boxing us. That's what happens when you fight on your terms."

Virgil taught Dre what he called the "slip-'n-slide," a Texas style of boxing that could trace its roots as far back as Jack Johnson, the first black heavyweight champ, in 1908. "It's not necessarily a crowd-pleasing style, when it emerged it wasn't respected. It has a lot of hidden components."

Dre's Olympic run in 2004, when the details are told, takes on a *Rocky* feel. Dre's father died suddenly, of heart failure, in 2002, out of the blue—one morning he was gone. Dre, at the age of eighteen, stood over the grave and promised to bring back Olympic gold. He struggled for a reason to continue, and his growing family and sense of faith helped rebuild the steel.

There were shadowy dreadnoughts in the mists of international amateur boxing. It was an uphill climb from the start, as Dre was dramatically undersized for his division. Virgil had made the decision, in January of the year before, to fight Dre at 178 pounds, because he thought that he was still in a growth spurt. But that growth tapered off. Dre fought his way through the Olympics weighing 170 in that 178-pound weight class. Virgil would make him drink a Gatorade right before the weigh-in so he wouldn't be too light, when most guys were probably cutting four or five pounds to make 178. And not only that—they were men; in the European system boxers will often spend eight years as an amateur, fighting in major competitions and culminating in the Olympics, while in the United States a good boxer (without the financial support) will go pro much quicker. Dre was up against essentially professional men who were much bigger and vastly more experienced.

The *Rocky IV* villain in this story was Evgeny Makarenko, a six-foot-five Russian fighter who'd won the world amateur championships for several years, with apparent ease. He'd beaten everyone he might face in the Olympics, including the perennial runner-up, Magomed Aripgadjiev, from Belarus. Makarenko was the heavy favorite to win gold but he had never fought Dre.

Both Dre and Virgil maintain this was "not by chance but by design," and not only was it God's will but also strategy. Virgil recalls during the run-up to the Olympics that every boxing coach he talked to told him that Dre had to go to middleweight, where "maybe he could medal." Virgil says he intentionally kept Andre out of the Pan Am games, and the Worlds, where he would have faced international competition at a top level. "I was branded a fool . . . even my wife told me I was 'messing with Andre's career.'"

Virgil had a plan. "I believed that if they've never seen him, if they can't game plan for him, they can't beat him in four two-minute rounds. There's just too much going on." Speed kills, and in amateur boxing, which focuses on point scoring, Dre's speed gave him an insidious advantage. The weight differences, which might have told over a longer, more punishing professional fight, weren't as crushing in the shorter amateur fights.

Dre remembers entering the arena, the enormity of the event all around him. The United States had just invaded Iraq and was seen as a power-hungry aggressor, and here on the world stage the boos were raucous, the disapproval given vent. The athletes had been prepped. They knew the boos were coming "and I didn't take it personal," Dre said. "But it was an eye-opener, that this is a big world stage. Any time the U.S. fans tried to get rowdy, they'd be booed down by the crowd, instantly. It was almost laughable." Dre stood under the wash of boos and shook it off like water off a duck. When he entered the ring he couldn't hear them, his focus was so complete. He went out and did his thing and blitzkrieged the first fighter he faced, winning through to the next bracket. He would face Makarenko in the quarterfinals.

The next day, Dre had to ride the same bus as Makarenko to the fight, and he can remember Makarenko smirking at him, laughing at him with a friend. Dre was dismissed as too small, too inexperienced for this world stage. For Dre, it was David and Goliath. "I would see those guys smirking at me, and I was reminded of when Goliath laughed at David and asked him, 'Who are you to come and fight me? Am I a dog?' and that fired David up."

Dre fought the fight of his life. He used his speed, bounding in and out from the much taller, longer fighter. Dre put it on him. Of the fight, Virgil muses that Makarenko "could win—but not in that time, he wasn't prepared to." Dre dominated the Russian, 23–16.

"That disrupted the whole thinking of all the trainers," Virgil recalls with a smile. "Here you got Makarenko who hasn't lost in five years. He's beaten every fighter in the division and so has the fighter from Belarus—but Makarenko always beat him by eight or nine points. What did this do to Magomed, the Belarus fighter?"

Virgil chuckles, "That was the best feeling, knowing what we'd done to the division." He remembers going back to the house he was staying at in Greece, on the beach, and listening to the waves crash and smelling the jasmine and lavender through his window and feeling exhilarated. "It was a great moment for me as a coach. We forced the entire division, all this world-class talent, to rethink its strategy."

But Dre was exhausted, emotionally. He'd burned out his adrenaline, he used up his tank to beat Makarenko. Dre drew on his faith. He took strength from it when he couldn't imagine he had any left and went out and won the semifinal in a hard fight against a tough guy from Uzbekistan. "For that fight, I knew it would be ugly, because Dre was so emotionally spent, so I said to him, 'Just go fight the guy and win, he has to stop you from doing what you do. Just win and it will recharge you.'"

Then the final, the gold medal match, against the Belarussian, against a fighter who had served as a gatekeeper to the best fighter in the division. Dre talks about the necessity of changing plans in a fight. "What I had done to Makarenko wasn't working as well, the getting in and out. He was timing me. I'd go back to the corner between rounds and be a point down, or a point up. In the third I made an adjustment and started to really put pressure on him, using my speed up close, and he went downhill, he got winded. He was in his comfort zone out there picking me off, and I pushed him out of it."

The international crowd had stopped booing Andre and cheered him. The *Rocky* cycle was complete.

Dre's faith continues to be his bedrock, his source of strength. "It's everything," he says, "and it's not just faith in faith. I have faith in Jesus Christ. This game, boxing, is so brutal—mentally, physically, financially—that me and Virg always joke we wouldn't dare be in this game without God. But it's the truth."

When Dre has a fight, he goes into camp, moving in with Virgil. He has a lovely wife and two children he misses badly, but camp has to be all about training—it is a purely selfish place. The fighter has to be focused on himself. This is the worst part of boxing for Dre. "Being away from my family my heart aches every day. But I use it for motivation. When I run sprints on these hills, if I slow down, I think of them. This is how I make my living, and that, coupled with faith, helps me out. I know God has called me to do this, I know God has called me here for a reason. It's a platform to where I can put God's voice on a worldwide stage."

I interviewed Dre after we both worked out, and he stretched and I sat there with my tape recorder, growing cold. He still has some of that boy in him, even as he relaxes into a man. He's only twenty-four but he's been through a lot. His face has that strange combination of youth and wisdom. There's some of that eternal kid of the professional athlete, who's so specialized that he may not function well in other arenas, but on the other hand he's an experienced father, and Dre's been in the deepest waters an amateur fighter can be in.

"If God has brought you to it, he'll see you through it." He smiles at the stock phrase, but to him it's not stock.

"Although God has given me the power to do what I do, I have to get out there and do it. It doesn't just fall out of the sky. You have to make your destiny happen. After I won the gold medal, I saw God had given me the power to do this. God is *real*, it's not faith in faith. When I have bad days, when I'm tired and worn down, I can take strength from God and I can come in here and have the best day I had all week. I need God's strength, his divine enablement, his *unmerited favor*—that's what grace is."

I am reminded of some of the thoughts I'd first had about Dre, about his faith—it's a way forward for him without ego. If you are so much faster than everybody else, if you can see that power as being *for a reason,* not for your own glory but for something larger than yourself, it must be a great relief. A powerful tool.

Hanging around over the next few days I was reminded how quiet and watchful Virgil is as a trainer. He's watching his fighters without talking to them much, listening to them, analyzing them. Later, at night, we would just talk. He would talk about what he was seeing, what he was looking for. He had no concerns about Dre, but there was still Antonio Johnson back in camp, and Heather Hartman, and Karim Maceo. Virgil's "adopted" son Cymone Carney-Hunter was a devastating puncher as an amateur, and Virg also had a promising heavyweight named Marlow Dion. I always thought that Virgil would be a good trainer for a heavyweight, being tall, but also because Virgil wouldn't accept that a heavyweight has to be slow and just powerful. Why can't a heavyweight have the quick feet of a middleweight?

Virgil talked about the necessity of consistency in training. "You got to be screwed up in a lot of respects to fight anyway— I mean to take it to the pinnacle. To find those reasons, day in and day out. The ability to know that somewhere out there, all those days ahead"—his voice slowed and drawled for emphasis—"hundreds of days, thousands of days. That one day is *yours*, somewhere. You work hard for it, for that one day, then everything changes, and you have to be ready for it."

Fighters live in preparation for instantaneous flashes, that one brief span of time that will define them for the rest of their lives. That moment when everything they've done, everything they will do, and everything they are is evaluated. There's really nothing like it, nothing with the same level of preparation and risk.

"You can sense the change coming, like with Andre, for him, the day is at hand." Virgil means that this is Andre's breakout year, this is the year they come into the limelight. He means fighting and winning titles. "That day you transform from getting to keeping. You have to be prepared for it."

Virgil talked about the recent Ricky Hatton/Floyd Mayweather fight. He looked at me and said quietly, "I was paying close attention to Ricky Hatton. He had accepted losing—by decision—as a possibility. He knew that was a very real chance. He wanted to lose on his terms, so he fought the way he did. Because Ricky knew he wouldn't *lose* anything by losing a decision. But getting knocked out, that wasn't on his script," and Virgil shows me a flash of that small, ruthless smile. "Ricky didn't think that could happen, so that's why it did. You always have to be aware that you could lose. I could get knocked out, or tapped out. Anything is possible in the ring, don't stop short of anything. You train ninety-nine percent of eventualities in training camp, but missing that one percent could get you knocked out. Your whole camp is serious disillusion."

Virgil leaned toward me so I could follow. "If you and I were over in Iraq right now, we're thinking about bullets flying. We're not thinking, 'Hey, I might get wounded,' you see? You can get *killed*. And you react as such."

Virgil continued, leaning back. "That's the one thing that intrigued me about *The Book of Five Rings*: there was no trophy. It was understood there was a winner and a dead man. Which makes my approach to training totally different if I'm going to die. It's impossible for you to train the same way, I don't care how much you practice, I don't care how sharp your sword is or what famous smith made it. If you go into a sword fight for points, you'll never obtain what I'm obtaining with a dull sword against somebody that's gonna die."

I thought about that, about how my own training had always been compromised by a lack of sincerity, a lack of life-or-death intensity. I had been wasting Virgil's time when I trained with him, and he had seen it and treated me accordingly. He'd done the best he could with me, without overly investing his time, because it was obvious that I wasn't going to win titles.

Virgil continued on his riff. "When I think about Hatton, that's what I think about. He didn't have respect for his opponent. He never thought about Floyd knocking out thirty other guys, and Floyd knew this, he had it all together in his mind. This isn't the best fighter, the best boxer. This is a person who has it all in *perspective* and he reacts accordingly."

Successful professional fighters are the ones who achieve perspective at an early age.

Virgil smiled. "If I tell you my intent is to kill you in the ring, I'll get labeled all sorts of things. But that's my intent, within the rules."

This is a serious business, and you have to recognize the underlying truth that fighting is a "hurt business," as Mike Tyson, the poet laureate of rage, once said.

Virgil and I kept talking, and he moved on to Andre and his last fight in St. Lucia, where the promoter, surprised, said, "I never realized that this kid was *mean*."

"He was looking for something conventional," Virgil said. "Was Mike Tyson really a killer because he went out and got you in two rounds, or did he just punch well and he was scared? We found out later on in Mike's career. He fired his weapons out of fear. When you fire out of fear there's a demolition effect—it's crude, panicky. When you fire out of calculation it has a slower effect. That's what I'm getting at with Andre. They haven't woken up to the fact that he's a killer in the ring."

Opinions on Andre vary in the boxing community, but many critics agree with *Ring* magazine, which named him "the most protected prospect." This is just fuel for Andre and Virgil.

Andre said, "Fernando Vargas and David Reed, both good friends of mine, went for title shots early, after twelve or thirteen fights and it didn't turn out good. The thing is, at this weight class, guys can be as fast as a welter but hit as hard as a heavyweight. At smaller weights you can take more chances. Look at Pavlik—it took him eight years to get his title shot, and he was ready. He made it to the Olympic trials and lost to Jermaine Taylor . . . but because I made it a little further in my amateur career, I'm supposed to go twice as fast as a pro? You want me fighting for a title in two years?" Andre smiles and shakes his head. He's sure he's on the right track. As of this writing, Andre is still undefeated, with a pro record of 17–0 and the WBO NABO super-middleweight title. He's been developed in an old-school way, brought along slowly, exposed to different styles, without chasing a big payday. But now he's in his prime, and ready, and looking to fight the best guys in the world.

Virgil later told me why the critics and the press have a hard time with Andre.

"It's hard to recognize what you're watching, at first," he said. "He's developed into a fighter who kills in stages, like the lethal injection. You know, with multiple shots. One goes in and sedates you, the next one shuts down the nervous system, the next one stops your heart. It's not a firing squad.

"That's what's unfolding. People go to fights and look for the wrecking ball, but instead you have this totally helpless person. I watch the ref watch the other guy. After the second round the ref never looks at Andre again—he starts watching the other guy closely. He's getting steadily blasted and he can't do anything back, and he's starting to shut down. The ref sees and feels it first. I watch the faces of people around the ring, and there isn't much cheering or yelling. It's almost somber, like we're witnesses to an execution."

Virgil leaned back and looked at me. "And they ask me if he can do that to everybody. And I say, *yes*. To everybody. It has nothing to do with their skill. I saw it back when he was getting whipped by Glen, back when he was ten years old. He was never afraid. He couldn't wait for the day when he could do it back."

CAPTAIN AMERICA

Randy Couture

Another man's sword is your sword.

—Yagyu Munenori

Greatness in sports is born in the moment. It is situational. It's not inherent to the athlete with the most ability, or the most dominance, and it's not just about the championship (though that added pressure is essential). It's about the pure moment, the transcendence of time and place, when an athlete or a team performs miraculously under the most intense pressure, against insurmountable odds. The situation rises out of sports but speaks to universal truths and emotions, an attainment of the divine, touched by grace (indeed miraculous). The moment steps out of time, into history; it becomes important to everyone. Perhaps it's silly for sports to aspire to the grandure of history, but it happens to us here in the twenty-first century. It's what we've got. And in the end fighting is more than a sport.

The television announcers aspire to that moment and they pretend to see it everywhere. They try and force it, hoping for some lucrative historical sheen. But it can't be faked, or repeated. UFC commentator Mike Goldberg, calling "Down goes Franklin" in an attempt (perhaps subconsciously) to recall the iconic Howard

Cosell chanting "Down goes Frazier!" doesn't cut it. That guy who yelled, "How much more can you give us, big Mac?" when Mark McGwire hit his seventieth home run in 1998 didn't really nail it. It has to be genuine—like art, it requires sincerity.

The first true, "gee whiz" moment of modern American MMA is Joe Rogan calling out "That man is my hero." He was talking about Randy Couture, maybe the greatest MMA fighter to date.

Randy is not the best fighter we've seen, or even the most unexpected. And he would almost certainly disagree with my characterization. Nonetheless I will stick with it. Randy is the first Great American MMA fighter. He earned greatness in the moment, not through hype or hyperbole, and not through dominance; his record is 16–8. He's had his share of defeats. Randy earned it with upsets. Randy goes into fights as a serious underdog with regularity, and he pulls off genuine shockers. He does it often enough to make it familiar, and feel inevitable as you see it unfold—yet each fresh time, it seems he must succumb, and we relearn his greatness.

My background, such as it is, is in striking. I have learned a little jiu-jitsu late, and never really liked wrestling. But the deeper I got into MMA, the more I realized how important wrestling is. At first, when I saw the good wrestlers doing well, I thought it was because of their athleticism and ground control. They don't have a professional avenue open to them after college, unless they're huge and can go into the WWE or the NFL. It made sense that wrestlers would be great ground fighters, and they're already practiced at cutting weight.

After several years of MMA, I gradually came to the realization that, in fact, of all the disciplines wrestling is probably the most tactically important—for the simple fact that if your wrestling is better then YOU decide. Meaning if your wrestling is better than your opponent's, you can either A) take him down, or B) prevent him from taking you down. So you decide where the fight goes, and you can make that decision based on where you feel strongest. Randy uses his wrestling—his trapping clinch, dirty boxing, and filthy Greco—to put fighters where they least want to be and then absolutely smothers them. He drowns fighters right before your very eyes.

I realized from Dan Gable and Randy and all these other wrestlers that there is another great edge that elite level wrestlers bring to the MMA world—mental toughness and conditioning. Mental toughness is a dominant factor in wrestling, and wrestling practices are the hardest in sports. Wrestling has such a huge conditioning factor that the guys who excel have developed extraordinary mental toughness—indeed, much of the training is focused on pushing through internal walls of exhaustion and breaking your opponent. Wrestling is by design a "game test," a test of will and conditioning. It's harder than fighting in some ways, because there are so many fewer options; it's man on man and muscle against muscle for the whole match.

Randy Couture was an all-state high school wrestler, and he married young, after high school. Struggling for work, he joined the army and wrestled on the army team. Still, the athletic path was a rough road. Randy was never given anything; he worked for every little step. Eventually he became a student at Oklahoma State, he was an NCAA all-American, and then he coached at Oregon State, but all the while he fought to make the Olympic team in Greco-Roman wrestling. Greco-Roman (as opposed to freestyle) is all upper-body takedowns and clinches—no attacks on the legs. Randy struggled for eight years in the international wrestling world, often ranked number one but never quite winning the right tournament to earn a spot on the Olympic team. He lost critical matches through overtraining or overconfidence.

I talked to him at his gym in Las Vegas, Xtreme Couture, a mecca for fighters. Randy's got a genuine goodness about him that even the cameras pick up—an honesty, an openness. He has a craggy, noble face that creases into a smile like an old cartoon of the sun.

When Randy started fighting, it was almost an afterthought— let's see if I can do this, have some fun. The Olympics had been an albatross around his neck, a crushing weight of expectation and disappointment. He didn't put any pressure on himself in fighting; that was saved for the big wrestling meets. Fighting was just a gas he was doing on the side, and he performed better than anyone thought possible. He was so good they called him "the Natural."

Randy arrived at the UFC at the ripening age of thirty-three, and after one fight he upset the seemingly unstoppable Vitor Belfort. He beat Mo Smith for the title in only his third fight. This was for the heavyweight title, which topped out at 265 pounds. Randy had a contract dispute and was stripped, but he won the title back two years later. Randy then lost to the much bigger wrestler Josh Barnett, and the heavyweight division was full of guys who had to cut weight to make 265 while Randy fought at 220 or so. Feeling the squeeze from these behemoths, Randy moved down to light heavy (205 pounds) and beat Chuck Liddell, another upset. Then came the biggest fight of his career, against Tito Ortiz, when Tito was at his peak, the young, unstoppable killer who would bound nearly out of the cage in his prefight warm-up. Randy was forty years old and he dominated Tito for five rounds in a win that solidified his myth of defying reputation. Overnight, his nickname changed from the Natural to "Captain America."

Randy then lost twice to Chuck Liddell, who had adjusted his style to perfectly counter Randy. After the second loss, Randy retired from the sport, working as a commentator. He couldn't stay away, and after watching Tim Sylvia defend the heavyweight title in what he felt was lackluster fashion, Randy came out of retirement at the age of forty-four. The six-foot-eight, 265-pound Sylvia seemed a lock to destroy Randy and fans worried for Randy's health—until the first few seconds of the fight, when Randy (with the perfect game plan) knocked Tim Sylvia on his ass and put it on him for the rest of the fight. Randy defended his new title once against Gabe Gonzaga, with a clinic on how to use the cage as a tool, and then resigned from the UFC. He was chasing the biggest fight in the world, with Fedor Emelianenko, the Russian heavyweight, who was somehow (essentially) unbeaten in MMA and was generally held as the greatest MMA heavyweight of all time. The UFC, with its restrictive contracts, couldn't sign Fedor but wouldn't let Randy go, and hung him up in court until Randy was forced to come back. No organization will let its heavyweight champ fight someone it doesn't have a contract with. What if their champion loses? What's the belt worth then?

For his "welcome back, champ" fight, he was matched for the title against Brock Lesnar, a wrestling goliath who outweighed him by fifty pounds. Lesnar is a huge man, built like a silverback gorilla, and a terrific athlete, an NCAA wrestling legend. The first round was classic Couture, Randy in control, chipping and scrapping, and the air was pregnant with the possibility of a further demonstration of Couture's greatness. But it was not to be; in the second round Randy got caught. Brock is unreasonably fast for a man his size, and Randy's head movement had slowed down that last little tick, putting him in reach. Brock punched and Randy moved a second late, got clipped behind the ear, and went down.

Maybe at forty-five the end is finally on Randy, but it should never detract from what he's accomplished, and when he fights again don't bet against him.

"One of the things about being an underdog, there's no pressure. Nobody expects you to win. It frees you up to go out and compete. We often complicate things with fear of failure, all that baggage of winning and losing. Being an underdog is freedom." This knowledge hadn't come easy to Randy; he'd earned it. We sat in his office at Xtreme Couture, the Vegas sun spilling like liquid gold outside on the pavement.

"I realized I get way more nervous for wrestling than for fights. Way more keyed up. When I realized that, I thought, *That's odd.* This guy could kick my head off, but I'm not worried about that at all. I'm having fun, I'm enjoying learning all this new stuff. I stopped and thought, *Why the hell am I so nervous for the wrestling matches?* I'd lost perspective, and I was putting all this pressure on myself. It came down to one match—everything hinged on it—so I'd forgotten that I loved to wrestle and why I started wrestling—because it's fun."

Randy had been dealing with the systemic pressure that elite athletes face, the overwhelming pressure to succeed. The Olympics is particularly grueling in that respect—there are no seasons, no multiple game series, not many chances to fail. When you've worked every day for four years (or a lifetime) for a goal, and all that work comes down to the next ten minutes, it's hard not to feel pressure—shattering pressure. But it is precisely how you deal with that pressure that dictates your chances of success. It is the catch-22 vise for Olympic athletes.

Randy has found his way through. He's regarded as the strongest mental competitor in MMA. He develops uncanny game plans and sticks to them. He knows in his heart that he has as good a chance to win as his opponent.

"The first thing is perspective. I frame things in a positive way and stay reflective. It's almost a cliché, but in the grand scheme of my life, if the worst thing that happens to me is I lose a wrestling match, even if it's the Olympic finals, then I'm doing pretty damn good." A fight, even a title fight, barely registers.

"Right away that takes some of the pressure off. I know I'll survive it, it's not the end of the world. I won't like it; I don't like to lose, but the people who really care about me don't care about me because I win. They care about me and want me to be happy. I think this helps me overcome the classic fear of failure that most athletes set themselves up for. They're so worried about looking stupid, or making a mistake, they don't do what they've trained to do. They get in their own way."

Randy understands what I'm looking for.

"You have to put a positive frame on things. In wrestling, in a heated match, sometimes the difference in the match is that you got called for 'passivity,' or your opponent did. You know you're working your ass off, and then the referee decides for whatever reason that you are more passive than your opponent, so the ref gives him the choice, and your opponent sticks you in the disadvantaged position. And it would get to me, because no one was as active as I was in matches. It would really mess with me when I got called for passivity." He shakes his head in remembered frustration.

"Then I figured out, with my coaches, that it was okay, it was a coin toss. The ref was going to call it on somebody. So why am I getting upset? It was taking me out of my game, and I was losing matches because everyone would put you in the disadvantaged position, and I'd get turned and scored on because I was pissed off.

"So I started framing it as 'out of my control,' what the referee does. It's no big deal, this is just another thing to beat. Now my opponent will put me at a disadvantage, but he's still not going to score on me. So, psychologically, that will have a big effect on him, *it's one more place where I can break this guy*. Who gives a shit what the ref thinks? It's all about my opponent.

"Once I wrapped my head around that, I started savoring those situations, not that I ever stalled, but when the passivity call came I looked at it as a positive. Here's a place where he can't turn me, another place for me to attack him, wear him down. By creating a different perspective on the same situation, then *technically* things went a lot better. I thought better, my defense was better, and I had more success."

When Yagyu Munenori (the legendary swordsman and contemporary of Musashi's) wrote that "another man's sword is your

133

sword," he meant just that. If your understanding is deeper, his weapons are your weapons, and you can turn his weapons against him. His own sword is more dangerous to him than to you.

The importance of coaching and cornering is not lost on Randy. "The corner has to have a real understanding of his fighter, seeing things that he can do. You use a word or a phrase, when he gets distracted, when he gets flustered or hit, you use the word or phrase to get you centered, bring you back to your training. Maybe 'move your feet' and that goes to your game plan, footwork.

"A guy gets caught, his bell gets rung, he needs a place to go mentally, to get him back to safety. For Chuck it was, *Chin down, hands up.* For Tito it was, *Scramble, don't concede,* because I didn't want to give up the takedown. The Tito fight became about who was going to give up the takedown. If I got it he was going to have a bad night, and if he got it, I would probably have a bad night.

"But you have to be careful with saying *don't get taken down* because that's a negative statement. I was coaching this kid who was winning by one point with thirty seconds left in the match. All he has to do is not get taken down so I'm screaming *don't get taken down!* And whaddya think happens? What did I put in his head?"

Randy frowns and shakes his head ruefully.

"Instead of giving him positive things to do—*get an underhook, tie him up, stay in his face,* the things that got him to this point of winning—I give him something negative and he gets tentative.

"It's the same in fights. *Don't get hit by the right hand,* well shit I just got nailed by it."

He pauses, musing, and then picks up his earlier thread.

"So that positive phrase will refocus him, keep him on track. You want to be calm and focused, not emotional and excitable. But if he needs a slap in the face to wake him up, you gotta do it. All fighters are different. Forrest Griffin needs to be slapped around the locker room or he'll have a slow start. Karo Parisiyan is the same way. You gotta jack him up. With Mike Pyle I try to settle him down. If he's smiling and joking he'll do well, and if he's intense and inside himself something's wrong."

When you hear Randy describe what he's going to do in a fight, or talk about another fighter, his language is interesting. It's technical and dry and devoid of emotion. Randy sees a problem, a technical problem, not an emotional fight filled with fear and rage. He talks about solving Tim Sylvia's reach advantage like a plumber talks about coming at a leak.

There's a reason for this dispassionate observation, and it goes back to wrestling. Even from the beginning, in high school, Randy found what worked was an "in-your-face" type of wrestling, which required he outwork his opponent. In his book *Wrestling for Fighting,* Randy said, "My style certainly wasn't the prettiest, but it proved quite effective. During my senior year in high school, I plotted and pounded my way . . . to the State Championships." You could say that he's been plotting and pounding ever since.

Randy can't deny his own genetic gifts—he's a natural athlete whose longevity has defied all conventional wisdom on aging. He single-handedly keeps about a dozen aging fighters from retiring. They see him win and think, *Why not me?* But they're not Randy. He was featured on a TV show, National Geographic's *Fight Science,* where they measured his lactic acid levels (the acid that builds up in muscles as they fatigue and burn oxygen; that tired feeling is lactic acid buildup). Randy was straining and choking a training partner—and his lactic acid levels actually *dropped,* as did the jaws of the monitoring scientists.

Randy may not have been the fastest or most purely athletic wrestler, but he loved to train and he could train harder than just about anyone. He's smart—at Oklahoma State, after the army, he had a 4.0 GPA and was an academic all-American as well as a wrestling all-American. Although they called him the Natural, Randy never felt that way about himself. He titled his autobiography *Becoming the Natural,* and it shows how his career, his success, was a process, that it was worked for—it wasn't a free ride on talent.

His brain has been his biggest asset in his fighting career. Most other fighters will express admiration for how scientific he is, how technical. Randy was always developing his "plotting" skills as well as his "pounding" ones.

These skills—watching opponents closely, studying tape, and crafting game plans—were honed to a fine point during that long Olympic chase. In the years that Randy didn't make the team, especially in '92 and '96, he was stuck in the unofficial Scrub Club.

"That's what we called the number two and number three guys, the Scrub Club. We'd travel with the team but wouldn't get tickets to many events. We were alternates but it was only until the first weigh-in, after that you couldn't enter. We scouted, we filmed matches all day long so that the guy we had advancing in the tournament knew who he had next. We filled out scouting reports and watched tons and tons of tape."

Even now, Randy sighs at the memories of monotony tinged with gnawing disappointment.

"That mind-set carried over into fighting. I watched because I liked to watch fights. I would watch how guys were technically doing things, making adjustments."

Randy had a whole professional life of scouting opponents and breaking down tape, and he applies those lessons to all his fights. He would see what he needed to learn and then hit the gym religiously, intelligently, to learn it.

"I had several of Vitor Belfort's fights on tape and I watched them carefully. I saw okay, he's left-handed and leads every combination with his left, and he's very straight-ahead, and he'll blow through you if you stand in front of him—so I've got to work on footwork. I had to learn to box because wrestling won't work, so I got a boxing coach and started circling left all day. I was confident that if I could get my hands on him I could wear him out, make him work harder than he wanted to work. No one gave me a snowball's chance in hell."

It was all the new knowledge, hiring new coaches and learning entirely new disciplines, that really excited Randy. "I love to train and learn. For me a that's like a kid in a candy store. The things I was learning in wrestling at the end of my career were so minuscule, tiny technical variations, little changes to grips, things like that. But fighting had so many dimensions, new techniques, it was as exciting as hell. When I'm done learning I'm done winning."

Randy learned from his own teaching of wrestling. "The more I taught, the more I dissected my game. And the more I dissected my game, the more technical I became. A lot of wrestlers never truly take the time to analyze how they do what they do, which makes it difficult for them to go down on all fours with a fine-tooth comb and refine their game," he said in *Wrestling for Fighting*.

He could have learned from Dan Gable, especially Gable's "back-off-to-win" experience, how Gable had been winning his last match in college but kept going for the pin and lost. Gable learned that lesson, internalized it, and won with it.

In the '96 finals for a berth on the Olympic team Randy was wrestling against his "nemesis" Mike Foy. He was winning by 9 points with forty-five seconds left and could have "run all over the mat and he never would have beat me." But Randy "wanted to tech fall his ass. I wanted to *beat* him, so I stayed on him, aggressive, went for that last fall and I ended up on my back and pinned." Like Dan, that loss is ever fresh. Watching the match today, it's hard to believe that was a pin. Randy was pushing Foy all over the place. In the final seconds his shoulders brush the mat as they roll over for the briefest moment.

But just as Gable probably never would have had the fire to have the Olympic career he did without losing that final NCAA match, Randy might never have had the fire to succeed in the way he did as a fighter if he'd won a medal in the Olympics. And it's something Randy is tangentially aware of.

Even to this day, Randy's wrestling matches are more important to him than his fighting career. When I ask him about losing in general, he talks solely about wrestling. Maybe he thought I meant wrestling—but the mind-set is revealing. "I lost the NCAA finals twice, and the Olympic trials four times when I could have made the team. But I learned to put it in perspective."

Randy went into one of his favorite topics.

"I started thinking about the differences between being nervous and being excited—they're very similar. The physical attributes you assign to each are real similar, and one has negative connotations. Nervousness means something bad is happening and you're not enjoying it, and being excited makes you smile, you love what you're doing and good things are happening."

I had gone through a similar experience years ago, when I first thought about being a writer. I was anxious about the future, about not knowing where I was going to be living in three or four months, never having a salary. I realized that I couldn't do that—not if I wanted to be a writer. I couldn't live in a state of anxiety, it had to be excitement. I tell that to friends or people I meet who want to be writers or artists, anybody who wants to do something different, a job without security. Don't let it be anxiety; let that uncertainty generate excitement. If you can't make that switch you shouldn't be a writer, or an artist, or a fighter. You won't enjoy it.

There have been plenty of scientific studies that show how laughter and being relaxed reduces stress hormones and performance inhibitors. Smiling changes our brain. It's common sense, sports psych 101. Randy's own relationship with fear is distinct, studied. He turns his opponents into athletic puzzles. It's not about them, personally, and he has no emotion about them.

"In the Tim Sylvia fight, I knew it was going to be a little problem for Tim—because he fights on emotion. He has to generate a little dislike, a little anger. And Tim and I are friends, he stayed at my house. I knew that would make things a little harder for him, because he respects me."

Randy has no problem fighting his friends because of where he comes from, the wrestling; it's not personal.

"It's problem solving. With Chuck Liddell, I knew there was a distinct risk that if I did what I had to do to beat him I could get knocked out. So at some point you have to make friends with the worst-case possibility. But hey, if the worst thing that happens is you lose a fucking fight, you're doing good. So risk it."

Randy is a competitor, it's something that gets said a lot. He loves the process, the training and learning, but the "pinnacle of competition" for him is when you see your opponent break. "Once you do it . . . you realize that's what it's all about. I never even really saw it until I went to Oklahoma State. But you open a guy's eyes to that mind-set and it changes him.

"The first time that I felt it was with Vitor." Randy smiles avidly. Here's something he enjoys remembering, trying to quantify. "It's almost a noise. I liken it to a stick snapping. You can hear it, feel the stick break."

He mimes snapping a stick in half.

"Tito was close, he struggled with it. From the third round on I would take him right to the edge, I would feel the will start to go, and he screamed. He'd find a way. He knew he was close to giving up but he'd come storming back, he'd try and fight and find a way to fight on. He never really did break, he was right there teetering and I couldn't push him over.

"You need to have the conditioning and mentality to stay one step ahead, make them work and keep scoring, and frustrate them, until they try and stop it some other way. With Vitor I felt the tension leave him, and shortly after, he fell over. There was no big shot, but all these little ones. Physically, he'd reached his limit."

Randy talked at length about breaking a fighter's will, saying "the way you do it is through conditioning, being one step ahead of them . . . keep making them work, keep scoring, at some point they'll break and give in to you, they'll try and make it stop some other way. In wrestling, our national coach was big on 'grind' matches. You'd do your own warm-up for fifteen minutes and then wrestle with one partner for ninety minutes straight. You didn't stop, drink water, or do anything but go for ninety minutes, and I saw more guys break in that time. I saw guys start crying."

Randy talked about watching Rulon Gardner, a heavyweight, and his brother Reynold, who "didn't look like anything, athletically, but they'd flat push guys and break their hearts."

I asked Randy if he ever broke in those grind matches, and he smiles a little smile. His special secret.

"You know, I never broke. I got beat up plenty but I never broke. I go with the heavyweights like Rulon and they physically beat me up, and I couldn't score, but I never got to the point where I quit trying. I have no idea why. Everybody has their limit. I'm sure I have my limit, too. I've just never reached it in a ninety-minute grind match."

Or in a five-round MMA title fight. There may very well be something that could break Randy, some limit, but you get the feeling it's not a fight.

IT NEVER ALWAYS
GETS WORSE

David Horton. (Courtesy: David Horton)

There is magic in far-running. There's an aura, a mystique around the Paiute Indians, who could somehow make a hundred miles in a day across the Mojave, or the Japanese "marathon monks" of Mount Hiei, who cover a route of forty-nine miles every day for months on end. Today's ultramarathoners run races of more than a hundred miles in the desert heat or southern forests. These are mysterious, mythic figures covering such immense distances that mere mortals tremble in uncertainty and disbelief. It can't be, but it is—and so often dismissed, with a shrug or a shake of the head, into the realm of modern legend, half-believed, incomprehensible.

I remember as a child reading about colonial New England and Canada, of the French *coureur de bois* (the fur trappers, the "runners of the woods") making fifty miles a day in the winter, wearing snowshoes, and then wrapping themselves in bearskin and sleeping under a tree. It sounded outlandish, that they could be so different from us, so much tougher.

I took a Wilderness EMT course in New Hampshire in 2002 to help my Wildland Firefighting career. One of the instructors had been an Ironman triathlete. I had asked him about the absurd thing that was an Ironman race—to swim 2.4 miles, bike 112 miles, and then run a marathon. He had laughed at my attitude. The common attitude, *I could never do that it.*

"You don't know how fast you are," he said. "I ran my first half-marathon, and then a little while later ran my first marathon—in the same time. It's all mental, all in the push."

I fought fire with a guy who'd been a Division 1 cross-country runner, and he'd said with a shake of his shaggy head, "It's all mental, dude."

Kyle Klingman, the young assistant at the Dan Gable Wrestling Museum, had told me he wasn't a wrestler, but I could see he was some kind of athlete. He had a cadaverous look, a tinge of the fanatic in his eyes, that had initially puzzled me. Then I found out he ran ultramarathons. When I asked him about that mentality, Kyle led me to David Horton, a strange, legendary character even among the rogues gallery of ultra-runners.

Horton once held the Appalachian Trail record, that famous trail that runs 2,175 miles from Georgia to Maine. He'd run it in 52 days, 9 hours. I'd met fast "through-hikers" who did it in four months. Horton had *run* the thing, forty-plus miles a day for more than fifty days. He'd run the third best time in the Trans-America, a race from L.A. to New York. And he'd recently, at the age of fifty-five, crushed the record for the Pacific Crest Trail, 2,650 miles in sixty-six days, a feat well documented in *The Runner,* a film by another ultrarunner J. B. Benna of Journey Films. Ultrarunning is defined as anything longer than a marathon, which is twenty-six miles. Usually the races are either fifty or a hundred miles, or they take place over a series of days. What Horton does is on the far end of even that extreme category.

Horton was also a professor of kinesiology at Jerry Falwell's Liberty University in Lynchburg, Virginia, where he also taught running. He was a big Dan Gable fan. Kyle gave me his number and I caught up with him for a phone call.

We started talking about Dan Gable. Horton was effusive. "I think he's the toughest athlete that I know of. I can't think of anyone tougher . . . not only his wrestling but his coaching. Why was he like that? Sure his parents helped, and his situation, but I think he was just a tougher-than-nails little boy, too."

Horton's voice is accented and charming, with some of that southern courtliness and rhythm. He's eloquent, used to expounding and teaching, comfortable in that role, but pure and honest. Everything false has been burned away; like many great fighters there's mostly honesty and pure emotion. Like an asteroid falling to the earth, these people have endured so much beyond the limits of what they thought was human endurance that any falseness and cuteness, anything extraneous, got seared off.

"Do you feel that overtraining is a myth?" I asked him.

"Yes, overtraining is a myth," he said. "The harder you train, the more you train, the better you'll do. World-class athletes train on the verge of injury. A guy I know who finished second in the Trans-America Race said he took a leave of absence from his job and for two months, in preparation, averaged fifty miles a day."

The Trans-America footrace, of which there have been eight, is held in sixty-four stages, on sixty-four straight days, and the time is cumulative. This race was nine weeks, averaging 317 miles per week. Day after day of 52 miles, 44 miles, 36 miles, back to 52 miles. How do you prepare for something like that?

"I said to him, 'I feel that was a little too much.' And he agreed with me. For two months I averaged a hundred and sixty miles a week, about half what he did, and I ran the third fastest time ever. Was that too much? Nope, that was about right . . . but who knows, maybe if I'd done more I'd have done better . . . but the only way to find out is to do it again!"

So maybe overtraining isn't exactly a myth, I thought. You should just behave as if it is, until you can prove otherwise by injuring yourself. It's not a myth but you need to pretend it is.

Horton's voice swoops and swirls over the phone, animated. I bet he's a good teacher. He understands that to teach you have to entertain.

"Ted Corbitt, the father of ultrarunning, a black man, just passed away in the last few years. He was in New York and he'd train a hundred and fifty, a hundred and seventy, two hundred miles a week—and this is at a time when forty or fifty miles a week was thought of as outrageous. He found two hundred worked for him."

When I explained my project and asked him about the mental game in ultrarunning, I could hear him inhale thoughtfully down the line.

"It's a tough subject," he said. "If you asked me what percentage for the split between mental and physical, I often say it's eighty-fifty, which of course doesn't quite add up. Any sport like this, with a prolonged level of discomfort, it's going to have a strong mental component.

"Success in ultras depends on the ability to sustain discomfort for prolonged periods of time, whether it's hours or days or many days . . . it's just that. All it takes to relieve it is to stop—and that's what we're fighting against, all the time."

It was interesting to think about—winning the battle against the urge to stop, that's what it takes. It reminded me of the difference between a combat photographer and a soldier in a war. The soldier has no choice, he has to be there, while the photographer is facing a test of courage, an endurance test, that he can leave at any time and go home. Easier to be brave for the photographer, when it's a choice.

"The body can always do more than the mind thinks it can. In the first year of the Trans-America, running from Los Angeles to New York, a young man got a stress fracture in Missouri and for a period of a couple weeks he still had to run the average of forty-five miles a day, and he was just barely making the cutoffs. But he made them. And toward the end his foot started recovering, and he started running fast again.

"The first time I did the Appalachian Trail I was averaging forty miles a day from Georgia to Maine," he says almost in a singsong, he's told this story so many times.

146

"On days eight, nine, and ten I had severe tendonitis in one shin, and one day all day long I was urinating blood. For a thousand miles I was dealing with shin splints, icing, and using anti-inflammatories . . . but then finally they got well!

"Your body sends signals to your mind, *It's time to stop, let up, this doesn't feel good, it HURTS!* The mind has to override the signal.

"You know those little glass globe candles on the tables at restaurants? With a narrow opening at the top, just a few inches across? Now, you can put your hand over the mouth of that candle, and if you hold it there long enough the flame will go out. But it'll hurt. If someone bet you ten dollars you might try it, but it starts to burn a little and you jerk your hand away. Now if someone told you 'I'll give you a million dollars' . . . NOW there are all sorts of signals in your mind. That's what mental training is about, learning to deal with signals and what you can override, and what you shouldn't."

I asked him about the ability to override, where it comes from.

"It's not an easy thing, it's very difficult, and it doesn't come overnight. Any time I go out to do something extremely difficult, I always wonder, *Do I have the edge, this time?* Because I've done it before, does it mean I can do it again?"

I thought about Tom Brands, Gable's apostle, talking about the "mysteries of tough guys." You get the sense David Horton takes to the trail in some way to see what will happen, out of curiosity, to see where his mind and body will take him once he's gone farther than he thought he could.

"It's still about *how bad do you want it.* Once you've achieved some major thing, can you repeat? Sometimes you can, sometimes you can't."

I asked him about the athlete's dilemma—how to tell what kind of pain it is. Is the pain just hurting or is it from being injured?

"Trial and error, the only way. No book or magazine can tell you, and it doesn't matter what other people say.

"Say you sprain your ankle. Should you stop and ice it or keep going? Every time I've sprained an ankle I kept going. But does that mean everyone should? No."

He thought about it for a moment. "I've seen broken bones that didn't swell up, and things swell up hugely that there was nothing really wrong with. The only way to know is experience." And to have that drive to push through, that first time—to see, to go find out.

I watched *The Runner,* the documentary about Horton's record-breaking Pacific Crest Trail run from Mexico to Canada in sixty-six days with a 300,000-foot total elevation change. That's averaging more than 4,500 feet of change *a day,* which is horrific. It's an ungodly amount of up and down.

There were a few things that kept coming to mind when I watched the documentary. Here was a guy who wore his heart on his sleeve; his emotions and feelings are out there, in play. He obviously can harness them and put them to work.

When I asked him about using his emotions, David responded eagerly, almost confessing a dirty secret: "One of the things I do, it sounds strange, I sometimes will make myself cry. I'll think about my family, or home, or I'll start singing a sad song, and I'll start crying. Then after I cry, I feel better—not just mentally but physically. Physically, I FEEL BETTER." He constructs a cathartic release for himself, something the ancient Greeks thought would restore and purify you.

The other thing that struck me, watching the documentary, was the dual nature of David. Sometimes, at rest, he seemed frail, some fifty-five-year-old machine, too old to have a hope of success, already past his limit. But then, when he runs, there's a sense of iron running through his body. A large chunk of steel, woven inside that fragile, aging, human frame. Endlessly durable, wound tight.

"Commitment to a goal, that's a big part of ultrarunning. Doing what you said you were going to do. It's as simple as that. Part of it is that I tell people; I have a team that helps me." David sets himself up, he talks about his goals, to give him another reason not to quit later. He's told everyone he knows he's doing it.

"The Appalachian Trail, the Trans-America, the PCT—once I start one of those things, I'm totally committed. I don't view it as dedication. It's just something I do. It's like the light switch in my office. When I open the door and turn on the switch, the light comes on. That's what I do when I start running. I don't think about it. I just get up in the morning and go. To me it's not dedication, it's commitment.

"Once in a while, people crack. On these long things . . ." This was a term David would use often, "these long things," and he meant the incredible endurance races, or self-tests. There's something poignant about it, something loose and generic. He could be talking about something else, not a race but some terrible trial, an illness, a war.

"By and large, once people get into these long things, they don't stop. They just keep going. It's not dedication, or mental toughness—you just keep doing it."

I asked him about it, the kinds of games you play with yourself.

"There are two statements that I use," he said. "The first is simple: this too shall pass. It will end. It can't last forever . . . because sometimes things will feel that way."

David is one of the very few finishers of the Barkley Marathon, an ultramarathon that makes even professional ultrarunners shudder and cross themselves. It's sometimes referred to as "the race that eats its young."

In 1973 Gary Cantrell had been hiking in Frozen Head Park in Tennessee when he saw an ancient trail marked on the map, considered by the park to be impassable. When he went back later, Gary was thinking of the recent prison break of Martin Luther King Jr.'s assassin, James Earl Ray, who had made four miles through the woods in fifty-five hours, from a nearby prison. The terrain was too harsh for Ray to make it any farther. Gary thought he could do a hundred miles in that time, even in similar terrain. In 1985 he finally hiked it, and then he started the race the next year.

The Barkley was born, a one-hundred-mile race through the woods, five horrible loops up steep thorny mountains, over fallen trees, and under bushes, with very little support in terms of aid stations and water. Even the trail is easy to lose. There are eleven books, hidden along the way, and the runners must find the books and tear out a page. It became infamous in the small ultramarathon world as the hardest, baddest, most miserable experience in running. It breaks top professionals all the time, with a total vertical climb of 54,000 feet, trees down crossing the trail, mud slides. David Horton was one of the seven finishers (in under sixty hours), of the 650 who have attempted it since 1986. If you want to enter, you have to write a long essay about "Why I should be allowed to run the Barkley," even to get a chance to race. As Cantrell once said, "To run the Barkley is to know humility and fear." Horton had survived and triumphed because of his second maxim.

"The second one is very, very important: *It never always gets worse*," he said, and paused, reverential. He wanted me to think about that one.

"A lot of people think this way. If you said you just ran ten miles they'd say, "That's great!," or if you said you just ran a marathon they'd say, "That's fantastic!" He sighed.

"You run a fifty-mile race and they say 'That's stupid, it's crazy!' Now why is that? The reason is, people theorize, *I know how I feel when I run five miles, or twenty-six miles, and that hurts!* So fifty miles must be twice the pain and torture!

"But it isn't. It never always gets worse. Sometimes it gets worse, but then sometimes, IT'LL GO AWAY!" He seemed boggled with amazement.

"I've been in races where I was trashed, I was dog meat, and a day, or two days, later I felt chipper, I felt good. So when you're in a bad race, and it's ten miles into a fifty-mile race and it's hurting bad right now, what's it going to be at forty?" he breathed and changed his tone, his voice falling mellow and clear. "It may feel a lot better . . . and there's only one way to find out."

David was a professor at a Christian college and I knew that he'd been saved. I asked him about his faith.

"To me it's simple. I'm God's creation, the Earth is God's creation, and God gives us different talents and abilities. We're supposed to use and develop our talents, to get out the mission and the word. My calling, the things I do, God has enabled me—to teach, to run, to do long, long things. To me it's one ball of wax. I'm a runner and a Christian. I'm running on God's creation and I'm God's creation myself." It made me think of a quote from *Zen in the Art of Archery*: "For them [the masters], the contest consists in the archer aiming at himself—and yet not at himself, in hitting himself—and yet not himself, and thus becoming simultaneously the aimer and the aim."

"Who would ever have thought it? Did I think it would go this way? No, I never did.

"I think of two verses, Philippians 4:13 and 4:19. I can do all things through Christ, who strengthens me. If God wants me to do this, his strength is unbelievable. On the PCT I knew I would finish this thing. It was just a question of how long, how much torture and pain. I knew God wanted me to do it. God will supply all my needs according to his riches and glory. What percent of our brain, our strength, our lungs, goes unused most of the time? When you hear about a person lifting a car off a loved one, is that God giving us strength, or is that God allowing us to find the hidden strength we already have? The answer is yes. Both. We have a phenomenal amount of power and He can give it to us.

"I do know, in every person, Christian or non-Christian, saved, lost, that our bodies are capable of so much more than we think possible."

Watching or reading about David finishing the Appalachian Trail or the Pacific Crest Trail is strangely moving, even sublime, although the rational mind understands the endeavor to be absurd, ridiculous, pointless in the practical sense. It seems a twisted form of hapless masochism, yet it is also proof of the power of pure will, of a man's ability to do so much more than thought possible, and in some way this ennobles us all.

THE CONSISTENT
IMPROVER

Kenny Florian versus Pat Stevenson.
(Courtesy: MMAWeekly.com)

The Ultimate Fighter reality show began in 2005 on Spike TV, an offshoot and feeder for the Ultimate Fighting Championship, which had previously only been on pay-per-view. The show—specifically, the free fights—broke MMA into mainstream America. It was part of the reality TV craze, but in all honesty the show's popularity was due to the fights; at the end of each show, contestants (young hopefuls) would fight an unedited MMA fight. It was the fight that brought the viewers, a chance to watch MMA without paying forty bucks.

For fight fans, it was sometimes hard to watch, simply because of the inexperience of the contestants. Nerves play a huge role in fighting. Studies have shown (as Pat Miletich said) that a sky-high heart rate affects your thinking, vision, and hearing and that the only way to maintain a reasonable heart rate, in a fight, is by living through it. Fighters make peace with the terror of "fight or flight" and learn to harness it. But it takes time.

Fighting professionally, on a national stage, requires a tremendous amount of experience to perform well. Any boxing match you've seen on TV, most likely the fighters have had a hundred amateur bouts and at least ten or fifteen professional ones. After years of work like that the boxers look smooth and graceful, professional. The fighters on Spike, with the chance to win a shot at the big show, had records that were more along the lines of 4–1, or even 2–0.

The young fighters went through all the growing pains that often don't get seen by the public—freezing in a fight or completely abandoning game plans. The fights were very raw, and in some cases exciting. Hard-core fight fans watched (because they were free) but were critical, sometimes without understanding quite why—they just weren't used to seeing guys this inexperienced on TV.

Kenny Florian, an underdog on the first show, was a contestant with a Brazilian jiu-jitsu background and only a few MMA fights. He was drastically undersized, but tougher than expected, and he made it to the finals—where he succumbed to nerves and the relentless pressure of a hard wrestler, Diego Sanchez (an experienced MMA fighter with a pro record of 11–0). Kenny was an ordinary-looking college kid, and he was in fact ridiculously small for the 185-pound weight class. He moved down, from 185 past 170, and finally to his natural weight class of 155.

Kenny looks like somebody I could have gone to school with, a college kid from Boston. But he'd found and excelled in Brazilian jiu-jitsu, and then MMA. He'd taken two losses—two huge, grinding losses —and somehow come away stronger, come away a better fighter. Those losses had made him.

I met Kenny on the outskirts of Boston, in Somerville, at Sityodtong, Mark DellaGrotte's muay Thai school. I worked out a few times with Kenny and his strength coach, Kevin Kearns, and over a few weeks developed a conversation with him.

Kenny has an open smiling way and a friendly manner, and instantly we were laughing and joking. He's of the same humor background as I am, we did voices from *The Simpsons,* and other brilliant repartee. He's medium height, with a big head and a large, noble nose, maybe some Peruvian Indian in there somewhere, peeking out. Thick black hair and eyebrows, and an instant, open grin that squeezes his eyes to slits, familiar creases on his cheeks—

Kenny Florian laughs a lot. His sense of confidence is powerful, nonthreatening but complete. He's been in deep waters (he's swum with muscle sharks) and come back alive.

Kenny's parents are from Peru, although they're of European descent. So that nose is Italian, maybe. His father was a surgeon who came to the United States to study and stayed for the opportunities. Kenny talks admiringly about how driven his dad was, how he wouldn't take no for an answer when it came to going to the medical school he wanted. "He taught me a lot about determination, about proving people wrong—and never being afraid to work hard. Some people accept their limitations, but my dad never saw any reason why you couldn't be the best."

Kenny was recruited by Olympic soccer development out of high school, and he played at Boston College (which is Division 1), but he wasn't sure there was anywhere to go afterward. Professional soccer in 1999 wasn't established in the United States, and a hobby was starting to dominate his dreams.

As a kid he'd seen the first UFC and thought it was awesome. The real deal. Kenny had the young boy's fantasy that I and so many other American males had, of being Bruce Lee, able to beat up fifteen guys without getting a scratch. "When I was a kid my older brother Edgar would have me fight in what I called the 'Pankration Olympics.' He was the Don King in the neighborhood. He'd set up fights between all the kids. He was an instigator—he'd get them to footrace, and then box with the gloves on, and then, 'Well, let's see who's tougher, take the gloves off.'" Kenny laughed.

It was much later that Kenny and his other brother, Keith, stumbled into jiu-jitsu. They saw Royce Gracie do the unthinkable. "The moves made sense to me," Kenny said about his early affinity for jiu-jitsu. It became his secret other girlfriend, the one he was thinking about when he should have been thinking about soccer. She was always on his mind.

Kenny is in many ways a difficult figure for me to reconcile, personally. He's not a huge, ripped, preternaturally fast guy, and although he's an obvious athlete he doesn't seem like one. Instead, he's a guy who *believes* in himself, in an interesting way. He makes me embarrassed about my own mental limitations.

"My goal is to beat the hell out of the last Kenny Florian I fought," he says over lunch. "I'm going to look at his game and blow him out of the water. You can't compare yourself to Fedor, to BJ Penn, or to those tippy-top guys. You really want to be as good as *you* can possibly be. You want to be able to be the most amazing fighter that you could ever be, someone who can do things that Fedor or George St. Pierre can't possibly comprehend."

I always felt like I started too late. I didn't find muay Thai until I was twenty-six years old, and I'm not a beast, I don't have great hand-speed or power that can make up for a lack of experience. I would always justify my shying away from turning pro like this: I'm not that good an athlete. I could play and practice basketball every day for my whole life and I'd never be Michael Jordan, right? What Kenny is remonstrating is that, sure, you'll never be Michael Jordan, but you could be something else, you could be a great professional NBA player in your own style. Maybe a great passer, or a three-point shooter. It comes around to an important facet of fighting: acknowledging your identity and working to make it the best version of *you*.

"We all could be great, but we have to open our mind to the way in which we could."

This attitude is not something Kenny always understood. He arrived at it over time, and part of it came from the two losses I was interested in talking about.

Kenny had come into the first season of *The Ultimate Fighter* with just a few fights and a long history of Brazilian jiu-jitsu competition. He was a gifted black belt who'd trained in Boston with Roberto Maia, and gone to Rio to train at Gracie Barra. He was the smallest guy on the show, some of those guys probably cut ten or fifteen pounds. Kenny did well in the practice sessions and had his eyes opened to what MMA training was all about. When he won his first fight on the show, it was a bit of a surprise, just because he seemed so undersized and one-dimensional. He made it to the finale, against the much bigger and more experienced Diego Sanchez. Still, he was there as the jiu-jitsu guy, to see if he could win in MMA with his pure jiu-jitsu.

"I was so nervous. The real ability now is that I'm mastering that fear. I've had way more fights in the UFC than locally, so I did my growing up in the UFC, which is a tough thing to do. It was a blessing and a curse. A lot of doubt and fear, and the uncontrol was scary, but now I use that fear. It puts the pressure on me in a good way." The ability to make fear work for you is essential, and there are no short cuts. It takes experience and time.

The fights on *The Ultimate Fighter* had been televised, but there was a crowd of only twenty or thirty people watching in the room. Here, at the finale, was a stadium packed with fans. The pressure and the shock of the new took their toll.

"During the finale, it hit me all of a sudden. I was warming up backstage, hitting mitts, and fifteen seconds into it I am dead tired. My hands and forearms are cramping, they felt like lead weights, and I started to feel panic. I was trying to pump myself up, but I felt terrible. There's a camera in my face and Dana White was wishing me luck, and all my friends and family, and the piss test, there's money—it was this huge blur. I couldn't understand what was happening. How did I get here? And then suddenly I'm in the Octagon, and I say 'What the hell?' to myself. And the fight starts and I'm circling, circling forever, and I think 'What am I supposed to do?' and by the time I realize I'm in a fight, and I know what to do, Diego Sanchez is mounted on me. What happened? The fight shouldn't have been like that—I got beat before it even started." It was a classic example of the big-show jitters, the nerves, for which experience is the only cure.

Kenny took that loss hard, but what really bugged him was that he knew he could have done better. He'd done better against Diego in practice, and he'd held his own against all those guys in the gym who were more highly touted. Kenny's brother and training partner, Keith, said, "The cameras, the pressure, they got him in that fight. He said, *That wasn't me and I can prove it.*"

"After the Diego fight I said to myself, 'I'm gonna try this.' It's not about the contract, whatever, it's about me really going for this. I can be that MMA fighter. I knew how I did against Diego in training. I performed so horribly in that fight. I need to do this for myself. It became personal." He used the loss twofold, both as fuel to drive himself and as an instruction on what he needed to fix.

Kenny felt like he'd let himself down, that he hadn't performed up to his potential, and it rankled him. He turned it inward and drove himself to become a professional *mixed* martial artist, as opposed to just the "bjj guy." He dropped down to the 155 weight class, for which he was still on the small side. Kenny laughs, "I usually end up cutting about two pounds, and I don't tell anyone because the wrestlers would all make fun of me—that's not a cut!"

At 155, Kenny proved a force and strung together a series of victories, and then he fought Sean Sherk for the lightweight title. Sherk, the "Muscle Shark," has a nightmare style for anyone in the division. He's a hulking, ballistic wrestler. He'd been a top contender at 170 pounds but had fallen short against the top few guys. So Sherk dropped down a weight class. He is a titanic lightweight, muscled like a comic-book superhero. He's a relentless takedown machine with great defense, good boxing, and limitless cardio. Stylistically, Sherk is a terrible matchup for almost anyone at 155.

I still remember Kenny's entrance for that fight. He came in wearing full samurai regalia, he was the ronin, the masterless warrior with a domed straw hat and a kimono. It was awesome, the kind of theater that is sadly lacking in the "all-business" utilitarian aesthetic of the UFC. He even had both the swords on, "because only the samurai was allowed to wear both swords."

"Before I even fought in UFC, I always had a love for the samurai culture—the warrior mentality. They lived a very peaceful life, they were gardeners, painters and poets, but when they went out and did battle they were fully committed. I said to myself if I ever got in the UFC I would do the samurai thing."

The fight went the way everyone thought it would—Sherk overwhelming Kenny with takedowns and ground and pound, although Kenny did land a slashing elbow that had Sherk bleeding heavily the whole fight. Kenny couldn't stand up, he couldn't get away from Sherk, but he never stopped looking for a submission, he never stopped looking to win for five five-minute rounds. "I got that determination from the Sanchez fight," he said. "It allowed me to keep fighting. Even when it seemed hopeless, it never was." Kenny had gone in with a bad back, a recurring injury, but he never took refuge in that.

"In the fight against Sherk, I couldn't adapt to the way he was holding me in my guard. And I thought, wow, I can't stand up. I should have worked on that. And he's not giving me enough to submit him. He's being consistent with his takedowns . . . but it's too late now. I have to try and open it up, to do something crazy to open the fight up. I didn't have the tools in place to adapt. I had a hammer and I needed a screwdriver."

It was a hard thing to swallow, and Kenny was depressed for a while after the fight. But it led him to rethink his approach. He had to become a complete professional.

"You need to have a brutal honesty with yourself. Did I do everything possible to win that fight? What didn't I do? And analyze honestly, without bias, from a technical standpoint. And then ask yourself, 'Did I do everything in my training to prepare?' It's about moving forward. We plague ourselves with stupidity, with bad thoughts. We put our brains in that prison. You can carry that fear with you, inside you, and it can keep you from changing for the better."

Kenny continued, "That loss drives me. Any loss I've had drives me. I don't think there's a day when I haven't thought about the Sherk fight. I never want that to happen again. It drives me in training. I changed a lot of things since that fight. Training happens all the time, every day, even without a fight in the future. It was a huge hole in my game. I didn't have a full-time strength and conditioning guy, and I needed to close that hole. Sherk was a real professional and I wasn't."

Since then, Kenny has worked with Kevin Kearns, his strength and conditioning coach, and made tremendous progress—he feels much stronger and more explosive. The injuries that plagued him have been rehabilitated. Against fighters that are supposed to be stronger than him, a deceptively stringy Kenny has shown plenty of pure strength. He's won several fights in a row, finishing all of his opponents. But Kenny's permanently dissatisfied, even in victory.

"I hate my wins, I just hate my losses more. I enjoyed the Sam Stout one—it was a coming-out party. He'd just beat Spencer Fischer, and I knew I could beat him easy and I did it. But I look back two weeks later and I think *that sucked*. That fight was a nice clean fight, no mistakes. But I don't think about the past too much. When I look at tape and I think, *That sucks, what am I doing, my hand is up here, I'm ducking all weird* . . . it's not pretty."

Kenny went to Afghanistan in 2007 to train with some of the troops, as part of a program to boost morale that a company called ProSport MVP put together, originally with baseball players. The troops had requested UFC fighters, and Kenny answered the call. He thought it'd be interesting. Like any true student of the game, Kenny learned more from those he was teaching and interacting with than they from him.

What impressed Kenny the most was "the guys with beards," the Special Forces soldiers who grew beards to better fit into Afghan society. The real, hard-core killers.

"They had the scars, the look in their eyes. They had seen the shit. But they were very professional about it." Kenny tries to verbalize the impression he got. "This is the reality, and we accept it. We've been killing a lot of people and we're satisfied with the job we're doing . . . they were matter-of-fact and passionate.

"They told me about their weapon loop: how you go to your rifle, then the enemy's rifle, then the sidearm, then your knife. In a fight, that's game plan A, to B, to C, but in terms of life and death."

"I looked around and thought, *These guys must be on alert twenty-four-seven,* they must be on alert *all* the time. They have to be. You see guys you know get killed and how does that affect your intensity? I walk into a cage and get it, but they're out there every single day with it. I thought about it a lot, that kind of mental focus and clarity."

Kenny remembers talking to Rob Kamen (a former muay Thai superstar fighter) about it. They were discussing the "self-programming."

"I'm nastier than I used to be. And the closer to a fight, I get worse. I feel that I need to go out there and do a serious job. I want to take him out, I want to literally beat him—not just win. It changes me. And it must change them [the soldiers] a lot."

Kenny mused aloud that it must be hard to come back to normal society after functioning on that level for so long. He can offer only his own example.

"I'm not the most fun person to be around, especially near a fight. You prepare your mind to suffer and inflict suffering. You delete a part of your compassion. There's a certain amount of brutality—to offer violence. Or you're vulnerable. I didn't always feel that way. Before the Sherk fight it was always just part of my job, just compete. Now I want to kill that guy. Whatever I can do within the rules with the utmost brutality. I won't hesitate. Every fight there's more wood on the fire, more bad intentions the closer I get. I've been programmed." Because without it you're a sitting duck.

Kenny recounts the conversation with Rob Kamen. Rob had trouble deprogramming after he retired. He'd beat up the guys he was training with the pads, or he'd knock them out sparring. He couldn't shut down the intensity. His students, who were paying him for training, couldn't handle him—he kept fucking them up.

Rob told Kenny, "Certain people have it or they don't, but you have to feed it. The fire may be there but it needs fuel. Some people don't have that spark, and you need it or you'll get hurt."

Kenny remembers one guy in particular, a Special Forces soldier who approached him for an autograph with his arm in a sling. The guy's eyes were so incredibly intense and his energy was so focused, and they just bullshitted, but the guy made an impression. His eyes, his aura stuck in Kenny's mind. Afterward, Kenny found out the guy was a war hero.

I remember Dan Gable talking about the intensity "in the room"—you had to have examples of it. For fighters to know what is possible, you need to have examples. These soldiers had shown Kenny a different kind of focus, and he'd soaked it up.

"For them it's life on the line, and I thought about that for my next fight—it's either him or me. Being ready to die, going back to that samurai mentality. Today is a good day to die. You have to be ready for that, to leave everything out there. I think I had some understanding of the mentality, but going into that fight now, I know I need to kill him before he kills me. It's life or death. I'm gonna destroy him."

I see some of this intensity in sparring, when Kenny becomes another person entirely: savage, focused, and explosive. His will is palpable. He seems like the biggest guy in the room. But afterward, relaxed and laughing, Kenny makes something clear.

"I focus on destroying him, but emotions have no place. They can be good or bad, but emotions always run out. You can't fight on emotion or adrenaline. At the end of the day, you have to have a love for it, something that lasts forever, because that will carry you. You can only be mad for so long. It can help you, but any-time you make decisions based on emotions you'll make a deci-sion without all the information, it's inconsistent."

He continues, "Whereas if I'm just focused on the techniques and strategy of the fight, on the fluidity of the fight, on what needs to be done tactically, then I'll make the right decisions. Instead of just being mad, 'Oh, he punched me, I'll punch him.' That changes things. You need to be able to stay calm. Okay, I got hit. That hurt, but I got to find the right way to hurt him back."

Kenny confesses a secret to me toward the end of our last day. It goes back to our shared youth, the infatuation with ac-tion heroes and the perfect fight—where all your punches and kicks land cleanly and none of his do. Kenny confides that "being the champ would be great but, for me, I got into this and it's grown into a monster. It's about me doing the perfect technique. Doing something beautiful, like a painting. With accuracy, speed, power, timing—the best kick, the best punch, the pur-est and best technique. Like the old Bruce Lee stuff, but real. I'm so far away from that, and it's bigger than the sport, bigger than a title or fans or anything. With that in mind, I'd much rather go for it with all my heart than run the clock out to grind out the win. I wouldn't feel good about the win, it wouldn't feel real."

I asked Kenny what is the last thing he thinks right before the bell rings and he's staring across the cage, and he smiles. He loves that moment. "I just get excited. Here we go, like I'm a painter with a blank canvas."

Since we spoke, I watch Kenny fight with newfound inter-est and respect, because he consistently improves so much. He is a fighter who changes dramatically from fight to fight. In his last fight, with Joe Stevenson (a fight I thought would be really tough

for him), he dominated—and looked beautiful doing it, graceful. His footwork was smooth, his punches and kicks crisp and
lightning quick, and his ground game simple, pure, and inexo-
rable. And he knew it. The moment the fight was through he
covered his face with his hands, one step closer to painting his
masterpiece.

THE EGO IS GARBAGE

Frank Shamrock

What is a good man but a bad man's teacher?
What is a bad man but a good man's job?
If you don't understand this, you will get lost,
However intelligent you are.
It is the great secret.

—Lao-tzu

There was a video making the rounds some years ago of former UFC champ Frank Shamrock working on a Pilates ball. He was doing things that nobody had seen before, flowing over the ball like water, flipping, turning, and spinning—balletic and pure. Was it related to MMA or grappling? It looked like something out of Cirque du Soleil. It was graceful, beautiful to watch, the weird private workout of a strange figure in the MMA world.

Frank Shamrock rides an unsteady place in MMA history—he was a dominant champion in the UFC before the sport fully evolved, and he retired from MMA early in his career when there weren't many good fights left for him. At times he seemed supernaturally good, working in a different league than everyone else; at other times he's been all-too human. He's retained some of that aura of effortless invincibility, even when he loses. He seemed like an athlete from the future, and indeed when MMA began to surge in popularity Frank emerged from retirement. Older and wiser, however, he took control of his career.

He never returned to the UFC, which he calls "U-Fight-Cheap." He's had a love-hate relationship with longtime MMA fans, sometimes coming across as arrogant and sneering, other times as the epitome of the humble martial artist.

When I drove out to San Jose to meet Frank at his gym, he was remarkably reasonable, relaxed, and businesslike. But every now and again a flash of a fighter's ego would shine through, the silly self-focus of celebrity would make its presence felt. His handsome battered face could split with a jackal grin, one tooth sharp and snaggled, and a slightly wild look in his eyes. I set out the tape recorder and sat down on the mats, and Frank stretched and started to talk. There is little mystery as to why Frank is the way he is—it's where he's from.

Frank was born Alisio Juarez III in 1972 in Santa Monica, California, and had a hard youth. "I was a pretty serious juvie delinquent," he laughed, but there wasn't any humor in his voice. "I left home at eleven and was a ward of the state until I was nineteen. The state was my mom and dad." There is something about how he said it, a catch in his voice, a veil drawn by a self-made man over a wound that will never quite heal.

"It was a joke. As long as you don't hurt anybody, you can do anything. We'd have huge parties, steal cars, wreak havoc . . . but as long as you didn't hurt anyone they'd just send you along to the next place." Frank wasn't a street fighter, though—he disliked violence and can remember only a few scraps that he couldn't avoid. He came to the idea of fighting late.

Though Frank hadn't played many sports besides partying, he was a natural athlete. You can tell he was one of those odd kids who had all the gifts to make it—brawn, brains, looks, but without the family support and stability to guide him. So he drifted, alone. He dabbled in volleyball, soccer, and even pitched in Little League, but he never fought much, or even wrestled. "I went to wrestling camp and the first day a couple of guys went out partying, had a great time but got in some fights and caused trouble, and they assumed it was me who led them astray," he laughs, this time with genuine merriment. "That was the end of my wrestling career. The coach kicked me out."

Frank eventually found his way to Bob Shamrock, who ran the Shamrock Ranch, a foster home for boys in Susanville, California. Bob had a favorite adopted son, who'd taken his name: Ken Shamrock. Ken was a promising athlete and the alpha boy at the ranch, and he would become one of the founding fighters of modern MMA. He lost to Royce Gracie in a couple of early UFCs and had a good understanding of the ground game from training in Japan for Pancrase.

Pancrase was a promotion formed by Masakatsu Funaki, a bored pro wrestler, a submission wizard who wanted to fight as the "first ever pro-wrestling group with no preordained finishes" (to quote Paul Lazenby, a fighter and a commentator). This was in 1993, the year the UFC started in the United States. The idea, like so many ideas, was floating in the ether. Ken Shamrock was one of their early stars. Ken was very much the image of a fighter, with a superhero body of muscles, a square chin, and a GI Joe haircut. Ken eventually went to pro wrestling and was billed (in his prime with some veracity) as the "World's Most Dangerous Man."

The three Shamrocks have had a tempestuous relationship over the years. At one point, when Frank was sixteen, Bob and Ken went to North Carolina to pursue Ken's pro wrestling career and kicked Frank back into the system. What that must have felt like to a sixteen-year-old boy is hard to fathom.

A few years later Bob and Ken returned to California, and Frank was formally adopted. Frank started training with his new brother and found he enjoyed the fight training. "I was very, very competitive. I go a hundred percent and I want to be good or terrible. I loved submission wrestling because it was singular, self-driven. In volleyball I'd go crazy and try to be everywhere at once, and guys were loafing."

Frank took to it like a fish to water, and remembers, "It only took a few months to start beating those around me. Ken, my first teacher, taught me the basics, catch-as-catch-can wrestling. It was the simple stuff—movement, position, submission—but I loved it and I studied it like a science and progressed fast. I wrote down everything. I took a very scholastic approach. I saw the whole thing as a game, just a sport—not a fight. I wasn't encumbered by the idea of winning or dominating." Frank swears he had never been a street fighter, and he often talks about how distasteful he finds violence.

Ken was a superstar in the early MMA world, and Frank lurked in his shadow, going to the big fights at the UFC and in Japan as part of Ken's posse. He began to fight, but "I had trouble, because I didn't want to hurt people. I didn't really understand the game." He was in awe of his brother, who "smashed me at will." The gym was called the Lion's Den, and the brutality of training (and hazing new members) has become legendary. It was the epitome of the old school macho MMA gym, the original—come get your ass kicked if you want to play with the big boys.

Frank smiled at me with that hyena grin and said, "I had to accept that if I am swordsman, if I pick up the sword, I have to swing it. That's the game. It is what it is. A punch is a punch, and there's a game element and an art element, but it's also a physical altercation and if I don't go a hundred percent something bad could happen. Being a professional fighter and not trying to hurt your opponent is the stupidest, most oxymoronic thing. I think it was a fear of being good, of having the skill to hurt if necessary. At the time I wasn't mature enough to realize that having the skill is wonderful, that it's a blessing. You just need to know what to do with it. Some will fight in the street, some will languish in the middle, wondering if they should commit, and some will be the best fighters in the world. I realized and accepted it, that I loved it, and I accepted what comes with it. I may kill somebody or get famous but, if I'm true to it, then I accept that. From that point on, I smashed everybody." Frank burst into laughter again, content.

I thought of Liborio, and Freddie Roach, and the importance of *acceptance*. Here I was hearing it again, in a slightly different context, perhaps, but it also played to Virgil's comments about perspective. Maybe I was finally getting somewhere.

"There was a fight early on, John Lober, where I got him in a bunch of different holds and every time I got something I'd look over at him and think, 'Hey, time to tap, I got you.' But he was *fighting*. He came from a different place, and he's thinking, 'Just break my leg or I'll get out.' He forced me to confront the truth of fighting. It was a big growth moment for me." Frank cackled. "Now I'll stomp the head of my closest friend if he's in the cage with me—that's the game!"

Frank's rise was meteoric. "I got really good and famous, really fast," he said, and he's right. He started fighting in Pancrase in Japan and suddenly he was matched, after only a few fights, against Funaki himself—the legend, the guy who had trained his brother, Ken. "I had to fight my teacher's teacher. I couldn't touch Ken. Ken could smash me at will. No matter how much I thought about it, or visualized, I didn't see how I could beat this guy. So do I just go out there and die?" Frank laughed again.

Frank taught himself to meditate in hotel rooms in Japan. "The logic wasn't there, of a way to beat this guy," he says, "and I had so much fear and anxiety. I had to try something. I got inside myself, just trying to calm down. I was sitting in the hotel, thinking, 'Oh my God what am I doing?' when I realized I had to relax. So I worked on it. Deep breaths, eyes closed, just thinking about individual techniques. I relaxed and it worked. I started to do technical visualization. Then I went out there and Funaki kicked the shit out of me." Frank dissolves into feral cackles, genuine deep amusement. "Yeah, he smashed me, but I came back and beat him later. And it never bothered me to lose like that. If I didn't try hard enough, or screwed around, or was out of shape . . . those losses really bug me. If somebody kicks my ass—that was all you, dude. I have tremendous respect for them. Truthfully, that's kind of what I'm looking for, someone who can do that and push me." A sincerity came through those pat sporting words, a deep underlying need to be *challenged*.

Without a challenge, the top fighter has a hard time staying motivated, staying in the gym and doing what he needs to do. It's fun at first, but after years and years of it, working out acquires a deadly dullness that needs a sharp point to pierce. And on fight day, unless he's facing a really tough challenge, chances are he A) won't get to show his skills and perform and B) won't mentally be sharp. Most great fighters perform well only against great challengers, and often they give lackluster performances against mediocre opponents.

"For my guys, my fighters who lose, I tell them it's a learning experience. I do my job as a trainer and make sure they're not in there with someone who's just way too good for them, out of their league. So I can honestly say to them, 'Here's the lesson,' and if you learn it, it was worth it one hundred percent."

Frank studied bodybuilding before he got into fighting. He brought a physical trainer's mind-set—an understanding of musculature, anatomy, and force—to his grappling and later his striking.

"I was looking at the body and thinking about the angles and applied force in the holds, the strength and leverage of a body part. I look at someone and can see where they'll be strong, where they'll be weak."

Frank's a self-made man. Without an experienced trainer raising him, he was forced to be his own sage and expert. "I came up in submission wrestling, but I'm at the point where positions don't matter in my world—not position for it's own sake. How much energy are you expending? How much damage are you applying and how much damage is being done to you? Those are the big three. I like the endless flow of attacks, because it evens out the technical aspects. You may have a good grappler who's a hundred times better than me, but when the flow never stops he has to have the muscular and vascular systems to keep up the pace."

Frank and I sat in the dark in a wrestling room and Frank stretched slowly. He was perfectly content and relaxed, all business. I asked him to describe his mental process, and he willingly lectured, handing out self-evident truths.

"The mental side is broken into three areas or levels. One: the idea, the visualization or conceiving side. It's hard to equate it to anything other than those positive-affirmation, self-help type of things. Olympic skiers visualize the course. For me, I do it for everything I do, not just fighting. Now that I'm commentating on live TV, I play it out in my head a bunch of different times, seeing ways it could go, making sure I hit the points I want to hit.

"The second part is replicating—just practice. It's hard to believe something will work if you've never pulled it off. You practice the moves. The fighting ones are obvious, but for this last press conference I rehearsed with the fighters, I walked them through it, got them used to the sound of my voice. It chilled everyone out.

"The third part is doing, and every time you do it you get better. It takes less energy and stress."

Frank paused in the dark. "So, one, two, three, and I end up with a result, but then I evaluate it. I think about changing what I did, and this is where a lot of people fall down. They go through a good process, end up with a result, and think it's just fine. I won but I went to the hospital afterward."

He smiled, his teeth flashing in the gloom. "Fighting is like a business. If you did a deal and you came away with twenty percent of the company and somebody owns you, you need to do things differently. If you won the fight but you're in the hospital, did it really work out for you?"

Frank maintained that this process has helped him check his ego. He knew he had a reputation for being an occasional egomaniac. "If my ego was so big, I would never need to visualize anything. I would just do it and everything would be a hundred percent wonderful, right?"

I thought of Eddie Bravo's discussion on ego, and Frank had a lot to say about it. "Ego is an evil thing. Confidence is important, but ego is something false. Humility is the way to build confidence, and ego is hugely dangerous in this sport, because if you're running on ego you aren't running on good clean emotions, or cause and effect. You bypass it to support a false idea. It's all garbage, the ego is garbage.

"The hardest thing about being an MMA fighter is the huge ego boost you get from winning—not only from yourself but from your community. I hear, 'Oh you're the greatest, you don't have to train all the time.' Marcelo Garcia made the exact same complaint.

"Your own community is the hardest on you, because they're in love with ego, too, and you have to fight yourself *and* them now. Anyone can fight, fighting is easy, but to sustain it, to remain normal and relaxed and grounded within yourself and your community, is really challenging."

This is related to the other aspect of fighting that Frank has found to be challenging: fame. "Being famous is hard to do—it amplifies everything negative and positive about you. It's amplified by your fans, whoever watches you. I see guys get famous and that's a big test for them: what will you do with your ego and power and influence now?

"False ideas about yourself can destroy you," Frank said. "For me, I always stay a student. That's what martial arts are about, and you have to use that humility as a tool. You put yourself beneath someone you trust. That's extremely useful.

"There is a belief in our system"—he was referring to his school—"that I came up with years ago, that it takes three people to make you into the best person you can be. Somebody better than you, someone equal to you, and someone less than you. People hear that and get freaked out, because they want to be better than everyone, or at least equal. The goal is actually to put yourself as the last person, even if you're the guy in the lead. You can *always* find something other people are better at. So teach me, show me, let's work on that. If you can accept the humility and understand why it's important, you'll grow so strong in every way. Imagine if you did that to every person you came in contact with? You put yourself underneath them to learn? I always stay a student."

Frank launched into one of his favorite topics, his own scientific approach. "I study the biomechanics of the human body and look for the angles of strength. Where energy is distributed— I break down techniques into how much energy they expend. I go through the technique in my mind, and if your mind sees it, it happened. Whether it's true or not, if your mind saw it, it happened. So I go through these techniques mentally. My confidence gets built up and I go in and try them, and then I evaluate it, think about how it worked. There's always something that could be better, so you stay a student."

One of the things I was interested in was the pysch-out games Frank played. He would very famously talk shit. He made it very clear that, at this level, anything was fair game.

"I listen to people," he said. "They will inherently tell the truth about themselves—it always happens. I amplify things they say about themselves, either right or wrong. But the truth is stronger than anything. If you know a guy has bad feet, then he's got bad feet! Just tell the truth. Some people, when they hear something like that, will fight it. They'll argue, 'Oh, no, it's not like that.' Now the game is on—because you've got a guy defending something you both know is false. He *should* say, 'You're so right, and I'm grinding in the gym to make myself better,' but ego jumps in, 'Of course I'm good and my footwork is fantastic!'" He gives me his now-familiar smile. "If someone says to me, you're hands suck then I'll be in the gym working on that extra hard for the next six months.

"Everyone has stuff they get nervous about, their personal shit, and if you hang around long enough they'll volunteer it, or they'll tell somebody else for you. I go after that stuff. Phil Baroni stutters. We know it, he knows it. Most people don't pick up on it. But Phil hasn't made peace with it. When I'd goof on him, he'd get mad."

In one press conference, Phil was almost in tears. I get what Frank is about. He's not picking on Phil out of nowhere, he's not just an asshole. Mental toughness is on the table.

"Now he's not in a peaceful mind, ready to fight. Now he's somewhere else, some other issue from when he was a kid. He's not focused on the task or the goal.

"I talk to people during fights the whole time. I build on what I said beforehand. I picked that up from Bas Rutten. We'd both talk to each other the whole fight, and the ref used to warn us. Bas was funny. He'd talk to me as a way to pump himself up, 'I'm so strong, I almost got you,' more like Muhammad Ali, to empower himself. What he did wasn't crafted to get into you, but I'm all about that privacy, that inner attack. It's distracting and confusing and it's supposed to be. If you hear it, it exists. Especially if you're in a high-stress situation, with uncertainty anyway. I look in a guy's eyes, and I talk down low, just for him. I don't want anyone to hear it but him, not his corner, not the crowd. So when he goes back to his corner, and his trainer is telling him things, there's another voice he's been hearing. It falls into what he thinks about."

This may be why some MMA fans dislike Frank; shenanigans like this are frowned on in martial arts. But Frank assured me that mental strength and focus are fair targets at this level of fighting. "It's part of the game," he kept saying.

Frank even confessed to a time when he was head-fucked by another fighter. It was the second time he fought John Lober, and Lober engaged in psychological warfare of a petty nature—ordering room service to Frank's room, sending him threatening e-mails, prank calling him, getting personal.

"It was weird, funny childish stuff, but it made me upset. I was young, I had to learn. I went out all angry and kicked the shit out of him, but when it was over I had a big sobering up. I realized *holy shit I exposed myself,* being angry and frustrated. There was a moment when I could have finished him, and I thought no, I wanted to hurt him, and that could have been really bad. I could have let him off the hook, and he might have come back. I could have hurt myself or gotten hurt. He got in my head, plain and simple."

I was reminded of Dan Gable talking about seeing a guy break, and staying on him—because if you gave him respite he could come back. Frank agrees wholeheartedly. "You have to stay on him when you see him start to break. My style is to break you. I try to get you to go anaerobic—change your fuel source so you're no longer efficient, or you're afraid of running out of gas, of getting knocked out. I fight at a pace that borderlines aerobic activity, which is hard to do unless you've got good technique. Don't worry so much about positions, but keep the fight flowing at a fast pace. It's a race. The person with the best conditioning and technique should win. I didn't hurt Tito, I made him tired."

Frank was talking about his epic battle with Tito Ortiz, one of the great early MMA fights. Frank fought the larger, younger, and angrier Tito for four long rounds, and in a superb technical display he finally started to take Tito apart in the fourth.

"Tito tapped because he was exhausted, and I was going to keep beating him. When you're dog tired that lactic acid builds up, and you get sick and nauseous, and you have to do something. You can't keep fighting. It's conditioning. If you push them over the brink, they'll lose everything. They break down, they feel like they could die. Fatigue makes cowards of us all, right?

"Anytime you can take a technique from somebody—absorb a big blow without damage, stuff a takedown—that's huge. I don't consciously do it, I technically do it. I train for it. If he's got a great uppercut, I shift my hand over and take that away from him.

I don't think about it, but I can feel his energy subside when he thinks he's done something good and it doesn't work. You can feel him deflate. I'm always in tune with his energy, his emotions. You fight in front of thousands, but there's only one guy. I hear him breathing, I hear the impacts, and I hear my corner, that's it."

Frank found spirituality in what he does, in teaching and training. "The core of every religion is a social structure that connects everybody, for the common good of society," he said in a rehearsed line that rolls off his tongue. "For me, that's what martial arts is. You teach children to make them better people, you teach adults to give them a better understanding of themselves, or of their partner. Some students will ask me to go to church with them on Sunday, and I say, 'I go to church Monday through Saturday and Sunday I stay home with my family.' That's how I look at it."

EVERYTHING IS ALWAYS ON THE LINE

Josh Waitzkin playing chess as a kid.
(Courtesy: Josh Waitzkin)

Josh rolling with Marcelo Garcia in preparation
for Abu Dhabi." (Courtesy: Marcelo Garcia)

I first became aware of Josh Waitzkin through a friend from New York who'd played chess with him when they were both kids. "Did you ever see that movie *Searching for Bobby Fischer*? I drew that kid in a game," he said, over a chessboard. "We were nine." Not only had I not seen the movie, I hadn't been aware that nine-year-olds played in chess tournaments. When I was nine I focused on tying my shoes and killing salamanders.

When I left Thailand, sailing across the Indian Ocean, I started reading chess books, just because I hadn't studied anything since college. Funnily enough, one of the books I ended up with was Josh Waitzkin's *Attacking Chess,* written when he was eighteen. I enjoyed the story more than the chess, which is a common thread for me; I buy chess books and read the introductions.

Later, when I was living briefly in Manhattan and studying tai chi with William C. C. Chen, I saw pictures on the wall of that same chess kid, Waitzkin, winning "push-hands" tournaments. Push-hands is the competition side of tai chi, a kind of flowing, standing wrestling where you push and pull, trying to either push an opponent out of the ring or "fall" him. It's pretty fringe in the United States but a major deal in China and Taiwan, and Josh had gone there and won world championships. Now, push-hands is not MMA, but it's also not a joke, especially overseas, where it's taken as seriously as judo.

I finally watched *Searching for Bobby Fischer,* based on a book that Josh's "Pop" had written about Josh's early chess career. It's a great story about a chess prodigy coming to terms with competition and life, and a fascinating look into the cutthroat world of child chess in New York, high-stakes pressure tournaments for eight-year-olds.

At the age of six Josh had been walking by Washington Square in Manhattan and was lured in by the commotion of "street" chess. The Square has a famous corner where hustlers play for money, raucous as any street basketball court. I've played there, and it's a little rough on the ego to get shit-talked to, then slapped around the board by a black guy with muscled arms bigger than your legs. Josh started playing with these boisterous characters without ever seeing a chess board before, and he started coming back every day, winning more than he lost. With this rough apprenticeship, he'd gone on to become one of the top young players in the country. His story is powerful, and made more so by his struggle to maintain his identity and hold on to his childhood in a chessic world without mercy.

I had picked up a new book Josh had recently written, a nonchess book called *The Art of Learning.* The back is covered with intimidating quotes, effusive praise by everyone from Cal Ripken Jr. to Deepak Chopra —you better like it. Fortunately, it's easy to like. It's a great book, an honest and open look into Josh's thought processes, and the lessons he'd gleaned from his study of the world. The book takes into account both his chess and tai chi careers, and I would recommend it to anyone. Josh has been in deep waters, at least in chess and tai chi, and he's drawn genuine insight from them. At the end of the book he mentioned he was studying Brazilian jiu-jitsu, and that drew my attention. I knew some people who knew him, so I managed to get in touch. We set up a time to meet in New York.

Josh had been a star from six years old, immediately labeled "special" in the eyes of adults, and different than most kids . . . but then a hit movie about how wonderful you are, when you're fifteen? What could that do to your ego? To be honest, I was pretty sure he was going to be an asshole. It was almost impossible for him NOT to be.

He was taking jiu-jitsu, though—with an eye on competing in the Mundials (the world championship). I thought, *Perfect, here's a guy I can talk chess and jiu-jitsu with.* If he was an asshole I could handle it.

When I met Josh in New York he reminded me of Caravaggio's painting of Dionysus. He's a good-looking, normal guy, medium height and thick, with the jiu-jitsu body, rounded and grounded. He had an amiable face, broad nose, and thick curly black hair, like an Italian farmboy. He laughed easily, things amused him, and he was intensely curious about the world. He didn't come across as an asshole—he was a relaxed dude with a friendly intensity.

We laughed and talked and had coffee, and he was very complimentary about my book, and I about his. We both meant it.

Through it all, though, you could feel him watching you with those soft brown eyes—he didn't look like a chess genius, he looked like a Mediterranean peasant. But in his eyes you could feel it—suddenly it made sense, the serious intellect behind there watching you, evaluating you, and cataloging weakness and strength, patterns. Listening intently, watching carefully without self-consciousness. "Tell me," he'd say intently about something, an MMA fighter I knew, some detail from the book, and I'd try and be precise. He was watching for later use, gathering information. Here's a kid who's been playing serious competitive chess since he was six—of course he's watching you like that, that's how he grew up. Not all the time, but flashes, here and there.

At the end of his chess career, Josh was sort of off-balance from the pressures of fame, combined with a chess instructor who tried to lead him down a path away from his natural inclinations. Josh also talks about his emotions. "Now I don't block them, I use them . . . I was brittle, locked-up, and now I can channel what I need to. It's liberating and far more resilient." He's an incredibly emotional, heart-on-his-sleeve guy, something he freely admits, and which fuels him and his writing. But he learned to use his emotions, let his opponents read him, and then apply tiny emotional changes to mislead. He learned to channel his emotions into useful pathways, to ride them, in control and with understanding. Part of that process was the intensive study of tai chi.

Josh is aware of how tai chi and push-hands aren't taken very seriously in the United States. "It's about ten percent real dudes and ninety percent people with mystical delusions. But that ninety percent gives the rest of it a bad name," Josh said ruefully over sake and sushi. "At least six times I've had guys tell me they can't spar me because their chi is so strong they'd kill me."

He shakes his head and laughs. "They brainwash students. The better the student, the farther the master sends them flying with a bump of the wrist. I watched this one guy send his top students bouncing off the walls. He even knocked his prize student around without touching her, but when I asked to spar it was 'I'm sorry, I'd kill you.'

"In Asia, there are real athletes training hard, like real martial artists. It's so different."

Toward the end of his tai chi career Josh became aware of Brazilian jiu-jitsu. He studied jiu-jitsu in the gi, and he was a brown belt when I met him—he'd already come a long way. He was highly motivated, trained every day, and loved it. "A lot of guys would have come in and tried to jam tai chi ideas to jiu-jitsu right away," he said. "I knew that would be a mistake. I was out in L.A. and I went to John Machado's school. I had done all these push-hands competitions, so in the stand-up I could handle them, but on the ground I was getting tapped every ten seconds. John knew about me and about chess, too."

Josh studied with John Machado in 2005, for nine months, twice a day, and then back in New York with Marcos Santos, eventually getting his brown belt from Marcos and Rigan Machado. I asked him about learning jiu-jitsu.

"The biggest error I see in any discipline is people taking on too much, too fast. Depth over breadth, man. I believe in diving deeply into a small pool of information. For instance when you learn a new move in jiu-jitsu. Learn something on one side of the body, learn it very deeply, then learn it on the other side when you've developed that deep feel."

Josh is no superman, gifted with extraordinary speed and strength, but he's no shrinking violet either. He's not a skinny chess nerd with the glasses taped together; he's an athlete. But he was also without illusion. He was aware that he had a big advantage in the psychological game, because that is such a major part of chess. He'd been evaluating and psyching out opponents his whole life.

It was clear that his true strengths are in his intensity and his focus on learning, his "art of learning." From his books you come to understand his drive, his commitment to incredibly hard work. He put in the time. As a child playing chess, he put in the time studying endgames, mastering them, and it gave him the confidence to survive the killer openings that other children memorized. He puts in the time not only in chess but in tai chi and in jiu-jitsu. He blazes for his "ten thousand hours" with pure gameness. Sure, he's gifted, but he's immensely driven underneath his sunny exterior. There's a subtle difference to, say, Gable's intensity, which feels joyless, from a deep relentless place. Josh's intensity is easier, colored with excitement. It's playful. Of course, I'm not sitting across the board or rolling with him.

Josh had a funny story, well polished but useful, about observation. We had been talking about "tells," when an opponent does something that subconsciously reveals his inner state. The classic use is in poker, when someone is bluffing and they always act a certain way, maybe tap their fingers; they have a tell. When you pick it up, then they try to trick you with it.

In chess, an opponent might lay a trap and hope you fall into it, pretending to have made a bad move. When Josh was a kid he remembers acting, slapping his head, but as he got older and his needs more subtle, just a change of breathing, a slightly tense expression, might suffice.

"Guys were very aware of their tells at the high level. So they'd use them to mislead you, but off the board they weren't as aware. So I got good at reading people off the board.

"In Bermuda every year there was a two-week tournament where a dozen world-class chess players would live in this resort together and play chess all day. So everyone is walking on the beach, swimming, and studying each other. And some of these guys are truly brilliant people, but watch them get caught in the rain. There are these squalls that rip through Bermuda, and I would sit on a cliff and watch other players get caught in the rain. Some guys would stand there, breathe it in, and get wet. They'd look out at the ocean. Other guys would put their hands over their head and run desperately for cover. When you observe that kind of moment, when people are caught off guard, you can start to see how they are as humans and competitors.

"If they put their hands up and run, they're controllers. So, over the chessboard, you take a critical moment and make it chaotic, out-of-control. Make it so they have to embrace the unknown to perform.

"But if they stand and just get wet and enjoy the rain, then maybe they embrace chaos—that was the kind of player I was. So for them you create a position where it takes painstaking, mind-numbing calculation to succeed.

"Of course you can't always control the board to that extent, but often you can give them a choice, where the correct decision is to go a certain way and the incorrect decision is to go to their own style, and often they'll take the disadvantage. They'll shy away, and give you a slightly better position."

It may sound odd to nonchessplayers to hear talk of the "correct decision" when chess seems so open and free-form. That is one of the big surprises about chess, when you start to study it—there is almost always a correct move, a "best" move. To the beginner the chessboard seems a vast, mysterious place where an infinite variety of things could happen. But as you learn more you start to see how the game plays, and where the best move is. At the very high level there is sometimes uncertainty between a few best moves. Most of the time there is a right decision, though, and one best move.

There is an interesting correlation with MMA, where I've observed "better" strikers getting outstruck by tough grapplers. The reason is slightly insidious. It's not that the grappler had better striking; it's that the striker was so terrified of the takedown, so concerned about being outclassed on the ground, that he constricts his striking game; the grappler, unconcerned with being taken down, can let it all hang out and swing for the fences.

Josh has refined these psychological manipulations in chess, has used them in tai chi, and is starting to apply them to jiu-jitsu. As you focus on the opponent, his emotions and yours come into play. Josh talks of "shared illusions."

He remembers playing in the under-eighteen world chess championship tournament, in an important round against the Vietnamese national champ. They were deep in a very positional game when his opponent "hung a rook." Basically, his opponent made a beginner's blunder; he gave Josh a piece on an error. The error that was so weirdly obvious, so big, that it was almost impossible for Josh to see. When you read the game now, it's simply mystifying. They were both embroiled in computations of this deep position, getting deeper and deeper, and missing the obvious, but feeding on each other. Josh sat there calculating for fifteen minutes and then moved, missing the blunder that would have handily won him the game. Eventually his opponent saw the mistake he'd made but Josh never did. "One of the U.S. coaches almost had a heart attack," he confessed ruefully. "I ended up winning, but I could have taken his rook," Josh muses. "It's astonishing at that level." He sighs.

Now although I am far, far below that level, I have been in similar situations in chess many times, where I am so focused and calculating I miss an obvious change that the opponent's new move has created (or a position has gotten so complicated that I remove a base without realizing it's supporting my whole house).

It's not just that; it's that *both* of us missed it, and we feel each other. I've made a move and sat there waiting and watching and suddenly realized I made a huge mistake. But if I don't react, if I successfully conceal my emotions, sometimes he won't see it either. But usually, just me noticing it, the change in tension, will give it away. Josh talked about shared illusions in jiu-jitsu—"once you beat somebody once, they sometimes get convinced that you're just better than them, and now you're tapping them every fifteen seconds, when in the beginning there was a real struggle." You see it in MMA fights all the time—one fighter avoids the takedown a few times, and both fighters become convinced that the guy can't be taken down.

Josh talks about variations on the psychic connection between two opponents. "You might prepare these openings, and have a thousand variations thought out, but there is one problem that is haunting you, one off-beat line you haven't prepared. It's a needle in a haystack so you play the opening hoping your opponent won't find the hole—but he will if he's a grandmaster. It's like he smells it." At the high levels, the minds connect.

It reminds me a little of my friend Javier Calderon, a filmmaker who is also a professional boxer. Javier has been a sparring partner in camps with some of the best fighters in the world, and he is a regular at the Wild Card Boxing Club. He recalls he was sparring a young kid, who was a better boxer, who moved well. But Javier was stalking him for three, four, five rounds, chasing him around the ring. Javier said, "Because he can't hurt me, I'm stronger, and *he knows I know it,* or even *he knows I know he knows it . . .*" The level of connection went deep.

When Josh was competing in the push-hands in Taiwan, he ran into an opponent who could read his intentions so well that Josh was sure the guy could read his mind. No tricks could fool him. Here was an opponent whose skill was so great, and perception so powerful, that he was inside Josh's head with him. But Josh beat this wizard—by turning that very sensitivity against him. He started to just *think* about feints, instead of feinting. He used his intentions to mislead. *You're gonna read my mind? Okay, well, I'll use that against you, I'll think about the wrong thing.* Another man's sword is your sword.

"People are usually too aware of tells. You're looking for them but they know it, and they're going to be illusory. They'll be manipulating you with their own tells. So I plant 'minipatterns' on an opponent, in tai chi and jiu-jitsu. I give them dogma, a false construct. I convince them that A leads to B, A leads to B, and then suddenly when A doesn't lead to B anymore they're fucked. False assumptions."

He laughed, but that was exactly what striking is often about. How do you open somebody up to a punch or a kick? You lull them with something else, convince them they're out of range, or the jab is coming, and then you walk them into a head kick. How did George Foreman beat Michael Moorer? He gave Michael a false construct: you can stand there, I can't hit that hard, my jab is pawing and weak, the right is nothing to fear. You can handle my punch.

"You have to control your side of the board before you start messing with his," is a chess truism, meaning maintain control of your own emotions, tells, and psychology before you begin the head games. A bit like the poker saw, "If you can't spot the sucker at the table in ten minutes then you're the sucker."

In his book, Josh talks about pondering Wu Yu-hsiang in a "typically abstract Chinese instructional conundrum":

If the opponent does not move, then I do not move.
At the opponent's slightest move, I move first.

Josh had a hard time with that. How could you move first at his slightest move? But he eventually came to grips with it as being about "reading and ultimately controlling intention." He programs reactions into an opponent, he convinces them of things, and then he sets them up for the knockout. It plays to his ideas of tension.

"My vision of martial arts, of fighting, is that it relates to dual currents, the psychological reality and the technical reality—the position as it actually is. Very often in chess you'll have a moment when one person will have a superior position, but the other person has a greater clarity of mind. The one can transcend the other. The Gracies' always talk about jiu-jitsu and using breathing, yours to control his. If you're breathing slower, your clarity is better.

"There's a big misconception about how to win a chess game. If you have material or a positional advantage over a world-class opponent, it doesn't mean you've won. You don't just take a winning position and win it. A good defensive player can always swat away lunges for the throat." I have always been amazed at the opportunities for defense that chess contains. Things may look bad but, if you look hard, you can often find some piece that can save you.

"The way to win a game like that involves maintaining and increasing the tension. The person who makes the first break, who releases the tension, it's going to go against them, partly because they've broken the tension and now the other guy has the first move to exploit the new play dynamic."

In his chess tutorial, Josh talks about "cat and mouse." When a cat stalks a mouse the tension mounts as the mouse sees the cat coming. They are frozen, staring at each other, but the cat is comfortable, relaxed in the tension; "present" is the word Josh favors. The mouse is not, and it leaps first when the tension becomes unbearable. The cat reacts with the advantage of seeing which way the mouse is running.

"If I have a slightly better position, and I'm improving my position, then all the tactics are hovering like potential energy. I'm increasing the tension. And so are you. The tension mounts and there will come an inevitable explosion point, when the character of the game shifts. From abstract plans to precise calculations . . . usually whoever is in the worst position has to make that shift happen.

"What's interesting is that pretty much without exception there's a psychological component that is parallel. The tension is mounting on your brain, and on mine, the complexities and wildness. In a big game against a world-class player it feels like your brain is in a vise. The stronger player is better able to maintain and be at peace with the tension . . . they convert it into peace." Josh calls this ability *presence*. Just like the cat.

"In the mounting tension, eventually it has to explode, and in that moment everything hangs—you can be incredibly close to winning but also losing. Just a slight miscalculation or overconfidence can lose in that moment.

"You can see that tension in jiu-jitsu, when a guy goes for a submission too early and the other guy escapes. You're in cross sides, and he's rolling away from you and you've got the kimura grip on his top arm, so there's an armbar there. But it's not supertight and a lot of guys can escape from there. So instead you hook the arm and play against his neck and increase the tension, make him roll onto his stomach, make him give you the armbar . . . so you convert with the double attack, increase the tension, and win. Or you lunge for something and maybe he escapes and reverses you."

A fighter friend of mine named Chad George does something he calls the Gumby guard pass—he lies in your guard, on top of you, like a fish, loose and completely relaxed. But he's poised to explode, and he waits for you to try something, some sweep, or a submission, and then he explodes. It's hard to outwait the opponent; when I try it, my inclination is to get moving and try something. But the key is to wait, wait, wait for the guy on bottom to commit to something, and then explode in the opposite direction. Chad exploits that exact tension.

Josh continued.

"There's some real simple similarities, too, like the two ways to beat someone else who has a good game. Either you squelch his game, shut it down, or you push it and overextend it. Most people tend to squelch—if he's fast then slow him down. But the other way is to get him to run out, run his game too fast for him to control. In Taiwan, I gave my opponent the feeling in critical moments that his power was overwhelming."

I was reminded of Pat Miletich; sometimes the best way to beat a guy is to go into his strengths, not his weakness, to go where he doesn't expect you, where he feels so confident he's vulnerable. If you can get him to show a weakness, a flaw, a tiny crack in his strength—like Gable said, "loosen that wire in his brain."

Josh laughs. "In terms of the pysch-out game, chess was so hard and so highly developed that martial arts seems easy. I mean, these guys are great athletes, even incredible, but the mental pysch-out game is so much less developed. They can be dominated, pressured."

The way to survive and thrive under that pressure is through presence. Josh wrote in *The Art of Learning*:

> In every discipline, the ability to be clearheaded, present, cool under fire is much of what separates the best from the mediocre . . . if one player is serenely present while the other is being ripped apart by internal pressures, the outcome is already clear . . . We cannot expect to touch excellence if "going through the motions" is the norm of

our lives. On the other hand, if deep, fluid presence becomes second nature, then life, art and learning take on a richness that will continually surprise and delight . . . The secret is that everything is always on the line. The more present we are at practice, the more present we will be in competition, in the board room, at the exam, the operating table, the big stage.

Josh is a close friend of Marcelo Garcia, and he says that Marcelo does jiu-jitsu with wonderful, pure tai chi in it.

"There's the universal player versus the stylized player. Marcelo is stylized—he doesn't study his opponent and shut him down. Instead, he expresses his game. He makes you play with him. A universal player observes the opponent's rhythm and builds a game plan around it.

"Marcelo doesn't talk in shades of grey. Everything is black and white." Josh was with him at ADCC in 2007, and when he lost to Drysdale, Josh had talked to him about why. Was it that he needed more training against the darce (the choke Drysdale used, now much in vogue) or was it that he needed a game plan for long-armed opponents? Had Marcelo gotten too predictable with the single-leg takedown? "I need to be faster," Marcelo said with a smile.

"I'm more of a grey-type of guy, so it can be frustrating, because at times he seems overly simple. But it's incredibly powerful for him. In the chess world, there were plenty of guys like him who I envied, guys with pure clarity and no existential dilemmas, without angst." Josh laughs. "I was all angst. I was a tortured soul, until I started to really learn to use my emotions, to channel and get them to work for me.

"People talk about Marcelo as if he thinks ten moves ahead, but I don't think he does. People have the same misconception about strong chess players, that they see ten moves ahead. They don't, but they know where to look. They think two or three moves ahead but in the right direction. The computer has to look at every legal move. So if there are forty legal moves, and then each of those moves has forty moves following, quickly the play goes into the trillions, right? The strong chess player only looks at two or three moves but because of his intuitive understanding, his pattern recognition, when he analyzes just those two or three moves he gains insight into the position. He thinks thematically. In chess, you don't need to think of everything, just the *right* two or three moves, and you're *golden*.

"Same with Marcelo. I don't think he's thinking that far ahead, but he's a few moves ahead in the right direction. I've studied him closely, both his DVDs and as a human being, as a teacher and a training partner and a friend.

"That thing about how he gets the back from everywhere, that seat belt thing?" Josh is talking about Marcelo's uncanny ability to "get the back" on opponents, to take a great position on their back. A universal experience of opponents rolling with Marcelo is they think they're safe, and somehow he gets their back from a seem-ingly odd position. He does it with a grip he calls the "seat belt." He reaches around you and starts cinching himself onto your back.

"It starts his squeeze. You think you're passing his guard, but you give him a little angle, and he starts that seat belt thing and BAM he's chest to back on you.

"His squeeze is deadly. But it's not the pressure, it's more the commitment, it's always getting tighter. He even says 'once it starts in, it never comes out.' He tightens millimeter by millime-ter, inching it in. You're defending and think you're okay but it's never backing off, it's just getting tighter all the time.

"He commits to the idea of never going backward, in terms of chokes. That seat belt squeeze that precedes the choke is trippy. It comes from all different places and starts and then pretty soon he's got your back and he's going to choke you without hooks in.

"But he's always letting people out in practice, especially guys under him. He plays in transition. It's very important. His whole life is spent in transitions. He's a ball, but when you roll with

Marcelo sometimes it feels like you're very close to getting a position, and then he rolls out and you're not quite there. He's the purest tai chi I've ever seen, deflection, letting attacks roll off. Everything tai chi is supposed to be, that's what Marcelo is doing."

Before meeting Josh, I thought about what happens to a fifteen-year-old kid who has had a movie made about his life. It could easily destroy someone. Josh writes that he had at first enjoyed the attention, especially from girls, but then it had gradually derailed his chess career. He'd play tournaments and the organizers would pull out a life-size poster of the movie and stand it next to him. Grandmasters would come after him with long knives. Lesser fame than that has ruined lives; the narcissism that celebrity seems to generate can cripple people.

I had noticed a similar thing at Harvard, on a smaller scale. Kids finish high school, seventeen or eighteen, and right at that moment of learning their place in the world they get into Harvard and their inflated sense of self-worth (that most teenagers have) is validated. *I am that great.* A friend of mine married a movie star who was on the cover of *Time* magazine when she was eighteen. Miraculously, she recovered, a testament to her intelligence and wisdom. And also grit—there's an essence of grit to fight through something like that. You have to get down and dirty and battle with yourself. *I am just like everyone else. My work can be great but I'm nothing special.* If you don't win that one, you're finished as an artist, a student, a fighter. Josh won that battle, maybe his most important fight.

Josh is no asshole. He had fantastic parenting or his own internal compass saved him (or maybe both) because he walked away from chess when it started to make him miserable and dove into tai chi—and he rode that out until he won a few world championships in Taiwan. He came up for air, wrote a book, looked around, and saw Brazilian jiu-jitsu, and that took him back to square one. He really *is* that kid from the movie: he's managed to dodge bullets of fame and celebrity. And that is a testament to his intelligence as much, or more, than any annotated chess game or book. He genuinely wants to help people see and learn what he's learned.

Josh and I got along smoothly, each cloaked in honesty. Both of us, to a certain degree, hide in plain sight. He's a good dude, mellow and friendly, although intensely competitive and driven beyond belief in his chosen areas. He's got a lot of gameness, as a little kid on the beach his sister would set him to cracking coconuts and he'd be at it, doggedly, for hours, while she sunbathed.

We talked about innate ability, how a six-year-old gets drawn to chess, and he said, "There are a lot of people who could do it . . . maybe not everybody, but you'd be surprised—a lot of different minds, if taught in a way that used the natural strength of that mind, could be great at chess."

With goals like that in mind, Josh writes and thinks and clarifies his world, and he wants to make it a better place.

Once a simple inhalation can trigger a state of tremendous alertness, our moment-to-moment awareness becomes blissful, like that of someone half-blind who puts on glasses for the first time. We see more as we walk down the street. The everyday becomes exquisitely beautiful. The notion of boredom becomes alien and absurd as we naturally soak in the lovely subtleties of "banal." All experiences become richly intertwined by our new vision, and then the new connections begin to emerge. Rainwater streaming on city pavement will teach a pianist to flow. A leaf gliding easily with the wind will teach a controller how to let go. A house cat will teach me how to move. All moments become each moment. This book is about learning and performance, but it is also about my life. Presence has taught me how to live.

That's where Josh ended up. He's doing something right.

CONVERSATIONS WITH
THE DESERT FOX

Greg Jackson

A shadowy figure lurks at the edge of the known MMA world. A coach, a trainer, a quiet unassuming man with a bald head, a thin blade of a face, a beard, and assassin's eyes. I started seeing him everywhere, in every other corner, at big events, walking behind this contender or that champion, with no clear connection between the fighters except the man. His name started to circulate. Greg Jackson. Who was the dude? He had no MMA record at all. He wasn't a former champ like Pat Miletich or a world-class jiu-jitsu player like Ricardo Liborio.

Jackson claims ten world champions (and, as of this writing, two UFC titleholders), and his grapplers have won all kinds of competitions. He is the first MMA trainer famous only for his product. His fight team has the "highest winning percentage," so rated by some of the MMA Web sites, and his stable of fighters has fought on all the big shows—Pride, the UFC, and all the new upstarts. Fighters as disparate as George St. Pierre, Joey Villasenor, Rashad Evans, and Keith Jardine—fighters with no stylistic or otherwise observable connection—all train at his camp.

I knew Greg's wrestling coach was Mike Van Arsdale, a superstar at Iowa State who'd been an Olympic alternate a few times and a formidable top level MMA fighter (Mike has since moved, for love, to Arizona). I'd heard about Michael Winkeljohn, his kickboxing guy who was an old-school ISKA standout, a multiple former champion. But Greg was a mystery.

Strange stories were cropping up about his gym in New Mexico, tales of fighters being made to run in the mountains carrying each other. It suddenly seemed like the major new crop of talent in the UFC all subscribed to Jackson with enigmatic devotion. All these rising superstars would gush about him. But Greg? He said very little.

He wrote a scholarly article for *FIGHT!* magazine that compared the quest of the modern fighter to the tactics of General Sherman—stressing the need for a "two-pronged" attack. What kind of trainer was this, who exhaustively and publicly mined military theory? It only deepened the mystery.

Albuquerque, New Mexico, is a big flat city in the true southwest desert, on the edge of stark hills. I'd been there, years before, on a bender as a hotshot firefighter. We'd driven the five hours from our base in the Gila National Forest to go to the only punk bar in New Mexico. The night had not ended well; Albuquerque is a rough town. A law enforcement friend once said to me, "The cops in Albuquerque fire their weapons more times in their first year than most cops do in a lifetime."

I landed at the airport in the morning, and already the temperature was in the triple digits. Jackson's gym is just a few miles from the airport, down a side street in a semi-industrial part of town. The sun was an incandescent weight in the sky by ten o'clock. Walking into the unfamiliar gym, it had the same old feel—the smells, the watchful glances, the sizing up.

I found Greg Jackson in his back room, and he shook my hand with some wariness. He wasn't quite sure what I was doing, but he was interested. I spent a moment in that adjustment period when you meet someone you've seen many times on TV and silently catalog the differences. His beard and shiny bald head make him seem much older than he really is—he's only thirty-four—and up close in person, you can see his youth.

We sat in his "office," his private sanctum strewn with coaches and toys and even a bunk bed, a place where he could get out of the eye of the gym. We chatted with his assistant and family friend, Julie Kedzie (a good-looking young fighter with incredible mental toughness and an appetite for pain—it was her scrap with Gina Carano on prime-time TV that put women's MMA on the map); the gym manager, Van Arsdale; and a few others in a constant parade. I sat down into a wash of banter, a barrage of jokes and comedy routines that people who spend a lot of time together develop. Over the next week I sat in there every day for hours and listened and learned. Greg and I talked when he had quiet moments, and sometimes we did formal interviews with the tape recorder going. But other times we just bullshitted and came to recognize we were *un poco simpatico*.

I had nowhere to begin, so I started with the basic questions. I wanted to draw some kind of picture . . . where was Greg from? Every hero needs an origin story.

Greg was raised in Albuquerque, "the only white kid in the poorest part of the poorest state." His parents were hippies and practicing Quakers. "It's Christianity, but without preachers," he said. "In church it's just chairs in a circle, and you sit and talk to God directly, without help. My parents converted in Albuquerque."

The Quaker tradition had one huge problem for Greg: pacifism. "Pacifism taken to extreme is ridiculous. In the circumstances I found myself in, even in kindergarten, it just wouldn't fly. If the British had the resolve to wipe out Gandhi, then all the pacifism in the world wouldn't have kept them from mowing him down. A big part of my young life was coming to grips with the ideology I was taught, and the reality I had to face.

"It was a huge deal, when you're taught one thing and it doesn't work as a little kid. My parents kept telling me 'this is how you deal with the world,' *but it didn't work*. It was as if I went to school in one language and spoke another at home and no one would admit it. One set of values didn't hold in the other environment. I'd get in a fight at school and come home and feel terrible, and then sometimes I needed to fight and I wouldn't, and I'd feel just as bad.

"My parents would tell me to defend myself, but fighting isn't only about hitting or getting hit. It's about standing up to bullies, for yourself or others. Once they bully you once, they'll do it every time. In middle school it got harder, the consequences and the fights got more extreme—and the disparity between what I was told was the right thing and what *was* right got harder to reconcile."

Greg shook his head demurely. "That was probably the hardest thing in my life to deal with. Anything taken to extremes is insanity. Pacifism at all costs is as bad as saying violence is the answer to everything. But I was a dumb kid. The struggle with pacifism created a rebellion, an opposite swing. I hurt people I shouldn't have, I did a lot of things." He sighs.

"I was especially stupid. For instance, I grew up in a community that spoke Spanish, and I could and *should* have learned it so many times, but because I was endlessly picked on for being the white kid, I said to myself, *Fuck Spanish*."

He shrugged. "I was constantly in fights, and getting challenged, and then my world would get bigger and new groups would come in and I'd have to do it all over again. I dedicated my life at an early age to combat. But I make up for my sins now. I help-help-help." He laughed.

Greg's family had a strong wrestling background. His father and uncles all wrestled, his little brother was a state champ. Greg grew up wrestling but in his own words he was too busy being a "dumb kid" to wrestle in school. In West Aurora High, there's a giant picture of his father, who was a wrestling champion and valedictorian. "I've always been in his shadow and happily so," he said quietly. Throughout all this the love and respect—even awe—he has for his parents is very clear.

"My parents are geniuses, but they didn't understand my circumstances. They were from the Midwest and didn't see what I saw. I could have switched schools, but that would have been running away, and I wasn't gonna do that."

He smiles.

"My folks put me in aikido, which was the worst martial art to fight with, but they liked the philosophy of it."

Greg started teaching fighting in 1992, at the tender age of seventeen. It was at Frank Trujillo's martial arts school, a place that taught kajukenbo—a kind of early form of MMA that drew from karate, judo, and boxing.

"I never really wanted to run a school, but I got into my share of scraps and scrapes and people wanted to know how I did what I was doing. I wasn't a big street fighter, but I did what I had to do," he laughed, "and I was always in wars because I couldn't KO anybody." Greg is reflexively self-effacing, and his humility isn't fake. He's smart enough to really be humble.

"My only real strength is that I'm reflective. I learned enough lessons young and thought about them, and that's why I'm a decent trainer now. Of course, I still make mistakes."

He was a self-taught martial artist, particularly on the ground. He'd never studied jiu-jitsu with a Brazilian. That was a surprise. He taught himself from books and competitions. He was paying attention, and when Royce Gracie did his thing at UFC 1, Greg was watching and studying. But he has no belt, and he never trained in the gi. Yet his guys have always done well at no-gi grappling competitions, winning big shows, competing with the best in the world at Abu Dhabi.

At the same time, he began training with Michael Winkeljohn, a fighter from Albuquerque who had become a serious kickboxing star. Winkeljohn had been at it since 1980, had even boxed professionally, and was winning renown as a striking coach.

Greg elaborated. "When I started with him I could kick a little, but I had no set-ups, no real understanding of the kickboxing game. He gave me all that. I call him my big brother and he taught me about business, kickboxing . . ." Greg assumes a hammy, hoary voice, filled with false tears, "*a little bit about life.*" Winkeljohn was infamous for his grueling desert runs, a tradition Greg carries on. Apparently, in his prime, Winkeljohn would get dropped off on the far side of the mountains and run ten or fifteen miles back to town, through the desert heat. Greg often has his fighters run the mountains on routes Winkeljohn discovered— but Greg sometimes has his fighters carry each other.

I followed Greg out into the gym and watched him lead a practice. He worked on technique for most of the hour and a half, but at the end he had his fighters doing flutter kicks for grueling five-minute rounds that seemed endless. He kept them in the dark about when it would end. Just when they thought it was all over he'd tack on another round. I was happy I'd decided to just sit and watch this one. We chatted while they suffered in near silence, and then afterward we retreated back to his sanctum. Everything he did was for a reason.

"Mental toughness is learned. It's not a skill that everyone has, or is born with. There are people that are born tougher than others mentally, or figure things out earlier in their life. But if you have motivation you can acquire mental toughness, it's just about what your body gets used to putting up with.

"Sure, some people are already tougher and some folks just won't get tough, but those are the novelties, on the statistical fringe. Most people are of average toughness and can get tougher. I saw it all the time as a kid. There were these guys who were *supertough* growing up. I looked up to them because they could take a crowbar to the face and keep fighting. But as I grew up, they stayed the same level. They were scrappers to the core, don't get me wrong, but they never got any tougher. It was from their environment and they never worked on it. I could outdo them, outwork them, and they'd tire and break. It was a real revelation to me, that you can train mental toughness and work harder, that it doesn't have to be born into you."

He pauses, thoughtful. "Your mind is a muscle and you have to exercise it. And I don't mean crossword puzzles, though that helps. What we did today, those flutter kicks? I can get them in shape any way, a treadmill. But that's not why you do those exercises. You do it to acquire mental stamina as well as physical toughness. You do brutal workouts to get used to suffering so that suffering doesn't become a huge defining deal."

Greg is a diehard advocate of learning to function under pain, under duress. The idea is to develop resistance to the pain affecting your mental or physical abilities.

"You do those workouts to get tougher, you have hard sparring to get tougher. So when it happens in a fight it's not this foreign, unfamiliar thing, *Ohmigod I'm so tired now, I've never felt this tired and he wants to hit me in the face . . .*"

Greg continued. "Fighting is a selfish thing but at its core it should be unselfish. If you start thinking about yourself, then your mind is off your opponent. You're worried about what he's doing to you instead of focusing on hurting him, and you've lost the fight if you get there.

"We work on never accepting the takedown, even if he's in deep, never think, *I'm going to start working from the bottom now*. Make him fight for every little thing, even if you don't know how you're going to get out."

I thought of something my friend Rory Markham had once said to me. I asked Rory why he fought like hell to get out from under a guy when there was only ten seconds left in the round. It was taking a lot of energy, and if and when he got up, he wouldn't have time to mount a real attack. He smiled and said,

"Because I'll gas him, and it eats him mentally, when he can't hold me down."

Greg continued his train of thought.

"What are you going to do to him? How do I get to him, open him up to damage, push or pull or cut that angle? As soon as you say, *Oh shit my rib hurts,* you're not going to hit him. You'll focus on keeping him from hitting that rib. You've lost the initiative. Nothing worse than getting into a protracted war because you've lost the initiative." Greg shakes his head at me.

"Aggression is important. You have to refocus from yourself to your opponent. You practice staying focused through pain. I watch my fighters start out at one level, and I watch them get stronger. Things that they used to do that would just kill them don't kill them anymore." He barks a short laugh at me.

"Any fool can fight fresh," he says like a motto. He paused, drummed his fingers on the table.

"We call it the *emotional roller coaster.* You see it all the time, especially in the younger guys. You start winning, your emotions start peaking, and you *almost* finish the fight. You put everything into it, hitting as hard as you can, and you are really going to win—yet your opponent somehow is still there. And now you're exhausted. If he comes back at you you're smoked.

"So you need to maintain a constant line. Your emotions need to keep increasing on a steady line on the graph. If you get mounted, if you escape, no matter what happens, you keep climbing—but slowly, steadily. Stay out of the peaks and valleys. Keep it as 'just business' and stay strong.

"You recognize it in training and work on staying calm and focused. Every fighter knows the feeling when you're winning, or you're getting close to finishing somebody, especially in wars. It'll sneak up on you. Suddenly you've got an ankle lock and you've GOT that ankle—and it's all over."

Greg mimes the cranking on the ankle, pretending tension and excitement, his face squeezed in a rictus.

"I just got to get it a little tighter, a little longer, and I'm putting everything I got into it . . . and *whoosh*, now I'm tired. Now he survives, and he starts hitting me, and I accept dominance, and now it's over."

He shakes his head.

"We do drills applying the squeeze with different muscles, to keep that same squeeze going with dynamic tension—so you breath hard and deep while squeezing—but the main thing is to keep emotions out of it. At its core, if you keep emotions out you can have maximum oxygen exchange as well as full muscle squeeze—and not gas." Techniques like this—increasing squeeze while controlling breathing—are the things that Randy Couture pioneered and the reason his lactic acid levels actually drop when he's squeezing.

"But what about going for the kill, knowing when to finish?" I asked him. Certainly some fighters are great finishers and some struggle to do it. It's almost an art form in itself. You see certain fighters, when they get an opponent hurt, know how to overwhelm to get the finish. Other fighters who struggle with the concept can attack and attack—but ineffectively, and the round ends. Now they've "punched themselves out," meaning they worked so hard in their excitement that they have exhausted themselves. They built up a huge oxygen deficit in their bloodstream by attacking on a wave of adrenaline. But the opponent survived and now he's coming back.

Greg frowned a little. "You can develop it, and you need it, but basically you have to do your job. Like Clausewitz [the Prussian military officer who wrote *On War*, a book on strategy that defined military thought for the twentieth century] said, 'War is a continuation of policy by other means.' Your policy is to win, and killer instinct to finish when a guy is hurt can be a part of that. But just wanting to finish somebody can bite you in the ass. When Joey Villasenor lost to Ninja Rua, he had too much killer instinct. He saw Ninja hurt and blew his gas tank trying to finish him.

"Killer instinct has to be trained—you have to understand how to stay on a guy who's hurt, but without blowing your gas tank. Joey did it beautifully in the last Baroni fight. He just kept applying high-intensity pressure, but he was calm and controlled. That needs to be taught, developed. It's not just about jumping on a guy and finishing him. That's a myth that fighters who aren't sure about themselves perpetuate, this holy grail of 'killer instinct.' If you go into a fight to knock a guy out, chances are you won't. But when you see a guy hurt, pick up the pressure and the knockout comes. Stay calm. Pick your shots. Just apply your pressure."

It's what Josh Waitzkin said about increasing the pressure, the tension, the cat and mouse.

"People fall in love with the idea of *when he's hurt I'll finish him* and it makes it too big a deal. As soon as anything becomes a big deal you'll have problems with it.

"There's always a point at which people will break. That's why you train mental toughness. Everyone will break—there's not a man alive that can't be broke. Your job, with all that mental training, that suffering, is just to push your own line of mental breaking so far back your opponent can't find it. Then you take your opponent and get *him* to cross his line, because once he starts breaking he accepts your dominance, and once he accepts your dominance, you can finish him off.

"It's a skill to see if people are hurt, so I train guys not to show as much as you can—not to look tired or hurt. It adds layers of protection, because you can come back, too, if you break, but your opponent can't capitalize, that's strong for you. He had you, but you're still okay! And it's bad for him, because he's thinking, *Oh man, I can't finish this guy.*"

"So you watch his eyes?" I asked.

This was a matter of some debate. My friend Javier, the boxer/ filmmaker in L.A., and I often discussed this very point. Javier had been in training camp with Pernell Whittaker, Arturo Gatti, Hector Camacho Sr., Vanes Martirosyian—all legendary, world-class fighters. Javier sparred regularly at Wild Card with the best in the world. He and I had been friends for a while and we sparred together and did drills. He taught me a tremendous amount and was extremely thoughtful about boxing. He had forced me to start looking in his eyes as we sparred. I had never done that, but Javier maintained that *that* was the big shock at the high level, with the top fighters in the world. They locked eyes.

"For the good guys, it's all in the eyes. I can't remember any-one, any top guy, without constant vigilant eye contact."

Javier told me, "You learn to *see through the veil.*" His point was that before you make any physical movement, whether its conscious or subconscious, the maneuver first manifests in the brain and you can see it in his eyes. The eyes are windows on the brain. You can feel what he's thinking. Once you get sufficiently sensitive—you develop "pugilistic sensitivity"—you begin to pick up on visual indications that the eyes give you as to what punch is coming. You can feel what they're thinking. Jav would laugh and say, "It is microcosmically subtle. The eyes do different things, and you can't really say what they are. But you can see them. You discern that paradigm."

Javier was something of a counterpuncher (he waits for you to punch, makes you miss, and then counters with his own punch). For him, proper eye contact is useful for allowing the read, but useful also because keeping proper eye contact facilitates the overall body posture that is necessary to counter. Locking gaze with the opponent keeps your head, neck, everything set prop-erly, to see the openings. So you can take advantage of windows that are open for only fractions of a second.

To me, when I started sparring, looking at the opponent's eyes, I found it disconcertingly personal. But fighting *is* personal.

For someone who started boxing in a college environment, it's okay that boxing is a kind of athletic endeavor; you look for openings, try to score points. But fighting in a real gym, at the professional level, you have to be aware of what you're about, which is hurting and getting hurt, hitting and being hit. Dominating someone on a personal, intimate level is the goal. Smashing.

Javier would take it even further. "Locked into eye contact, you get a ton of information about the individual you're engaged with. Not just what maneuvers and feints, but emotions: shyness, aggression, confidence—and it can be really disconcerting. For instance, the guy I was sparring the other day has got a lot of pro fights, a ton of professional experience. But I was walking him down. He was good enough to maintain eye contact, he made good maneuvers, but I could feel a difference in the level of maturity. He's doing well but not enjoying himself."

I've had this same experience sparring with Javier, 'winning' rounds due to the fact I outweigh him by thirty pounds and am four inches taller, but both of us knowing I'm getting tired, that I'm worried about getting hit in the ribs. I barely have enough power to keep him off me, and he's fighting at about 60 percent, slowly coming on, and by the third or fourth round he'll nail me with a few hard shots, just to show me he can.

Javier continued his story, "There's a power differential and a maturity differential we can both feel. He was very good, came from a great school with wonderful sparring partners, but he wasn't as experienced as them. I could feel that he was fearful even though he was good and effective. Not only could I sense that but I can sense that he *knows* I can sense it."

For Greg, as for many MMA trainers (such as Miletich, for one), eye contact wasn't the way. Maybe the addition of all the weapons—kicks and knees and the threat of the takedown—forced you to be more focused on the man's body. But I remember even Virgil saying, "He don't hit you with his eyes, man!"

Greg's opinion was that "the eyes don't attack, but you check them to see if he's hurt. Keep your eyes on his chest, his body, to see what weapons are coming at you, when it comes time to throw. If I hit him twice with a body shot, I'll glance up and see the re-action. If he's good, I won't see anything. If he smiles, I know I hurt him, and he might even be rocked. Then I add pressure. It goes back to my fighting days. I hit like a sissy and always had to check," he chuckled.

We took time out to commiserate over the horror of body shots. Greg, like me, would rather take ten to the head than one to the body.

We started talking about the problems in training fighters. "The big one is motivation. If they're motivated, it's just a matter of time before they break through," Greg said. "Each problem is unique, just like the fighter. Training fighters is like jazz—each unique piece has to be pushed sometimes, pulled others. It's improvisational. You're responding to situations, and there are so many factors. At the core of everything is respect. If they don't have it, they're unhappy. Keep that principle in mind.

"Sometimes, when they get too big-headed, they start think-ing they know everything." This is one I've seen before. We used to call it "champ-itis" at Pat Miletich's place.

"Now they're not giving respect, and they're demanding too much. I usually have a talk with them. I say, 'I've seen other guys do exactly what you're doing and it always ends bad. If you want me to keep coaching you, you have to abide and respect these principles, and if not there are a lot of other good coaches out there.' If it's in my house, it's gotta be done my way."

We started in on fighters and ego.

"You don't make it far if you have a big ego. The guys that come in here with huge egos get smashed until they learn. Verbal reasoning won't work, that's where those guys live . . . you just gotta smash them until they get humble. And build them back up, if they can stand it."

213

Greg also has thoughts on the reverse side of that coin—those without enough ego or belief in themselves.

"For the fighters without enough ego I try to talk to them about idealism and believing in yourself. It's simple. Either start believing in yourself and you win—even if you lose, you're on the path to winning for the rest of your life—or you don't, and sit where you are. It's not just about learning the moves, it's about learning to believe in yourself. If you don't win, you should feel like you did."

I asked about all the top guys in his camp who were facing such massive pressure because of the explosive surge in popularity of MMA in the last few years. The media scrutiny had become inescapable.

"The way things have grown, every fight is always the biggest fight. Every week here it's the *biggest fight ever*. It's ridiculous. I do my best to remind them it's just another fight. The media, the fans, will all fall in love with the fight, and they'll convince fighters that 'if you win, everything will change, and if you lose, your life is over.'"

Greg ruminates on his early days, and all his problems in school. I get the sense of how it molded him. Greg versus the world from kindergarten on.

"The thing about being young, it's all so relative. You're in school and you've got to fight this guy tomorrow who's enormous. He beat up two friends, and the whole school will be watching. As a kid you have no perspective—it feels like the end of the world. Fighters do the same thing. They make a fight into a huge mountain, and then they've already lost.

"You just have to let it all go. Accept that it sucks and do the job. I know you're nervous and you'll be scared, but when the cage closes none of that matters anymore. All that matters is him.

"I don't always read the pressure that a fighter is feeling. I'll see him fight and realize that he had too much pressure on him, because he's not relaxed, he's tight, he's not performing well. After the first thirty seconds I'll go 'aww, fuck, I should have seen that, why didn't I read that in him?'"

I asked Greg what he would have said if he had read the tension properly. How would he deal with it?

"You remind people why they're doing what they're doing. Tell him the sun will rise tomorrow, even if you get knocked out in thirty seconds—the same is true for all your teammates. You got to let it all go and do what you love and fuck the rest."

One of the key elements of any successful trainer is the ability to create game plans for specific fighters and successfully implement them. It's not just about seeing a weakness but getting a fighter to exploit it. Greg has an individualistic approach—just like all the best guys I spoke with.

"Game plans vary in complexity. Some guys I get superspecific with—when he does this, you do that, your foot goes here. Other people it's more situational—stay out of this situation, try and get him into that situation. And then we train it—here's how we do it.

"I try to train my fighters to be as versatile as possible so the game plans can be as versatile as humanly possible. Being a standup guy who's decent on the ground isn't good enough—you got to be great on the ground and great on the feet. They're all in the process. Everyone has a personal development plan so when they get to the top level they're all like George [St. Pierre]. Game planning is fighter specific.

"Once you're a pro fighter you have an individual growth plan, so every time you train with me or on your own, you know what you need to be doing.

"For specific things, we drill it over and over. If you're fighting somebody at a high level, you worry about tiny technical details—they drop the jab, they pass to the left. At the lower level it's bigger stuff. Training partners fight like the opponent might. Often it doesn't go exactly as you want, and then it's up to the fighter to improvise.

"The ideal length of a training camp varies, but I like six weeks. Too long and you get burned out. Not long enough and you can't peak well. Most of my guys are in shape year-round. But if you work out eight hours a day your intensity is shit." Greg means that if you actually train for eight hours during the day, you can't train hard. A lot of fighters will claim that they do—with technique, sparring, and conditioning all separate workouts— but usually they train for six hours total a day, maximum. Or less. In Thailand we trained twice a day, but usually only for an hour and a half or two hours, tops, plus a long run in the morning. And that was governed by intensity—it's better to go harder than longer. You're only fighting for twenty-five minutes or less, right? Fighters might be at the gym for eight hours, maybe, but there's a lot of downtime, stretching, wrapping hands, watching, goofing.

Training camp is a specific term. A fighter "goes into camp" to prepare for a fight—and the bigger the fight, the longer the camp. An eight-week camp is considered normal by professional MMA standards. It's a ramping up of all training, moving away from technique and focusing on conditioning, getting the fighter in peak physical condition. You might learn a trick or two but you won't become a massively different fighter, so now let's just get you in top shape and get you sparring hard so the timing is right.

Pro MMA fighters will train at least twice a day, maybe three times. Strength and conditioning would be one session, then technique followed by hard sparring that night. Part of the relentless overtraining comes from the fact that there are so many disciplines to train, but another big factor is the wrestling mentality—where more is always better—inherited from the likes of Dan Gable. Often, fighters train too hard, too long, and either fight injured or miss paydays because of injury.

"Overtraining in this sport is an enormous mental issue. I tell fighters to get the fuck out of the dojo . . . because it just leads to burnout, mentally and physically. That's why a shorter camp is better. We went through a bad patch here one summer when everyone was overtrained and everyone lost. It was crazy. But I learned my lesson."

What about personal burnout? Greg has an interesting way, unique to New Mexico, of recharging his batteries. He grew up with a strong sense of local history, and one of his favorite hobbies is "ghost towning," where you get maps and track down old ghost towns in the New Mexican wilderness.

"It's incredible, these abandoned towns. Such hard work went into it and now nature is reclaiming everything. You come over a ridge and find a town that has been essentially unchanged for 130 years. It's a window into history. I get a sense of my own mortality. You find shoes, and books—they just up and left everything."

I spent only the week there but I felt like I connected with Greg. Probably everyone feels like this; it's part of what makes him a great trainer. We talked about books, about history, about warfare and Zen. Greg's interests are enormously varied. He reads and reflects on a range of subjects from military history to musical theory. You start to understand the little "cult of Jackson" going on, because he's a deeply intelligent, caring guy who's involved in a rough business with often damaged souls. Greg made a critical point—that the gym gives you a social circle. "We have kids in here that are borderline mentally ill, who wouldn't get any respect anywhere else. But they work hard in here, and they get better, so they get respect." That is true of every fight gym I've ever been in.

"There's an old Celtic proverb that I follow: *See much, study much, suffer much is the path to wisdom.* It's not sitting and suffering. You've got to have a goal. You're not just making yourself miserable, you don't self-flagellate and become world champ. It's suffering and functioning, focusing. You learn about yourself. You increase the amount you can take."

I sat there nodding at his words like an idiot. I have a tattoo on my arm—MUNDIS EX IGNE FACTUS EST—which means "The world is made of fire," and it basically says the same thing to me. It's a reminder that suffering and struggle are the ways to truth, to understanding, and the only way to save your own soul.

"I'm an adventurer," Greg says lightly. "I still go out there and suffer. You can't let fear be a factor. I wrestled crocodiles with Steve Irwin, and I still get in there and spar, and run, and go hard."

Back up a second. You did what? Out comes a fascinating side story, and an unexpected mentor—Steve Irwin, the Crocodile Hunter. For those who live in a deep dark cave, Steve was an Australian naturalist who came to fame as the TV personality who "wrestled" crocodiles. Steve had grown up in his father's Reptile and Fauna Park, and he would chase all manner of dangerous animals around Australia and bring the cameras with him. He wasn't just a self-promoter; he had a deep love for what he did, a joy in conservation and a genuine spirit that made him into an international celebrity. He was killed in 2006 by a stingray barb while filming. It was a tragic event that gripped the major media for some days.

Greg laughed at my curiosity. "Steve and I were friends for years. Now, I wasn't his best friend, but I was his friend, and I'll always be in debt to him. I went to Australia with Joey Villasenor, who was fighting Steve's bodyguard, a guy named Danny. After the fights I asked Danny which zoo I should go to. I didn't know much or care about Steve. But I was lucky enough to meet him and become his friend. He'd fly me out and we'd train together— and he hit like a freight train. He could have fought. He was an amazing human being. A week before he died we caught crocs for nine days in northern Queensland on the Kennedy River." Greg pauses, nearly tearing up.

"He taught me a lot about fame. He said, 'I always thought I'd have certain people around me my entire life, and then they'd be gone.' He meant that people change, that fame changes people.

The fighter I train now won't be the same person in six years if he's successful. Steve was down-to-earth, but he used his fame to get his message out. He stayed positive, he stayed away from the negative stuff on the Internet, which used to bother me. I use his lessons for my fighters that have success. If you do your art well, fame is something that you deal with.

"Steve taught me how to feed the crocodiles, how to get into a little tug-of-war so they'd death roll. He was a phenomenal guy. It really satisfied an ancient urge for me. I used to watch horror movies and think about how to beat the monster. Ever since I was a kid I always wanted to wrestle a dinosaur."

There was a deep lull while Greg and I were just chilling in the office, and I asked him about some of the pictures on his wall—George Washington, Abe Lincoln, and Ernest Shackleton.

"When I make mistakes I look at those pictures. Burnout is my number-one enemy. I have to look for inspiration to stay on the cutting edge.

"George Washington, losing battle after battle? How the fuck did he keep the army together? The man is a genius, not the greatest field general but *no one* could break him. His line was non-existent, but no one could *break* George Washington. Same with Lincoln, no one could break him. With Shackleton, he got broken once with Scott, and he learned from it and you could never break him again. There was a summer when all my guys were losing, and I was hearing 'Oh, Jackson's went from the glory of Rome to the last days of Pompeii in a week,' and I was questioning myself. But I come in here and look at these pictures and slap myself, *Shut the fuck up, you're not leading soldiers with no shoes through the snow to death.*"

Greg smiles but he says a picture is missing—Genghis Khan. Greg makes a point to pronounce the name correctly, with a soft 'g,' *jhengis*. He can't get the one that he wants shipped to him, of old Genghis wearing a simple *gi*.

219

"I walk around thinking, how can you be that smart? Genghis was the first mixed martial artist. He utilized everyone's talents and brought them into the fold. He took siege war craft from China and used it in the Middle East. He borrowed what worked and didn't discriminate. He united all kinds of peoples, every nationality, and I try to emulate that with a real 'hive mind.' George St. Pierre has a phenomenal wrestling coach, but all this together, this hybrid is better yet. When I read about Genghis I think about how somebody could be so smart and it makes me want to punch myself in the face."

He laughed ruefully.

I remember reading a book that said something along the lines of "imagine a Negro slave in colonial America gaining his freedom and eventually conquering North *and* South America with an army—that's still not as astounding as what Genghis did." To this day, no modern empire or nation has been as large in terms of landmass.

Greg muttered, "The only thing that kept Genghis from conquering Europe is that he died. If he'd had another two lifetimes he'd have done it, easy. But when he was just starting out, he was being hunted in the mountains with his last twelve guys or so, and they had no fresh water so they drank dirty, brackish water. Years later, when he'd conquered the world, he always brought his loyal guys with him, the guys who had *drank the dark water.*"

It's a line Greg goes back to when he talks about his guys, the fighters who have been with him for so long, who were around when he started his gym on the dusty streets in this desert city.

Greg has a genuine softness when it comes to caring for his fighters. I hadn't expected it, but it made sense, in terms of the fanatical loyalty they showed him. He loves his guys, those guys who've drank the dark water.

"It was drilled into my head, that happiness comes from helping people. Since day one. So now I'm just helping. It doesn't matter if they live up to it, they fight for themselves, the win is for them. I'm outside the cage, safe, and they're the ones getting punched and feeling pressure. I'm about the process—the process is for me. I always train to win but the process is important. If they lose, I get broken up and emotional, but I recover and go back to the process. The fight is only fifteen minutes, the process is months, years. If it was just about the fight I'd have a miserable life."

I see Greg get choked up a few times, discussing his fighters. He *cares* and cares deeply. He's young, not burned out. His initial wariness was about protecting that softness.

Greg's father is the second tenor for the New Mexico Symphony Orchestra. "We had two traditions in my family—wrestling and music. I wasn't really musical, but I love listening to it.

"Bach to me is the greatest composer who ever lived. He did exactly what we do in the martial arts, with all the complexity . . . but his genius was far greater. He hid his name in the music. He worked the trinity in everywhere, in layers. It's beautiful and so intricate, so counterpoint, the crab canons with one going this way and one going that way." Greg dances his hands like opposing crabs running.

"In the same way, you can find beauty in an ant walking up a hill. At first you think, wow that's beautiful, and then you start to think about the mechanics and it blows your mind. I do that thing where I stomp around the room wondering 'how can somebody be so smart?' I love the way Bach turns things. You know how we do a kimura from on top, in side control? The same thing works from underneath. Bach does that with his music. It's the exact same thing but upside down."

Greg sighs deeply.

"If we have a night where all my guys win, all four or five, then my treat is Beethoven's Ninth, 'The Ode to Joy,' the most beautiful and emotional thing ever written." He smiles.

I have a plane to catch. But if I was going to fight again, I'd come here.

THE GUNSLINGER

Renzo Gracie catches Pat Miletich in a guillotine,
September 23, 2006. (Courtesy Zach Lynch)

"You must hold the drawn bowstring," answered the Master, "like a little child holding the proffered finger. It grips so firmly that one marvels at the strength of the tiny fist. And when it lets the finger go, there is not the slightest jerk. Do you know why? Because the child doesn't think: I will now let go of the finger to grasp this other thing. Completely unselfconsciously, without purpose, it turns from one to the other, and we would say that it was playing with things, were it not equally true that the things were playing with the child."

—Eugen Herrigel

The Gracie family is the first family of mixed martial arts—their contribution to the sport is nothing short of fundamental. In postcolonial Rio de Janeiro, the vibrant maze city that hung like a jewel of water on a spiderweb between the deep blue sea and the green jungle, a Brazilian politician and businessman of Scottish descent, Gastao Gracie befriended a wandering professional fighter and Japanese judoka master, Mitsuya Maeda, in 1917. Gastao helped Maeda do business in Rio. In return, Maeda agreed to instruct Gastao's eldest boy, Carlos.

Carlos and his brothers embraced and reinvented what they'd learned, and since the 1920s they've fostered an atmosphere of innovation and real-world combat in Rio. They challenged any and all comers, and nearly always won in the *vale tudo* ("anything goes") matches. The philosophy of *arte suave*—constant innovation and relentless testing, all on the ground—made for a revolution in the fighting world.

Brazil is a modern nation of frozen colonial power structures and wealth disparity. The Portuguese came to steal, exploit, and find gold to take home, not build a nation, and Brazil still suffers from those rapacious intentions woven into the cloth of her identity. In some ways, Brazil lags behind today's world by a full century; in others it is inescapably modern—educated, monied. The nature of jiu-jitsu reflects the dualities of scientific technique combining with old-school Latin-American machismo, a need to fight to prove who is the toughest, along with another Brazilian trait, the love of play.

While Royce (pronounced "Hoyce," as all 'R' sounds are 'H' in Portuguese) Gracie was the standard-bearer for jiu-jitsu, chosen by the forward-looking Rorion ("Horion") Gracie to lead the way in the initial UFCs and showcase the family's art, and Rickson ("Hickson") is the legend, the undefeated greatest who lives shrouded in mystery, to me the truly greatest Gracie is a younger cousin, Renzo (yes, "Henzo")—who fought anyone, anywhere, and took his losses and his wins with equal aplomb.

Renzo seemed apart from the convoluted family politics. He put himself out there, and he embodied what the Gracies claimed to be about. He fought anyone, anytime. When you step back and look at his fighting career as a whole, Renzo is probably *underrated*. In the beginning, when Royce won the UFC, not many people were aware of what he was doing. He was armbarring fighters who didn't know the danger they were in. The legendary Rickson has always been criticized for not fighting the best available, but in truth (being a generation older) he came up at a time when there wasn't as much competition, especially outside of Brazil. Rickson was retiring as international MMA blossomed.

Renzo consistently puts his money where his mouth is, and he fought with the best he could find. He fought and beat much bigger guys, and not clueless boxers but seasoned mixed martial artists such as Maurice Smith (235 pounds), Oleg Taktorov (210 pounds), and the like, most of whom outweighed him significantly and knew his game. His natural fighting weight would have been 155—and he was fighting heavyweights, *good* heavyweights for the time. It's unimaginable now. What I also love about Renzo is that he kept doing it, even through losing fights to bigger fighters like Sakuraba or Dan Henderson. Royce and Rickson seemed protective of their legacies, but Renzo was never precious about his. He would risk it (and himself) at the drop of a hat. In his last three fights, Renzo has beaten three former UFC champions—Pat Miletich, Carlos Newton, and Frank Shamrock.

Renzo was never a muscular freak of an athlete but a normal guy with a head of thick black curly hair and an open honest face. His standup wasn't his strength, but it was effective, and he was a fighter—he'd force opponents to respect his hands, just a little. His ground game was superlative. To this day (in the twilight of his career) he still has to be considered one of the best in the world on the ground, and an elite-level fighter, for despite the sport's quantum growth he has grown with it. Renzo still sometimes throws in his hat at Abu Dhabi, one of the very few MMA guys who will compete in pure grappling competitions.

Renzo has done it all with an incredible lightness of spirit, a human warmth and ease that makes him one of the best on-camera interviews in the business and one of the great teachers and most respected men in the fighting world.

Renzo was born into fighting. Fighting was the family business. His brothers and cousins and fathers and uncles were all dedicated to jiu-jitsu. The Gracie family had decided to go that way, to make their bones in that world, as a family. Renzo makes it clear that it wasn't forced, that nobody had do to anything they hated.

"We all grew up like champions, eating right, thinking right— we were built and forged to be the best. But everything came very naturally. We were never forced to fight. It surrounded us. Everything began as play. We spent time as kids at the academy, my brothers, cousins, everyone. Many in the family don't follow fighting as a profession, but they are still very strong-minded." The Gracie family is huge, and not everyone fights professionally, but almost everyone has logged some mat time.

"You start seeing your relatives, the people you love and admire, involved in jiu-jitsu and so you end up embracing that. It becomes a way of life, and then of course you want to excel and be the best. It comes naturally. And the way jiu-jitsu is, you want to win. You start to know that to be second place is just to be the first loser. That appetite is such a big part of the game."

Renzo sometimes seems a man out of time. There's something about him of the nineteenth-century gentleman, to whom honor and respect are far more important than life and limb, something about the feudalism of Rio and the nature of what he does. Brazil in the 1970s (when he was a boy) was still governed by colonial ethics, with the remnants of the Portuguese romanticism. There's a great new documentary film, called *Legacy* (made by Gethin Aldous), about Renzo, and in it Renzo's brilliant loquaciousness is on full display, bon mot following bon mot. Renzo talks about his father, Robson (also a jiu-jitsu *mestre*), who at one point took to the streets in an attempt to change things for the better and nearly lost his life. The Gracie family name saved him. Robson was obviously another iconoclast in this family of warrior monks. All of these factors combine to make Renzo a more unique individual than even he realizes.

I came to New York to talk to Renzo and hung around his school until he showed up. "Meet me at six," he said, and showed promptly at ten, classic *carioca* (the slang in Brazil for someone who lives in Rio, where punctuality is not a virtue). But once I got hold of him, Renzo understood what I was after and showed me why he was the most fun interview in MMA. The next day I drove out to his house, where he made me welcome.

Renzo laments the rudeness in America, even while he agrees it makes life simpler, the hermetic modern life where you never acknowledge anyone you don't know.

"Back in Rio, on the beach, I used to fight three or four times a day. And no one really held a grudge. The police would just send you home, maybe yell at whoever started it. But here everything is so serious. A guy insulted my wife and kids at a gas station"—here the mind reels—"and I went over to talk to him, to get him to apologize, and so he insulted me and I slapped him. He throws himself on the floor, crying for the police, says his neck is hurt. I had to go to court five times, pay fifteen hundred dollars, all for this damn slap we do harder every day in practice." He pauses and shrugs, then says with a hint of melancholy, "Life here is simpler. You don't waste time saying hello to everybody."

Respect—the essence of the fight game—was a huge part of Renzo's growing up. "My father, my grandfather, I respect them so much I am very quiet around them. I wanted to make sure that anything that came out of my mouth made sense. I idolized them, but I saw they were human, too."

Renzo's father, Carlson's brother, was an integral part of the family and eventually president of the Federation of Jiu-jitsu in Rio.

"I recently realized how important my father was, because he was always telling me that the impossible is nothing. Even though I was extremely weak physically, and small, he would always tell me that I was so smart and technical that without time limits I could finish anyone in the world." The old *vale tudo* fights were often fought without time limits, as that was closer to a real fight. The Gracie style could be played in a safe, defensive,

AM SHERIDAN

relentless way that would eventually yield a choke or submission, given enough time. Fighting without time limits is something they miss.

Renzo laughed hard, something he did about every third sentence, with a face like a cherub. His heavy Brazilian accent is iconic. It's not only his accent but the rhythm and variations in tone that are so signature Brazilian jiu-jitsu, *my friend*. He's almost cartoonishly animated, his eyes flaring wide, eyebrows reaching for the heavens.

"Now, that wasn't true back then. When I fought good guys who were big, they could give me trouble. But my father was always placing little pearls in my brain. And I believed him!"

Renzo grew up in the perfect environment in which to groom a fighter, and he fell deeply in love with jiu-jitsu and with competition. He would be a warm-up to best guys as a kid. His confidence grew. By the time he was a man he knew as much jiu-jitsu as anybody in the world (with the possible exception of Rickson).

"Every time I step in the ring, or onto the mat, I always feel that there is nobody that knows this better than I do. It's not a magic box. There's no surprise for me, no situations or positions that I can't understand. So I am very relaxed for fights. I even fall asleep before fights. A few times, in Pride, I bring a pillow from the hotel . . . and they have to wake me up to get me to warm up!" He finds that hilarious.

Renzo's career is unique—he is astride the transition of MMA. He fought in Brazil in the "old days," in the *vale tudo*. He fought in Japan in Pride, in front of forty thousand fans, and he fought for the UFC, for the IFL, for Elite XC . . . he's outlasted most of these promotions. He shrugs when he thinks about it. "It's been an unbelievable ride up to now," he says.

Early in his career Renzo had come to America. He wanted to teach in New York, and he struggled. He was doing okay but was having problems with his native partner. "My worries had a

230

base, because in the end he kicked me out of the country. He tried to call immigration on me and my visa was under him . . . it was a mess. I had to go home with my tail between my legs. That's one thing when you are alone, but another thing when you have a wife and three kids."

He needed money and took some fights, first Eugenio Tadeu, a *luta livre* star; and then two weeks later, Renzo was fighting in Japan. "So I fight, jump in a plane and then fight Akira Shoji at Pride One. I needed the money. I give it straight to the lawyers and split from that partner and get my green card."

He glosses over it blithely, but I press him. I know about the Tadeu fight, one of the last famous *vale tudo* matches. *Luta livre* basically means "wrestling" in Portuguese and it was the name taken by Gracie students who split off from the family (and the *gi*), often poorer guys from the favela in Rio who couldn't afford the *gi*. They wrestled and grappled no-*gi* and fought *vale tudo* and of course had a deep and undying enmity with the Gracies. I used this opportunity to ask Renzo about the age-old question: *gi* or no-*gi*?

MMA fights are not allowed with the *gi* on, so is it better to train without one all the time, or for jiu-jitsu do you need to practice with it? Greg Jackson's guys have high-level jiu-jitsu and they never train with it. Eddie Bravo threw away the *gi* but still wears the *gi* pants (and let me just say this: rolling in *gi* pants is NOT no-*gi*). Usually, the answer is pretty standard. The wrestlers feel like you don't need it, and the guys who come from traditional jiu-jitsu feel it's important. Renzo's take was interesting.

"If you want to be a really good grappler, you *have to learn* with the *gi*. With a *gi* on, everything is so much harder, a hundred times harder. With no-*gi*, you take a good wrestler and in three months he understands where the danger comes from and his game will be fine. The moment you put on a *gi*, the opponent has handles to grip, so everything is much harder—harder to pass guard, to defend guard—so it teaches your hips to be extremely active to get out of the way.

"What I see in MMA now is a lot of guys go straight to no-gi and then MMA. So their guard is a joke. *Poja,* I been on the bottom in every fight that I did and I never get hit. You see BJ Penn, he never takes damage on the bottom—and he trains in the *gi* all the time. He comes from my brother's school. I see these other guys go in there and lock their legs but they get hit the whole time they're in guard.

"When you train in the *gi,* your hips are better, sweeps are better, your escape from the mount is ten times better. With a *gi* on, the mounted guy has a hundred attacks, and without it, he has two or three. It's a joke.

"In Brazil, the *luta livre* guys trained with us for a while. They were purple belts when they separated off and stop training in the *gi.* They were big guys, taking steroids. They were tough and strong-minded, but we never lose to them. We beat the shit out of them, and we train *gi* all the time and only no-*gi* right before the fight."

Renzo was fighting Eugenio Tadeu in Rio, in one of the last *vale tudo* fights without gloves, pure old-school.

"I took the fight on last-minute notice, and the money wasn't good, but I had to pay lawyers in New York. I just wanted to make sure that the floor was canvas, because I knew he was going to come full of oil. Whatever his body touched on the mat, I couldn't stand on it." Renzo means Eugenio would be greased up—making him much harder to submit.

The *luta livre* guys and the Gracie family had a long feud and had met many times before in *vale tudo* matches and informal fights on the beach that could turn epic.

"It was an interesting match because I always dislike him, his attitude, his way of being. He was always with the wrong crowd, surrounded by criminals and drug dealers. I was always on the police side. I train a lot of police. I was on the sport side. He was always playing the role of being from the ghetto, so it was an important fight for me because I don't like him." You can see the class difference coming out; the Gracies had long trained only the upper echelons of Rio society.

"My only pleasure in that fight was going to be to punch him in the face, because I knew right away he was completely greased up and hell to hold on to, like trying to hold a fish."

This was a grudge match, and the *luta livre* guys had been filling up the arena for hours—they'd come in early and taken all the seats around the cage. And here the danger of Rio and Brazil starts to appear. It's not that all Rio is so dangerous—in Ipanema, little old ladies walk on the street at night—but it is a place where shit can go wrong, really wrong.

"Now his people had invaded the event. He brought two hundred guys with guns and knives and they surrounded the cage. Even before our fight they wouldn't let nobody get close. We were afraid of a riot, so we sent our guys up into the stands. When I walked out I saw the cage was surrounded by *luta livre* guys. There were no jiu-jitsu guys except my brother and a couple of others."

When both fighters were in the cage, they fell into a long, wild-west gunslinger staredown, both men frozen and staring across the ring for minutes. Totally still. Watching it, you can almost hear the theme song from *The Good, the Bad, and the Ugly*.

When the fight began, Renzo was having some success early on. He even took Eugenio's back a few times but couldn't keep him down. Renzo started to look for a little ground-and-pound, as he couldn't get any submissions going.

"I took him down, and every time I put my head against the fence—to keep him pinned down—they kick me through the fence. Someone cut me with a knife or maybe some keys through the fence, not deep but it was a mess." Renzo was bleeding from his shoulder.

SAM SHERIDAN

The *luta livre* guys were swarming outside the cage following the action, scuffling with the cameramen and ringside offi-
cials. Whenever Renzo and Eugenio got close to the edge, the sides
of the cage pulsed with screams and insults.

"I started seeing the guys outside the cage doing it. One time,
when the ref separates us, I see one of them hanging with his body
half inside the cage, talking shit. So I'm looking at Eugenio and I
move a little and get close, and then I land a straight shot right to
the middle of the forehead of the guy outside the cage. He fell
down and my brother kicked him in the face. So then the riot
starts."

Renzo laughs.

"It was such a mess. The lights ended up falling into the ring,
I started to feel this intense heat, and I looked up to see the big
lights have fallen into the cage, and people are screaming to turn
the lights off because it's gonna set the place on fire. As the lights
go out they pull out guns, they're shooting all over the place."
Renzo is bored with this story, "it was a big mess."

Then, two weeks later, Renzo flew to Japan to fight Akira
Shoji in the inaugural Pride show. "I was still purple with bruises
and cuts." It ended as a draw, this being the early days of Pride
without clear scoring.

I asked Renzo if these were his toughest fights. He declined to
answer, in a completely sincere way. I could feel what he was
thinking: fights that are in the past aren't tough anymore. Who
cares about those fights?

"Always I think the toughest one is the next one . . . every fight
is tough, a surprise box! You never know what's gonna happen.
Victory is certain, and then you have your arm broken with seventeen seconds left! Like the Sakuraba fight! I was thinking that fight
was mine, all I need to do is manage the time, and then I lost."

Renzo fought an epic battle with Kazushi Sakuraba, who was
a Japanese fighter and one of the all-time greats. Sakuraba was a

234

natural 185-pounder and much bigger than Renzo and they had one of the standout, fantastic MMA fights in history. The fight ended with Renzo's arm horrifically dislocated in a kimura, but with Renzo staring calmly, not tapping, hoping to continue.

"And there are fights when everything seemed lost, and I won. The toughest is always the next, because the other ones fade in my memory. I have to watch tapes because I can't believe I did this, it's so funny! Even my record, I have to check to see who I beat . . . but the ones I *lost*, those I always remember. I know exactly what happened, that's the difference.

"With my students, I always tell them that the loss is where you can get better. Once you make a mistake in a fight or a competition, you *never do that again*. It's burned in your brain. See those mistakes and cover those holes. That's why you learn more when you lose than when you win. When you win you forget.

"What is a champion but a guy that didn't quit? I always try to tell them there's nothing better than a day after another. Life is a continuous experience. You only fail by not learning.

"For jiu-jitsu, the smarter you are, the better you understand the leverage and positions and the *middle*. For instance, my head instructor is John Danaher, and he was a philosophy teacher at Columbia. He's a smart guy."

Danaher, or "New Zealand John" as he's sometimes referred to (being a Kiwi), is the head professor at Renzo's academy. He has a PhD in philosophy from Columbia and did in fact teach there. Renzo said, "He was one of my first students here, and I was able to bring him out of everything he believed in and get him into jiu-jitsu. It was one of the best things I have ever done."

I had heard about John, that he was the real genius at Renzo's—a master of jiu-jitsu, an innovator who never competed, a guy who was quietly changing the game with his private lessons. George St. Pierre and other notables took private lessons with him. Real guys knew what was up—Danaher was an open secret. Renzo said that even now, when he had questions about a move, he'd go talk to John first. Jiu-jitsu is a dialogue.

New Zealand John is a fine-featured man with a pale, narrow face, longish hair, a bald spot like a tonsure, and a muscular build. He has a deformed knee, a result of a childhood surgery gone wrong. He's so quiet and soft-spoken I practically had to put my ear to his mouth to hear what he was saying, sitting next to him on the mat. He's articulate in his murmuring Kiwi accent, and you don't want to miss a word he says.

John had come to the United States at twenty-four years old and gone to Columbia for his graduate degree. To supplement his income he'd worked as a bouncer—he'd been a gym rat and studied muay Thai in New Zealand, although his bum leg had limited his style to the clinch. He'd come to be Renzo's student the usual way, by word of mouth. He hadn't been a natural, or taken strongly to jiu-jitsu; with a wry smile John said, "I had an undistinguished entry into the sport." But when two of Renzo's top instructors left to form their own schools, he was asked to step up and teach. At that point he began to take it seriously and it took over his life.

When I asked him about his take on the mental game in jiu-jitsu, he turned professorial.

"The two most misused words in the English language are 'mental' and 'spiritual.' You hear people use the words so sloppily, with such an ill-defined manner, it's unclear what you mean."

John had studied and taught epistemology, questions about the nature of knowledge. He was concerned with semantics, specifically "knowledge" as opposed to "belief." He wasn't going to let me skate on some vague questions.

I sweated and babbled and eventually John took pity on me and helped me out.

"I see two things that fighters deal with, two emotions that create weakness—fear and anger. And for the first, it's not fear of injury. The idea of failing in front of a great crowd is massively harmful to us, as such social creatures." I recalled how David

Horton would tell everyone he knew that he was going to run the Appalachian Trail, or Pacific Crest Trail, because that added social pressure helped him continue.

"Anger just makes people inefficient. Their breathing gets shallow, they're too muscularly tense—they gas faster. Part of what I admire in a fighter like Marcelo Garcia is his ability to control his anger and stay focused. He often gets abused physically. He's a smaller guy in the open weight competitions, but you never see him distracted. He's like a laser, focused on finishing. He has one physical, cold goal in mind and nothing distracts him. The abuse is irrelevant.

"Anger can take you away from your goal. You can get caught up in a desire for revenge, which distracts you. Experienced fighters will create this in opponents."

To John, what sets the top guys apart is the idea of "relaxed poise."

"The single definitive feature of the überathlete is a sense of effortlessness in a world where most men grunt and strive and scream. It comes easy to the best, and what creates that? I think it's a sense of play. No fear or anxiety about their performance. Like when the first time you ever drove a car, you came out sweating and exhausted. Now when you drive a car it's effortless and smooth. Fear and anger are motor inhibitors."

Danaher reflects on his teacher. "Renzo has no fear of fights. He doesn't see them as serious events. He can't get mounted and pounded out. He may lose but he won't get smashed—there goes the gravity of the situation for him."

When I ask Renzo about Danaher, he gushes.

"He's completely unconventional, unpredictable, but he does jiu-jitsu the way I learned it: nothing matters but finishing. Position is just a way to get to the finish. His mind is good, and one of the most important things to teach is your own mind. If I just show you ten moves, you'll never do them like I do them. But if I show you why I get there, and how I think, then it's better for you. *And* almost more important, if I teach it the right way, then I have it pure in *my* mind."

Renzo fell silent, ruminating on that.

"The most important part of jiu-jitsu is the *middle of the way*. It's the path between one position and another—the transition—that makes the difference between a mediocre fighter and an unbelievable fighter. A bruiser, a guy who is just headbanging and pushing his way through, it stops when he meets someone stronger, and for every ten victories he'll have ten defeats. But when you have an understanding of the middle of the way, the ability to *think* and to see, your situation will get better."

I was instantly reminded of Marcelo Garcia, and what everyone always said about him—he was a master of the transition; he *lived* in the middle of the way. Renzo liked Marcelo's game because he's trying to finish all the time. "The beauty of Marcelo is that he developed such good defense, being the little guy at the academy, that he brushes off all finishing attempts on him, he's so efficient and focused on the finish. It's pure jiu-jitsu.

"I realize now that my jiu-jitsu is much simpler than when I was a purple belt. When I was a purple belt I tried the most amazing moves—I ran a marathon to get five miles away. Now, everything is much clearer, you don't waste time or strength, you just go straight to the point. I used to see this on Rickson a lot—his jiu-jitsu is very simple, he just goes straight for the finish. Even though everyone knows what he's trying to do nobody could stop him. He's very simple, with direct moves and objectives. He'll go *right there* and get you *right there*. Even though you knew what was happening, his precision and his tightness were so good that you couldn't stop him. The better you get the simpler everything gets.

"I always knew that nobody could control the situation better than I could, so that made me extremely confident. And nobody can make me give up. I remember a fifty-one-minute fight in Japan, the guy outweighed me by thirty kilos, and I thought,

I'm gonna be here all night. If I can't finish him, we'll be here tomor-row morning. Because I don't give a fuck, I'm not giving up. I'm going to see how he's gonna make me quit. It's impossible." The words are ordinary, but when Renzo says them they are moving, because he lives and dies with them.

"I think the jiu-jitsu mentality gives you that. From a young age we go—we believe that if we go until one of us quits it's never gonna be me!" He's almost shouting at me.

"I never could see myself being beaten. I could never ask for water, never ask for the bill." He laughs, "I could never be the one. If he's tired let him ask for the check." I remember Sean Williams, one of Renzo's students, who I studied under in L.A., telling a story about Renzo playing a video game. It was a game that Renzo had never played before, but he had it set at the hard-est level. "That's when he was having the most fun," said Sean.

Renzo continues quietly. "The mentality is from my grand-father, my father, but really it's the jiu-jitsu mentality, and prob-ably goes back to Maeda, his master. It's the soul of jiu-jitsu. Like that famous picture of a little cat looking in the mirror but he sees a lion on the other side."

Renzo sees the lion, believes it, makes it true.

DOWN THE
RABBIT HOLE

A quote used in my first book would often drift into my mind, wonderfully eloquent. *"These are forces played out on the physical stage—the raised white canvas is a blank and basic* platea—*which makes it possible to see great fighters as great artists, however terrible their symbolic systems. It may be, and perhaps should be, difficult to accept the notion that a prizefighter's work merits the same kind of attention we lavish on an artist's, but once we begin attending to and describing what he does in the ring, it becomes increasingly difficult to refuse the expenditure. The fighter creates a style in a world of risk and opportunity. His disciplined body assumes the essential postures of the mind: aggressive and defensive, elusively graceful with it's shifts of direction, or struggling with all its stylistic resources against a resistant but, until the very end, alterable reality. A great fighter redefines the possible."*

It's from an essay by Ronald Levao, in a book called *Reading the Fights*. I have always found the lines to be uniquely moving, and they seem particularly relevant to this project. I think we can and should consider great fighters as artists. We do, to belabor an obvious point, call it "martial *arts*."

Here we come to a fundamental question: is it interesting to talk to artists about how they think about art? Is there anything to be learned?

I have some unfortunate history with this question. I was an art major at Harvard, and I had a somewhat adversarial

243

relationship with the department. The central dissension (I thought) I had with my professors was about language and art. Simply put, I felt that art is visual and language is not, and so talking about art is something of a waste of time. Certainly talking about how artists think wasn't important; what matters is their work. I didn't care about the history of a painter, or what tradition he's refuting with subtle accuracy. Does his painting, does the picture on the wall, knock my socks off? If so, great. If not, who cares what he intended?

Well, I was an arrogant, callow youth, for now I find myself doing just that: discussing artists and how they think. Strangely, upon revisiting, I found that one of those same professors agreed with me the whole time. Maybe I was just a bad painter.

I tracked down Peter Schjeldahl, an art critic who had served a brief stint as my professor. Schjeldahl has written for the *New Yorker, ARTnews,* and the *New York Times*; his criticism has won awards. He'd been around the art scene in New York since the 1960s and known Andy Warhol and everybody else. David Salle, a painter, said of Peter, "He has a formidable ability to cast into lively prose the paradoxes and conundrums of looking at art. And his biggest influence was Red Smith," one of the great sportswriters of all time.

Peter and I had had a rocky relationship in college. I had been an admirer of his, and he had thoroughly savaged me in my final critique. But the past was past. I was over it, and I was curious to hear what he would say about this line of reasoning. Could talking to artists about how they think possibly be useful?

I finally caught up with Peter in Manhattan, at a café in the East Village. As I walked down the crowded streets to meet him, I reflected on the changes—in the heyday of the New York art scene, the Lower East Side neighborhoods were filled with old tenement buildings where artists hung out with poets (Peter had originally been a beat poet). Now it was the retail version of that, punks with faux-hawks and dirty clothing pushing shining bikes with solid disc wheels that cost two or three grand. I looked around for a real punk who might steal the kid's bike after stomping his face with a Doc Marten. No luck. Those days are gone from Manhattan. Now the prevailing feeling on the city streets is that everyone is wealthier than you.

Peter showed up much older, still vital, bemused by the changes around him. A refugee from the past, a stone in a whirlwind, New York was still New York to him. He had a hard time, at first, with the nature of my question. "Is it worthwhile to discuss how artists think?" He parroted my question, frowning. "I don't know. I *know* when artists work they don't think. It's a different setting in the mind . . . the purer the art the less they have to say."

We talked for a while, but to little effect. We parted amicably and agreed as writers that we should write each other about it. And so we began a correspondence of ideas.

"In each significant case," he wrote, discussing how artists might talk about how they think, "the answer will be idiosyncratically specific and, to us ordinary mortals, wondrously incomprehensible. It may seem scandalously dopey.

"Our tendency is to THINK, when our only hope is to NOT THINK. We get consumed with wanting to win or to do well and forget just to make the art or hit the ball.

"As a baseball nut, I have this constant fascination with the incredibly complicated task of seeing, assessing, and solidly hitting on exactly the right square inch of a round bat, a ninety-seven-mile-per-hour fastball, over a time span of far less than a second.

"It's amusing to read Ted Williams on hitting . . . he said he could see the ball compressing against his bat. He said he could smell the bat wood burn.

"I think that when we do a thing right, we feel joy—but an impersonal joy, not belonging to us. An example of personal joy is the joy of winning, which any true master will hold in contempt.

Considerations of success or failure don't enter the mind of a master, when the chips are down.

"Some artist [Peter thought it was maybe Philip Guston] said that when you start to work, every artist you ever cared about is in the studio with you. One by one, they leave. Finally, you leave, too. Then the work happens . . ."

I had a book of Peter's, a collection of interviews with David Salle, a painter who had become famous in the 1980s with his figurative work, rife with symbols, juxtaposing images from a wide variety of sources. He was a bona fide *famous painter*.

Peter recalled meeting Salle in 1980. "Fascination and suspicion, even fear, attended rumors of his enigmatic work, underground prestige and commercial success . . . I had seen a few of his pictures, with their bluntly drawn erotic and melodramatic images on fields of acrid color, and had been at first jarred then baffled, then increasingly stirred by them. They were like ready-made dreams, as intimate as if I had dreamed them myself, and utterly fresh."

I had a similar reaction to Salle's work—*I can paint better than that,* was my first thought. But, like very few paintings, they continue to get more interesting and *beautiful* the longer you examine them. The more you look, the better they appear, and they become transcendent.

With the help of my friend and agent David Kuhn I managed to track down Mr. Salle and spoke with him over the phone. As well as being one of the major figurative painters of his era, he'd designed sets for theater and ballet and had an appreciation for the kinesthetic. He'd even dabbled in boxing and knew the frenetic pace of early sparring sessions.

"What sets painting apart from other kinds of art making is that it's performative. In the moment, did you do it well? Or not?" he said over the phone from his studio in New York.

That was a shocking statement to me, because it was so obvious, yet I hadn't considered it. Of course, the athletic stroke of the painter is frozen in time for all eternity to witness. Sure, you can paint over it, but then that new stroke is the one we see, that new gesture. It's still frozen for all time, the minute you let it alone, the moment it's considered done. Some painters feverishly rework and repaint the canvas, trying to get it right, but they still have to get it right and then leave it. Just like a video record of a fight—you got knocked out and we can watch it for eternity.

"There's no such thing as conceptual boxing, or conceptual football. Either you complete the pass or you don't. Painting is obviously so much more than technique or brushwork . . . whatever it is, whatever mental, spiritual, or emotional thing you're bringing to bear, it's all expressed by the point of the brush, the paint left behind. It's bizarre how specific it is . . . like being a stunt pilot.

"What I try to do is a paradox, by consciously getting outside myself. It's hard to do with the consciousness, but the best paintings . . . one has a feeling that you don't know where they came from, they just happen. I always say that students need to get out of their own way.

"We're living through an intensely mental phase in the history of art. The scales often tip one way or the other, and right now they've gone into this extreme mental state and cognitive direction, but it's not always like this. The way art has been taught in the last thirty years is all about intentionality—and I would say intentionality is overrated.

So there, I thought with some satisfaction.

"I don't really give a shit what somebody *thinks* they're work is about. Students are expected to talk about *intentions,* and I think, Who cares? I don't even want to know, don't tell me . . ." Salle trailed off.

Schjeldahl had pointed out an article in a recent *New Yorker* called "The Eureka Hunt" by Jonah Lehrer (*The New Yorker,* July 28, 2008). It's a fascinating essay on the brain science behind insight.

The title comes from the shout "Eureka" (Greek for "I have found it"), when you suddenly realize the truth, the solution, and details the scientific pursuit for the location and "source" of insight, chemically and electrically, in the brain.

Mr. Lehrer endeared himself to me right off the bat by using the Mann Gulch fire as his lead-in. Mann Gulch was a famous "tragedy" wildfire in 1949 that killed thirteen smoke jumpers. I was a wild-land firefighter for two seasons, and this was a fire that every firefighter has studied, because it was an example of the first ever "burnout." A group of sixteen smoke jumpers were hiking along about midslope, flanking a fire on the far side of the valley, on the opposing wall. Then fire got in below them, on their side. Fire below you is death.

If you light a match and hold it with the flaming end up it will burn slowly down the match; fire burns down slowly. If instead you turn the match at a steep angle, with the flaming end down, then it will burn up to your fingers in a few seconds. Fire moves uphill at incredible, explosive speeds, and the smoke and hot gases precede the flames.

The crew was trapped, the fire racing up the slopes through the tall dry brush, pushing a wall of flame toward them. Their only hope was to try and outrun it, get over the top of the hill, a losing race. Men sprint uphill at four or maybe five miles per hour, while fire moves at twenty or more. The steeper the hill, the slower the men and the faster the fire.

Then the foreman, Wag Dodge, had a flash of insight; the finger of God stroked his brain. He lit his *own* fire and lay down in the ashes. He called for his men to join him, but they didn't understand what he had intuitively known—fire won't burn where it's already burned. This was the first intentional burnout, something that would later become standard strategy (of sorts) for firefighters—we'd call it "bringing the black with you." But Dodge's men didn't know him, and didn't trust him, and couldn't hear him over the roar. His men ran and thirteen of them died.

Wag lived. Norman Maclean wrote a beautiful book about it called *Young Men and Fire*.

Mr. Lehrer's article was about the cognitive action of insight, about where in the brain the activity took place and what that told us about flashes of genius. He chronicles the scientists mapping the brain first with MRIs, and then with EEGs, hats covered in electrodes.

While test subjects racked their minds for answers, the scientists watched. When insight appears there's a spike in gamma rhythm; "it's as if insight had gone incandescent." And they could trace the activity to a small part of the *right* brain.

The prevailing wisdom is that the left brain is more important, the conscious brain that controls language. The right brain is sometimes seen as minor; it seems more vague and unknown. The right brain is the creative side, which is great but nonessential, as the old clichéd brain science has it. Modern brain science has found that this is overly simplistic. The hemispheres are deeply connected and interdependent. But in terms of insight the old clichés hold water.

Lehrer describes insight as a balancing act: "At first, the brain lavishes the scarce resource of attention on a single problem. But, once the brain is sufficiently focused, the cortex needs to relax in order to seek out the more remote association in the right hemisphere, which will provide the insight." Lehrer quotes one of the scientists, who says "that's why so many insights happen during warm showers"—you have to relax away from your left brain. You have to cast your net wide, over all of your knowledge.

It's why, as a writer, I keep a notebook by the bed; often in a half-asleep state, my mind will see the connections I'm looking for. You can't focus too hard. "One of the surprising lessons of this research is that trying to force an insight can actually prevent the insight . . . Concentration comes with the hidden cost of diminished creativity."

This was all reminding me very strongly of a conversation I'd had with Greg Jackson. Sitting one afternoon in Greg's quiet office, between classes, I asked him about the martial arts from those dark times in human history, "traditional" arts, fighting styles and systems that had been discredited in the MMA ring.

Greg had responded, "Those were created to deal with a certain problem at a certain time and a certain place. It's not that it doesn't work. It does work against samurai. These guys weren't idiots, and it was a tough time. Our stuff is the pinnacle of unarmed personal combat. We're in the process as it keeps evolving, it's hyperspecialized. We don't have to deal with weapons, or arrows, or horseback."

When you think about it, I'm pretty sure in a battle during the Crusades or in medieval Japan you'd never want to leave your feet—you probably wouldn't shoot a takedown and work top position surrounded by guys with spears and swords. Leaving your feet would be death.

This was when Greg recommended I read *Zen in the Art of Archery*.

"I use that all the time when I teach," he said, "but I say it's *like walking to the door*. When you get up and walk to the door, you don't think about it, you don't put this foot in front of that foot and think your way through it. You just walk, without thinking. That's how fighting should be. The door is a metaphor for your opponent. Don't think about how you get there, just get there. And when you do that, you do things that are good—you hit somebody with something that you didn't even know you were going to throw, and he didn't expect it either because you weren't thinking about it. That's when it really happens, what Musashi calls 'the void.'"

I didn't get it. Greg laughed; he was aware of the trickiness of the concept.

"You have to be calm enough to get to the void—it's that weird fucking concept. Here's my problem with Eastern teaching: they're talking about experience, but they can't say experience. For some reason they won't say it, so they say 'unlearn what you have learned,' which you can understand when you're on the other side of it but what a terrible way to teach it. It's stupid. Zen's job is to break that filter down and get you to experience everything, to get that logic filter out of your brain. So I can see why they say it, but it's much easier if someone told me in Western language because we live in the Western culture. I understand that it's really cool to say 'unlearn what you have learned,' but teach in the culture you're in.

"So I prefer, *Find that place where you don't think about putting one foot in front of the other when you go to the door.*"

I thought about my own experience in sparring, and of the right hand. I fight orthodox, which means my left hand is the lead and jabs and my right is the power punch. I could land the jab okay, but whenever I threw the right hand it seemed like it was too late. Because I had to think about it, plan for it. When I started doing drills with Javier I started throwing it all the time, and then in sparring I would just throw it—don't think about it, just throw it—and lo and behold it was landing.

"That's why the mental toughness conditioning is important. As you get kicked or hit, and it starts to hurt, it forces you to focus on yourself instead of what you should be thinking about. It breaks you out of the place you want to be in. Not the void."

That made sense. I asked Greg about the spiritual side of fighting. Did he think there were a lot of things in the traditional martial arts that were good for MMA?

"The problem is, the traditional guys are holding on to their outmoded techniques. They've been doing reverse punches for twenty-five years. You're going to come and tell them they wasted their time? But all those traditionalists maintain the spirituality of what they do is tied to their art, that there's no separation between the two. But it's these jerks that have intertwined Zen and their old techniques, and so you say 'oh, it's all bullshit,' it doesn't work. It's no one's fault but the guys who won't let it go.

"I think we'll come back to it. Someday we'll say 'oh, these guys practiced for two thousand years, and they weren't stupid, there are lessons there.' I'm not going to go to war with a musket, but the lessons can be learned. It's the same bullet but a different gun."

We've all heard of "the zone," that heightened mental state in which we perform perfectly. I think I first heard it in discussion of basketball players, who would get hot and sink ten shots in a row, 'feeling it,' and 'in the zone'; probably in those old interviews with Michael Jordan when he would pin fifty points on the Knicks. It's a kind of a relaxed supercompetence, a place where you aren't nervous and make every shot, every right decision. You had it in postgame interviews: "I was in the zone," the athlete would say. That explained it.

A professor at the University of Chicago named Mihaly Csikszentmihalyi (Chek-sent-mi-hi, I think) wrote the definitive book of the zone, though he called it the "flow." Csikszentmihalyi gathered up twenty-five years of research and interviews and evidence for his 1990 book *Flow: The Psychology of Optimal Experience*, and the concept began to work its way into popular discussion, ESPN analysis, and sports radio.

I feel there is some connection here between the zone, and the eureka hunt, and the void that Greg was talking about. Being in the groove, that athletic place of peak performance, when the hitter can see the stitches on the baseball, when time slows down for a fighter and the left hook materializes out of nowhere and connects . . . it all seems related, these flashes of deeper understanding.

It's almost like using "the Force" from the *Star Wars* movies —but this is relaxing and letting go into muscle memory and action. Obi Wan says, "the Force flows through you." We talk about it all the time, in sports, even playing pool at the local bar, you'll run the table and laugh about being in the zone. The balls are just falling. Josh Waitzkin wrote about it in his *Art of Learning*, about "building triggers" to more easily fall into that state of easy attunedness. There's a chapter every fighter and trainer should read—about creating rituals to stay calm and clear before a fight. It reminded me of what Mark DellaGrotte intuitively understood, the fighter needs to feel relaxed and confident, his energies brought to bear on only one thing.

I got in touch with Jonah Lehrer in Boston and asked him about a connection between his article on insight and "the zone." He wanted to clarify a few things.

"Not the right brain per se. There is a lot of pop science out there about the right brain–left brain split, and the insight circuit is very interesting to me because it conforms to this cliché we have about the right brain being more intuitive and artistic and all the rest—but in general—the right brain is not necessarily always better at unconscious intuitve thought.

"Not right brain but the *emotional* brain I think is a better way to say it. Not just on the right side.

"When you talk about how athletes are thinking and the importance of not overthinking what you're doing, it's less about relying on the right brain than it is turning off the prefrontal cortex, the rational circuit behind your eyes—and relying more on the emotional brain, the intuitive, instinctive emotional brain.

"For a baseball player, how you hit a fastball going ninety-five miles an hour seems impossible, technically. The brain shouldn't be able to react that fast—you add up the time it takes from when the ball leaves the pitcher's hand to when the batter swings, technically you can't move that fast—yet obviously batters hit fastballs. So batters begin their swing before the ball is released, so they're relying on implicit unconscious cues, signals they're not close to aware of, body language, torque on wrist. Hitters pick up on that in nonconscious all-implicit ways—if they think too much it becomes paralyzing.

"Think about it this way. The emotional unconscious brain, the primitive brain we share with other animals, has been perfected by evolution for the last two hundred million years. It's like a very efficient supercomputer with all the bugs worked out. And then we've got the rational prefrontal cortex, which is ten million years old, so it's relatively new. It's like software version one-point-oh. It has bugs and makes mistakes. It's what lets us do algebra, and reflect, and what makes us uniquely human, but it's small and you don't want to rely on it for complex movement."

I started reading one of the sports psychology textbooks, *Applied Sport Psychology,* edited by Jean M. Williams. The guys at the Army Center for Enhanced Performance had told me to read it as a primer.

Poring over it, I thought to myself, "Geez, this is all really obvious. Athletes that think more positively, do better. Duh." And it is—sports psychology is fairly simple and self-explanatory. But the important thing to do is to realize it is obvious and make use of it. The conscious mind is simpler than you think; if you direct it, you can get better results. That's the basis of sports psychology, there's not a great mystery. The strategies are simple but labor intensive—make detailed lists of goals, not only in the short term but in the long. Enhance positive thinking with positive imagery—like Randy Couture, don't think in negatives, give yourself positive stuff to work for. Not "don't give up the takedown" but "get that underhook." Basically, take and develop the habits that successful top-flight athletes use.

I dug through the textbook for the "peak performance" chapters. The researchers take the experience of the zone, or whatever you want to call it, and quantify it through hard work and statistical analysis of athletes' responses. Although many athletes describe this euphoric feeling as involuntary, there is consensus among sports psychologists that this state can be achieved more often through analysis. Certainly elite athletes get there more often.

When *Applied Sport Psychology* describes peak performance, here are the notes it hits:

- Loss of fear—no fear of failure
- No thinking of performance
- Total immersion in activity
- Narrow focus of attention
- Effortless performance—not forcing it
- Feeling of being in complete control
- Time/space disorientation (usually slowed down)
- Universe perceived to be integrated and unified
- Unique, temporary, involuntary experience

These were common experiences described and collated by psychologists studying thousands and thousands of athletes, bringing together many studies. When I read through some of the literature on the zone and peak performance, and started to get a feel for what these athletes were going through, that line about the universe "perceived to be integrated and unified" caught my eye—that was some hippy dippy shit right there. C'mon, really, the universe is unified? In a textbook? It sounds like Eastern mysticism. Flow like a river, touching the leaf, step by step I quiet the babbling brook . . .

It occurred to me that what is Zen in martial arts but an earlier, far more exhaustive study of sports psychology? Sports psychology as a genuine field of study has existed for only twenty or thirty years; Musashi represents a tradition of study that covers hundreds of years, if not millennia. Greg Jackson's depiction of the void sounded suspiciously like getting in the zone to me, and so I reread Musashi and some others, *Zen in the Art of Archery* (recommended by both Renzo and Greg Jackson) and *The Life-Giving Sword* by a contemporary of Musashi's, Yagyu Munenori.

Here were writers and practitioners who had devoted lifetimes of study to problems that their caste had already devoted hundreds of years of study to, tested in actual combat, to the death.

The reason Zen and that Eastern philosophy is often pooh-poohed by fighters is that it sounds like bullshit. Pat Miletich had a fighter who studied Musashi and Pat thought that was his biggest problem—too much thinking.

The Western reader pretends there may be shortcuts to mastery, mysterious shortcuts. There's the *Karate Kid* idea—a few months of study, a few words of wisdom, and you can beat a black belt. Even the recent kids' flick *Kung Fu Panda* had the hero *realize the secret,* and then he could beat anybody. A lot of kung-fu movies have this idea of the philosophy trumping the physical. It's a misunderstanding of Musashi, that if you adopt that proper philosophy and "be like water" or "fear nothing," you don't need to practice ten hours a day for fifteen years. It's something that kung-fu movies with their trampolines and deafening punch noises pushed on the world, and it's attractive. Everybody loves a shortcut. Plus it makes a good movie narrative—a clueless hero gets beat up, studies for a few months, has a deep philosophical revelation, and emerges as a genuine badass.

That's all bullshit. As Miletich says, you have to take a lot of beatings.

Everyone I talked to, everyone I read, studied their own art obsessively. And all the Zen writing repeated this sentiment. "Much patience, much heartbreaking practice is needed, just as in archery. But once this practice has led to the goal the last trace of self-regard vanishes in sheer purposelessness" (from *Zen in the Art of Archery*).

Musashi says, "You must practice this" about every other sentence—a lifetime of study is not enough.

Josh Waitzkin spoke about Marcelo Garcia rolling with the "most beautiful chi" he'd ever seen. Now, Marcelo doesn't study tai chi, and yet he rolls with it, because his level of mastery is so far advanced that he has internalized those concepts; he plays his game. It's like the great boxers who can uncoil like springs and hit harder than men three times their weight—they haven't studied anything but boxing but their level of mastery is so high they intuitively do those things that Musashi talks about. There are no shortcuts but a lifetime of study. There are no easy ways but obsession.

But during that journey, that lifetime of study, one *can* recognize and feel these routes to the zone or the void. It's part of mastery. You can't start there, but you need to end up there. "Athletes who learn to be confident, focus their attention on the task at hand, control their anxiety, and have appropriate and challenging goals may experience flow and peak performance more often," says the textbook. There's an often-quoted Zen saying: "Enlightenment is an accident, but you can have more accidents."

Zen koans (those odd little stories) are in some ways about that—cutting you loose from your reasoning brain, the part filled with conscious thought and narration, tied up in the past and future and too slow to be useful in a fight. The koans don't make sense, on purpose. Those Zen masters are trying to get you away from you prefrontal cognitive reasoning brain, into the mysteries of the emotional and intuitive side. The wiser side, the big-picture side. Dan Gable throwing apples was a version of the Zen koan— he's teaching you a lesson, but first you have to come to the understanding on your own. What was the lesson? The same lesson Teddy Atlas was talking about when he said, "At a certain point, if he's going to get to the top of the boxing profession, a fighter has to learn the difference between a truth and a lie. The lie is thinking that submission is an acceptable option. The truth is that if you give up, afterward you'll realize that any of those punches that you thought you couldn't deal with, or those rough moments you didn't think you would make it through, were just *moments*." Pain is an illusion.

Zen in the Art of Archery was written by a German, Eugen Herrigel, who spent many years in Japan learning the practice of

Zen through the study of archery. He wrote: "Zen is akin to pure introspective mysticism. Unless we enter into mystic experiences by direct participation, we remain outside, twist and turn as we may. This law . . . allows no exceptions . . . Like all mysticism, Zen can only be understood by one who is himself a mystic and is therefore not tempted to gain by underhand methods what the mystical experience withholds from him."

You've got to wonder a little bit at the translations from Japanese to German to English, but I started to understand the Zen koan—deliberate mysteriousness.

So that's why the stories sound so magical and bullshity, because they have to be. They have to be somewhat mysterious—and you need to take that on as a reader, internalize it; to explain it would defeat the purpose. The purpose? I can't tell you, that would destroy it, but in some ways it's an embrace of mystery, at least in part. A strategy to help you move away from your tightly focused left brain. There's a reason that a lot of high-level jiu-jitsu guys smoke pot and roll.

We can revisit that old discussion of where to look in a fight—at his eyes or at his body? At the "T" of his chest? Musashi talks about the dangers of looking to only one place, even the eyes, because it limits you. If one place is stared at, the enemy can deceive you. Instead, Musashi favors looking *through* the opponent, "your stare should be unfixed . . . I think only of making the hit. I have no preconceived notions of which target is the one to aim for. I let nature take it's course and permit the spirit of the thing itself to express itself through me and make me the victor."

It's important to remember what Musashi was talking about—cutting another man with a sword, a man who is trying to cut you. Those legendary blades were incredibly sharp, horribly dangerous, and the duels had no margin for error.

Freddie Roach, the boxing trainer, told me, "Well, if you just stare at one thing you're gonna get killed. It's not realistic. As a fighter I see a whole picture of the fighter in front of me. I know when his feet move, I know when his hands move, he feints . . . it's a general picture. If you're looking at his feet he's gonna fucking kill you, I don't care what you say." And then he laughed his dry raspy laugh.

"You don't think about it," he continued. "You react and explode and it's automatic. I can't say I'm going to land one-two of a four-punch combination and realistically mean it. I won't land all four shots, but one punch will develop the next, and you don't know what that first punch developed until you're there. You become so accustomed to reacting to what your opponent does with that move, that now it comes natural. You don't have to think about it. Feel for it."

You can see that Freddie and Musashi are saying the same thing. And again there are no shortcuts or mysteries. These abilities come only with endless practice. Once you've devoted a lifetime to study then the important thing is to get out of your own way and not screw yourself up by thinking.

Herrigel describes the Zen experience, and it sounds just like being in the zone. "The soul is brought to the point where it vibrates of itself in itself—a serene pulsation which can be heightened into the feeling, otherwise experienced only in rare dreams, of extraordinary lightness, and the rapturous certainty of being able to summon up energies in any direction, to intensify or to release tensions graded to a nicety.

"This state, in which nothing definite is thought, planned, striven for, desired or expected, which aims in no particular direction and yet knows itself capable alike of the possible and the impossible, so unswerving is its power—this state, which is at bottom purposeless and egoless . . . can work its inexhaustible power because it is free."

Although the realization of similarities between the zone and Zen was a revelation to me, the ideas had been floating around for years. Andrew Cooper wrote an interesting book, called *Playing in the Zone,* and he wrote (from a far deeper Zen perspective) about the overlap between Zen and the zone. When I asked Greg Jackson to read this, he called me later to say with typical humility, "I must not have explained myself very well, because that's what I was talking about." Greg is way too nice a guy to ever say "duh."

I came across a clip of Dr. Michael Lardon talking about the "old samurai" and the similarities between *mushin no shin* (Musashi's "the mind of no-mind") and the zone experience.

Dr. Lardon is a celebrity sports psychiatrist, writing books, doing TV shows, and working with all sorts of top athletes—Olympians, pro golfers including David Duval, all kinds. But he's no empty suit; he's thoroughly accredited, a serious scientist and doctor, and a man with boundless enthusiasm and interest. There's a reason all these top-level professional golfers come to him.

Dr. Lardon's personal history drew me like a beacon. He'd been one of the best sixteen-year-old Ping-Pong players in the nation and had been sent to Japan to train in 1976. He told me the story over the phone—one of those stories he uses all the time, to good effect.

"I was training with a world champion, at Senshu University outside of Tokyo where we worked alongside martial artists, so I was exposed to a lot of the traditional martial arts, peripherally. There was this huge language barrier, but observationally . . . I would watch these martial artists do amazing things. I was fascinated with the idea of how they were training their brains, and what transfer of energy it allowed them to do. They were doing so much with mental focus . . . one of them even told me *you must leave no trace of yourself.*" One can imagine the impact that might have on a sixteen-year-old boy, far from home.

"In table tennis, you generate potential energy into kinetic, the ball comes out at ninety miles per hour and hits the table, spin takes hold on the bounce, and the ball shoots out at a hundred miles per hour or more in any direction . . . and you have to touch just the top of the ball. If it hits your racket straight up you can never control it. At Colorado Springs [the Olympic Center] a few years ago they tested reaction times of all the Olympic athletes and the table tennis players had the fastest time, no surprise—it's an eight-foot table and the ball is moving at a hundred miles per hour. It necessitates completely instinctual play, if you used your cognition at all, and thought about the shot, you couldn't hang."

At this young age, Lardon had his first real experience with the zone, back in the United States at the USTTA junior championship match at Caesar's Palace in Vegas. "I had been meditating, and I fell into this dreamy zone, the ball was moving in slow motion, I could do anything I wanted. I was winning everything. Then a friend started talking, and he said things like 'this is going to be a huge upset' and as soon as he said it, it was over. I fell out of the zone and lost the next three games and the championship."

Michael had gone on to Stanford and then medical school, all the while building his research around the zone state.

"In the early 1990s, I tried to look at the action of the brain, what was happening neurologically. Sports psychology doesn't do that too much. My hypothesis was that the top athletes were just getting more efficient at processing signals—we studied top Olympians, triatheletes, John McEnroe, all these guys who talked about time slowing down."

As the technology for testing got better, things got more interesting. Michael was working with the Scripps Research Institute doing EEG testing on athletes playing a video game they'd designed. There's a thing called the p300, a positive wave at 300 milliseconds when stimulus hits the brain—everyone has it. When a sound enters your ear, you can watch it on the EEG (after a mathematical manipulation making an event-related brain potential, or ERP). Everyone's brain does it, almost like a heartbeat on the EKG (think of that little squiggly jag, beeping on the monitor in hospital TV shows). It's the reaction time of electrical activity in the brain. People with dementia have it at 350 milliseconds, slower than normal. "Our hypothesis was that top athletes would have a *faster* time—that electric signals would move faster in their brains," Dr. Lardon said.

"The philosophy of the study comes from David Spiegel at Stanford, one of my heroes, a brilliant guy whose father, Herbert, was a scientific leader in hypnosis. David put people [hooked to an EEG] in a hypnotic trance, and then had two paradigms. One, he had them imagine there was a screen that blocked out a light that was being shot at them. What Spiegel found was that when people imagined this screen, there was a *reduction* in the p300 amplitude—as if the light was really being reduced. Then he flipped it, and had them imagine a giant magnifying glass that strengthened the light coming into their eyeballs. And there was an enhancement of the p300.

"I thought this was a landmark study, because what it tells you is that *states of consciousness* actually change the way you biologically process stimuli. So you think, hey, the baseball is coming and it is what it is—a ball moving ninety-five miles per hour, there's nothing I can do about it. But there is something you can do about it, you can affect the way you *process* it."

Ted Williams, one of baseball's greatest hitters, had always talked about how he could see the baseball hit the bat, and count the stitches, that was what Schjeldahl was referring to. In *Blink,* Malcolm Gladwell writes of a tennis coach who had studied these things and found that "in the final five feet of a tennis ball's flight toward a player, the ball is far too close and moving much too fast to be seen." The event happens in three milliseconds, far, far too short a time for the human eye to see it. But Ted *thought* he could. To him it was real. And just because it is "physically impossible" does that mean Ted was imagining it? I think the short answer is no. If everything else speeds up, then time slows down.

Dr. Lardon continued, "In doing this testing, we thought we were going to see a faster p300 from top athletes, but we didn't see that. What we saw instead was another wave, called the N50, a negative potential at fifty milliseconds that everybody has . . . but in great athletes, that potential came early, with more amplitude. So it wasn't the cortical process that was different, it was the priming pathway. It was as if they were picking it up earlier."

Michael talked about an insight he had, in terms of explaining this. His older brother had been deeply involved in very fancy stereos when they were growing up in New York. "He was into the high-end stuff, the twenty-grand stereos—the best stereos reproduced sound by making the circuit as fast as possible. Things we thought were cool, like equalizers, actually interrupted the flow and you lost depth of field, or lost the imaging quality of a great stereo. All those conductors with gold inlay were to make circuits as fast as possible . . . more beautiful was faster.

"I was John McEnroe's courtside guest, watching him and Andre Agassi, and I could just feel how they were both picking the ball up much quicker than you or I."

There have been plenty of studies that show that "experts" are much more efficient than amateurs at performing the same tasks. Their brains are more efficient and use less energy—giving you more energy to deal with anything outside of the practiced task. Of course, what defines expertise? Ten years of study or more, that same old line.

Dr. Lardon continued to an interesting further hypothesis. "In your brain there are these bands, alpha, beta, and then the gamma—they're brainwaves, electrical activity. Now, in schizophrenics, the gamma band is disrupted—they have trouble processing information. If you and I are talking, and you had a dream last night, you can differentiate between the two. For schizophrenics that boundary is knocked down. I have a little buzz right now in my telephone. A schizophrenic wouldn't be able to listen to you over that little buzz.

"There's something called a Kanizsa image. Like drawings by Escher, they fool you, visually. First you see one thing, then, as you look longer, you see another thing in the negative space. They discovered during studies on composers, at the moment of recognition of the other thing, the gamma band reveals itself in the brain. What's thought now is that the gamma band has to do with cortical synchronicity. When the gamma band comes then the motor and sensory parts are firing as one—like an in-tune engine."

I thought then about the Special Forces guys training with that M-wave monitor that showed coherence between brainwaves and breathing—again, like an in-tune engine. And I instantly started to think about all the pattern recognition, how a lot of guys in a fight would see patterns in an opponent and start cracking him up, inside his own pattern. It kind of made sense, in a grand, cosmic scheme of things—feeling and finding patterns without thinking about them.

"So right now I'm involved with Scripps and we're testing this further, trying to correlate the gamma band and the zone experience. I feel like it's the closest we've ever been to understanding what's going on."

Dr. Lardon told me an interesting story about watching a professional actress unwinding after an evening's performance. "I watched her backstage, and for twenty minutes she was coming out of this hypnotic state, it reminded me of the zone. I've seen it so many times in interviews with athletes after a great performance. They are in this trance—this sort of egoless place. They often don't have much to say." It seems Schjeldahl was right positing that to ask artists or athletes about their time in the zone would get you "scandalously dopey" answers.

Dr. Lardon talked about how he'd seen it in so many professional golfers who asked him for help. It was usually after they had done well and won a major tournament, and fame was upon them. "Suddenly the ego gets involved—and when it does, I bet there's no gamma band happening. Now, we don't know where ego lies, neuroanatomically, but my theory is that it interferes with your circuitry, like the stereo. The ego is treble and bass, you lengthen the circuit, and now it's not so fast or efficient."

Dr. Lardon had been working with a fighter and was very confused by the world of fighting, the intrusive promoters who were asking him to violate doctor-patient confidentiality. He mused, "The way that fighters are propped up in the media is basically antithetical to the parameters of the zone, of 'no-mind.' They have to badmouth each other, threaten to rip his heart out . . ." I could almost hear him shaking his head. It was a long way from the PGA tour.

I thought about Frank Shamrock's shit-talking—specifically designed to keep you out of the zone. During the recent "Dream Fight" between Manny Pacquiao and Oscar de La Hoya, head games and mental strategies were in play. Freddie Roach made a big stink, a few days before the fight, about the way Oscar tapes his hands, rolling the tape to create extra knuckles. He took it to the commission and got a partial ruling, and like in the old days he got to go watch Oscar get his hands taped prefight (which is how it used to be done; a trustworthy man from your camp would be in the opponent's locker room and watch him tape and glove up, making sure he wasn't putting a horseshoe in his glove).

Freddie said, "I had a real point, but if you can mentally fuck with a guy on the day of the fight, then you're doing your job. It's a mental game. Look at what Hopkins did to Trinidad. They say it never got to Oscar, but I know it did," he laughs his dry laugh. "Oscar reads the Internet." And Oscar's mental flaws were on display like never before—constantly casting about for a new trainer, someone to tell him what to do—and coming into the fight lighter than Pacquiao was surely a sign of machismo gone wrong. Manny, deeply in the zone, shut Oscar out and beat him up worse than anyone in his career. He fought perfectly, and seemed unhittable, a work of art.

Maybe it wasn't what art can tell us about fighting—maybe it was what fighting and sports can tell us about art. Art as sporting event? Was that what David Salle was telling me? Csikszentmihalyi had begun his research talking about the "flow" with composers and poets, not athletes. He talked about looking for places to find ecstasy, sports arenas and temples under the same roof.

From my very first real fighting experience in Thailand, I saw that the best fighters were the most humble. But, much like jiu-jitsu, you start to see it's a "chicken or the egg" question. Is it that great fighters lose their ego? Or is it that you cannot become great *unless* you lose your ego? Your ego keeps you out of the zone? Guys who can naturally control big egos do better?

"You have to live through it," Dr. Lardon said. "The eighteenth hole at the PGA West is all water up the left, and if you hit it there you don't have a job. When you're not at peace with that, then you're in trouble."

But what about the huge egos of guys like Michael Jordan, who needed control over the court? Or Kobe Bryant? Their monstrous egos obviously don't keep them out of the zone—Jordan's the defining athlete of the concept. I would imagine it's because they can compartmentalize and, in the moment, remove any trace of self-consciousness from what they do. They control it, like they control everything else. And they're at peace with it, with taking the pressure shot. They're at peace with failure or success; as Schjeldahl wrote, they take an "impersonal joy" in what they do. They see themselves from the outside, as impersonal constructs, which may lead to the oft-ridiculed referencing themselves in the third person.

Andre Ward told me, concerning his faith, "My faith and understanding is that God placed me here for a reason. He has work for me to do. That encourages me and keeps me going. I've said this before, and so does Virg, as a professional, that without God I wouldn't be in this business. I just wouldn't."

Andre paused. "God has me here for a reason, he's in control of everything and his will will come to pass. My job is to work hard, give him all I have in preparation, and leave it to him. It's everything, the centerpiece, the cornerstone of my career. He's brought me this far, he's not going to leave me high and dry. He won't pull the rug from under me, there's work to be done." I could hear in his voice two things—a way to avoid ego and a way to avoid fear. His faith was perfect for fitting him into the zone.

I thought of Liborio, of the importance of acceptance, of Manny Pacquiao, almost a kind of fatalism. The mentality that accepted the possibility of the worst, with a deeper understanding and without fear, because fear would keep you from attaining the no-mind.

What does all this mean, in a practical sense? You have to be simple, uncomplicated, pure, just to have a shot at falling into that zone state. And of course you need your ten thousand hours, too. Jordan and Kobe worked harder in the gym than everyone else. You can't just stay superrelaxed, talk a bunch of shit to keep your opponent out of the zone, or have the deep philosophical revelation and win the fight (the *Karate Kid* trap). You need to have outworked him in the gym. The more you immerse yourself in the subject, the deeper you go, the closer you come. There's no secret to the zone, the void. It comes only after mastery.

THE LONG KOAN

Paul Theroux, the great travel writer and novelist, calls it the "awkward question," when an innocent adventurer, back from some hellhole, gets asked, "Why?" at a cocktail party or on the street. Fighters and adventurers will go to great lengths to avoid answering. Dr. Horton replies, "Why not?," something I used with mixed results for years. Something I'd probably still be saying if I hadn't taken the money to write the first book.

Theroux stuck it to Gerard d'Aboville, about rowing a small boat across the Pacific in 1993, with "enormous personal risk." Gerard resisted the question, and then Theroux recounts the answer.

> "Only an animal does useful things," he said at last, after a long silence. "An animal gets food, finds a place to sleep, tries to keep comfortable. But I wanted to do something that was not useful, not like an animal at all. Something only a human being would do."
>
> The art of it, he was saying—such an effort was as much aesthetic as athletic. And that the greatest travel always contains within it the seeds of a spiritual quest, or else what's the point?

The *why?* of fighting is the elephant in the room, and I would be remiss if I didn't take a stab at it in a book about the mental side of fighting.

Any attempt to understand why begins with the nature of the beast, with understanding what fighting is. Paul Lazenby wrote an article about the Japanese fighter Masakatsu Funaki. This is the same Funaki that Frank Shamrock fought and who trained Ken. Now he was fighting long past his prime and getting beat up; the same old story. Paul had also lost to Funaki and was aware of Funaki's legend—he'd started the "first ever pro-wrestling group with no preordained finishes," called Pancrase, in 1993—the year the UFC started in the United States.

Paul's article was about the debt he felt was owed to Funaki. Funaki had recently fought as a shadow of his former self, just an old man getting pounded on. Paul was disgusted by some disrespect he overheard from fighters who couldn't remember what Funaki had been in his prime. As Paul noted, "It becomes painfully clear that the Herculean task of laying the groundwork for the sport that we know and love has taken more from Funaki than he could ever recover."

I had the same feelings when I listened to Thomas Hearns talk about making a comeback, with his mouth full of cotton, at the age of forty-six. Boxing writers, that sagacious lot, implored him not to fight. They didn't want to see him lose to a no-talent club fighter. A guy who couldn't carry Hearns's jock-strap when he was in his prime might get to say he beat Tommy Hearns? Why would Tommy want to fight again? But the pundits, fans, and outsiders weren't walking in his shoes. Hearns had lost some of his biggest fights, and the shadows couldn't let him go. I understood his need and felt like we owed him something.

What is the debt we owe great fighters? Is it owed them because of what they've shown us about courage and resiliency? Is it about what they have given to inspire us? The insight into the human heart and mind? The simple thrills? Why is there such reverential tragedy to Muhammad Ali, and now to Evander Holyfield? Why do I find such compassion and even love in my heart when I listen to Gabriel Ruelas?

The price you pay as a fighter is real, a throwback to the old days, the days when human life wasn't so precious. Throughout the past three or four centuries, a human life has become increasingly valued—but this is an exception not the norm of human history.

Prizefighting's roots lie in a time when life was cheap. The world has changed, and prizefighting has continued through it, undergoing paradoxical changes. The paradox of fighting lies in something Gabriel Ruelas (who knows better than most) asked me: "How safe can you make a sport that is about hurting people?"

Carlo Rotella wrote in his book *Cut Time*:

> Boxers hurt each other on purpose, a simple truth with unsimple consequences . . . In boxing, hurt is what people do to each other, an intimate social act, a pessimistically stripped-to-the-bone rendition of life as it is lived outside the ring. Hurting each other is all there can be between two boxers in an honest bout.

You, the fighter, you are paying a price. Fighters give us something irreplaceable—even the opponents, the bums, deserve to be respected for that. They can lose their wits, their intellect, their wisdom, everything a man has. Joe Frazier said, "Boxing is the only sport you get your brain shook, your money took, and your name in the undertaker book."

There is an element of tragedy in fighting, even in victory. We feel gratitude to fighters because we owe them for our joy and excitement—for showing us the truth of courage. There is acting in a prizefight, and play-acting and image, but there is also something very real happening, something that can't be faked. Even an expertly "worked" (fake) match isn't as exciting or enlightening as a great fight.

Fighting is tragic, even in victory. But that doesn't mean it isn't worthwhile. Most of us in the first world live in the safe society, as Jon Wertheim wrote, where "aggression has become a bad word and testosterone a banned substance. Danger is something to be avoided . . . something to be neutered." We have discovered that some things are worth the price. Fighters and those who train, who take shots to the head, they know in their hearts it can be costly. But there are reasons to fight and reasons to feel alive; there are prices worth paying.

Rotella again in *Cut Time*:

> Hurt changes you . . . hurt carries meaning, it can educate you . . . But it can also rob you of your capacity to learn or feel, or even to think. A fighter who gets hit too often can descend into dementia pugilistica; a heavy hitter can go blood simple; a jaded spectator can fall entirely out of the habit of compassion . . . the meaning can drain out of hurt, leaving only the nakedness of it.

We have to be on guard, to make sure that we never drain the meaning from our hurt. It requires vigilance and understanding, particularly in fight writers, those who study so much and watch so much, without personal investment, with a connoisseur's eye. The good fight writers and TV commentators never lose sight, entirely, of what this is all about, they never lose respect for the men fighting. The same can be said for any fan; never lose sight of what is happening when you cheer a bloody war.

Professional fighting is an awkward, uneasy thing. It falls in a strange place in society. It's entertainment, yet it serves the participants and the audience with an intrinsic need, scratches a primal itch. It's the manufacture of life-and-death situations for public consumption. The promoters and participants have to walk the line of entertainment and performance. There is some moral corrosion that happens, for the fans, for the fighters, for the promoters if they walk that line too fine.

One of the more interesting problems any trainer has to deal with is the difficulty of reconciling winning and entertaining. Mark DellaGrotte was the first guy I really talked to about it, in Boston. He has learned the lessons the hard way.

"I remember when Jorge Rivera fought Dennis Hallman, and Jorge survived and ground out a win. I kept telling Jorge, 'be careful, he's still dangerous.' When I ran into the UFC matchmaker, Joe Silva, later he was pissed off. He said, 'That fight sucked, Jorge coulda knocked him out.' I thought he was kidding. But he wasn't. And I had to learn the same lesson with Patrick Cote. I realized that the fights gotta be exciting, or else everyone loses, we turn this back into boxing. You have to fight strategically, to win, but not overcautious, because you're an entertainer. If people are turning off the TV, where are we going? Nobody makes money. Now the fighters themselves, the referees are slowly changing the formats, the 'standups' are getting faster and faster. It's not always about winning, it's about putting on a show, too."

The history of modern prizefighting traces back to the 1700s and James Figg's School of Arms and Self-Defense in England. It was an era of near-constant warfare, unbreakable class divisions, and personal violence. Europe was emerging from medieval darkness and practices such as dueling were gradually being outlawed because they were costing the Crown its best officers. Gentlemen of "the Fancy"—the gaming fans who went to prizefights, bull and bear baitings, rattings, and so forth—began to get involved in actually training and fighting. Their lives had value as members of the aristocracy. Gentlemen couldn't fight bare-fisted, like common ruffians. The life of the fighter began to acquire a different value, and the rules began to trickle in, culminating with the 1867 Marquess of Queensberry rules.

In boxing, because of its long professional history, performance and entertainment have become very close—the fans and aficionados, well versed in fine detail, want to see the very best in boxing compete, even if they never get a knockout. Skilled defensive work is appreciated. Andre Ward, criticized for being "protected," is picking his fights; he's trying to win a losing game, make a career in boxing without getting his brain shook or his money took. He'll take his risks when he has to—he'll fight for titles against the tough guys when the money is there—but he won't brawl for our thrill. And he is respected for it by anyone who knows anything.

MMA, with the dominance of one single promotion (the UFC) and an extremely varied fan base in terms of education in the nuances of the sport, features a bigger dichotomy between entertainment and winning. It's something that promoters, fighters, and trainers struggle with. For the promoter, fighting is about "asses in seats." For the top fighters, it's about winning and taking as little damage as possible while inflicting the most.

There are extremely boring ways to win in MMA, and the UFC has tried to eliminate those—either directly, through rule changes (like gloves and standups), or indirectly, letting fighters who "win boring" go. The strategy works; exciting slugfests draw in raw fans. But fighters in modern MMA have an incredible line to walk, a line of self-sacrifice and damage, where it's better to lose in an exciting fashion than to win. Promoters will actually tell that to the fighters. No one finds it disheartening—basically, take damage for our entertainment. Bleed for us. Wrestlers and ground fighters increasingly stand and brawl, hoping to be fan favorites or for the extra cash of a "fight of the night" prize.

The UFC uses images of a gladiator in its promotional videos, making the point that these are the modern-day versions. Of course, no one fights to the death. Still, death is a part of what they are doing.

While boxing has evolved to allow for top fighters to reap the rewards, the UFC has not. Fighter payouts are still an egregiously small portion of total profits. I hope MMA continues to grow and the fighters can be the ones making the money from people paying to see them fight. It's a simple thing. If the UFC is doing the numbers it claims to be doing, then someone is getting very rich. And it's not the fighters.

Clara de la Torre is a professional boxer in New Mexico and a great friend of mine, and when she went on a six-fight losing streak she said the feeling was like "surfing the apocalypse." She was in danger of turning into an opponent, even though some of her losses had been obvious robberies by hometown judges. But she was still game. Clara is educated, finished college, had been a firefighter who managed helicopters and a yoga instructor. Boxing gave her things that nothing else did. What things? you ask. Ahh . . .

A lot of the best guys in the world will claim fighting is merely a sport, but that is just the way they see it. In order to control fear, they take emotion out of the fight. But a fight is personal, it can't help itself; it's about you and me. Randy Couture is not *just* a competitor, as the pundits are fond of saying. He's a sportsman and a gentleman, but he's also a rough dude who plays rough and *loves,* in the fiber of his being, to break tough guys. It satisfies him in a way that nothing else does. If it didn't, he'd be coaching wrestling at OSU. There are mysteries left in the world, especially when it comes to the "arena of tough guys."

Man on Wire is a wonderful documentary about the Frenchman Philippe Petit, who walked a tightrope between the Twin Towers in New York City and was arrested after doing it. The reporters kept shoving microphones in his face, asking, "Why do you do it? Why?" He laughed, surprised, and answered simply in his light voice, his heavy French accent, "There is no why." He found the media's need to know why melancholy, bitterly amusing. He regretted that you needed to ask.

277

On the *The Daily Show,* Jon Stewart asked me why I went to Thailand to fight, and I answered, "It seems funny now, but at the time it seemed . . . normal." You'd think I would have prepared a better answer for that one. My why.

When I spoke to the army psychologists at Fort Bragg, I asked about teaching mental toughness—if that was part of the Special Forces training. The answer was an amused, "No." The men who were there had learned it already, somewhere else. They battled their way through training on their own. Their mental toughness skills had to be proved before they even got to this point—not taught to them now. It made me think of Tom Brands, how he talked about the "mysteries of tough guys, what makes them tick," and of an old friend in the dogfighting business, who said, "The right one is the right one," when asked about picking a dog to train and cultivate. There is no way of knowing, but you try and hope that you got the right one—only the result is the final proof.

Fighting plays to the instinctual nihilism in some men, the part that when faced with impossible odds, or certain destruction, says "Fuck it" and charges. It's not something easily understood, and here I think the sexes often diverge—not many women can be satisfied with "fuck it" as a real reason, but most men will understand it. Fyodor Dostoyevsky, the great Russian novelist, understood the value of such sentiment. He wrote, in *Notes from the Underground,* "What is to be done with the millions of facts that bear witness that men, consciously, that is fully understanding their real interests, have left them in the background and have rushed headlong on another path, to meet peril and danger, compelled to this course by nobody and by nothing, but, as it were, simply disliking the beaten track, and have obstinately, willfully, struck out another difficult, absurd way, seeking it almost in the darkness . . . And what if it happens that a man's advantage, sometimes, not only may, but even must, consist in his desiring in certain cases what is harmful to himself?"

We choose things that are against our own best interests because the freedom to make that choice is more important than those interests.

How many times do you hear fighters say, "I don't care who they put in front of me, I'll fight anyone"? Therein lies the appeal. Fighters will say, "I'm willing to die in the ring," and they are admired for it, for the commitment. In fact, that's an absurd statement. You're willing to die, in a fight with some guy you don't really know, for money to entertain people?

What is important is the principle of the thing. The fighter is saying he's willing to die rather than be dominated. He's valuing his free will over his life, something that we all admire. Fighting at its center is about making someone do what they don't want to do. Enforcing your will. We come to the fights to see that struggle as much as great technique—we want to see heart on display, we want a chance to see real courage —and it can be a costly show.

When I wrote my first book, I had to do "press," interviews and radio shows, things like that. I wasn't particularly good at it, but then my agent told me to start acting like a politician—have some points you want to make, and make them regardless of what questions get asked. One of the things I picked was that fighting is about identity, you are forced to learn who you are. The research for this book has convinced me even more of that truth. All the talk of game plans seems to play to it. Josh Waitzkin said, "I think organic game plans work the best," and what he meant by organic was natural—natural to you. The game plan has to come from who you are. When Jongsanan talked about being the "wooden man," when he spoke of de la Hoya being the Golden Boy, he was talking about the duality of the game plan and the fighter—you come to resemble who you have to be. You have to fight like who you are. In other walks of life, maybe you can get away with pretending, but not in fighting. You have to honor your true nature. Fighting forces honesty down your throat. You can and should deceive your opponent, but not yourself. It's why fight-ers are so forthcoming (although elusive), and trainers can see right through them. That journey of self-discovery is a major rea-son to why a lot of young men are drawn to the fight world.

Greg Jackson said, almost in passing, "I have guys here who are marginally functional. They wouldn't be respected anywhere else but in here, they work hard and get respect." F. X. Toole, the pen name for twenty-year cut man Jerry Boyd, wrote in *Rope Burns,* "The fight game isn't about being tough, it's about getting respect." One of Boyd's memorable characters is Danger Barch, so tragi-comic in the movie *Million Dollar Baby* with his absurd refrain, "I challenge the Motor City Cobra, Tommy Hearns." Danger is a familiar figure if you hang around the fight game—every gym in the entire world has a nut job like that, some marginal character. It's a place where you can belong if you put in the work. Nobody fucks with the crazy people who come to the gym, as long as they work. As Renzo said, the least physically gifted can become cham-pions with enough grit. Or at least get respected. In Thailand, there was a badly crippled ex-fighter who was a human ring clock, hoot-ing at the end of the rounds. He got respect, even though he could barely move. Freddie Roach's brother Pepper is a former drug addict. He's been in and out of jail, he'll laugh and show you his white power tattoos, 'bolts and swastikas, while he's giving fist bumps to all the black and Hispanic fighters that come through the door. Pepper's laugh is truly a joyous thing. He finds the world hilarious but, even more so, himself and his place in it. He's told me some of the funniest stories I've ever heard, and he belongs in the gym, and not only because of his brother. Pepper isn't even close to the craziest cat that comes in there.

When I spoke to Carlo Rotella about this issue over the phone, he said, "One of the things that always impressed me about the fight world, people want to feel like things they do in their life are meaningful and important. Fateful." That was a word Carlo would come back to often, *fateful.* People wanted to feel like the things they did mattered. He had written: *The primacy of hurt supercharges even the smallest detail.*

"It seems like the fight world is well set up to turn everything you do into something fateful and important. Every sit-up, staring at yourself in the mirror, every little detail of your day, whether you slept well, ate well, blinked, or not, standing face to face with that guy, is the most fateful, and important details matter in the epic that is your life. There is a whyness to that."

Carlo laughed and continued, "It helps explain why there is no money, because you get paid in satisfaction. It's not just spectacle. Fighters and trainers get addicted to big fights *meaning* something. Same for fight fans, and corners—corner men in the gym spend hours watching people do the same old damn things they do all the time."

Carlo thought a moment, and then continued, talking about opponents, guys with losing records who keep fighting. "A guy with a thirteen and twenty-seven record, is he there for the cheering? No. He thinks, 'I'm the guy who goes in there and mixes it up and doesn't get hurt, and this is my craft. I get through it, I'm a tough guy.'"

This brings me to the final note of a fighter's mind: what fighting is for, personally. It's always there, in the room with fighters, but never discussed, hard to understand.

I talked to Pat Miletich a lot about it. Pat himself had plenty of fuel, an abusive father who died young of cancer, and a lot of tragedy, brothers dying, going to jail, committing suicide.

"There are some guys out there that are from normal families, that are still animals and smash people, but usually it helps if you've had a shitty life. If somebody's starving, then somebody else is getting their ass kicked."

Many, many fighters come from damage. It is their why. I sometimes think of Rory and his friend who leaped to his death right in front him.

Rory's story, though unique, is by no means shocking. Most fighters are men who have come to the profession from fighting elsewhere, from fighting to feel good. After Ed's death, Rory went on a two-year jag of street fighting, where he religiously went out Friday and Saturday nights and got in a fight, every night. Which means (and he'll admit it) he was a raving asshole. But like all pro fighters, when they start fighting for money, they stop street fighting. They have nothing to prove to strangers on the street anymore. They have a sense of self-worth, they know what it is to be loved, to have responsibility. Their trainer needs them healthy.

Fighting provides, eventually, what you are looking for. (It could be anything—tennis, chess, ultrarunning—but you will bring that same intensity and need and make it into a fight. It's a fight you want, however you manifest it.) It can make you whole. People ask me, "Why fighting?" and I tell them, "There are a million different reasons, but they're all versions of the same reason." My attempt at a Zen koan. Why Clara de la Torre is still surfing the apocalypse. Boyd's line about respect is probably as close as anything.

The gym, where a fighter truly lives and is made, takes everything from you. It will take your mental pain away. Struggling and fighting you burn away all those hurtful emotions and emerge like an asteroid torched clean in the atmosphere and streaking toward the Earth. The world is made of fire.

I asked Freddie Roach. His Parkinson's (brought on by the wars in the ring) is descending on him without remorse, increasing the shake, and you see him fold his arms sometimes to hide his trembling hands. "I know you struggle with Parkinson's," I said hesitantly, looking for a way to proceed. I wanted to ask him about the price he was paying.

"I don't struggle," he laughed. For Freddie, it was worth it. "Maybe for guys who didn't do as well, who didn't have the same ride . . ." He shrugged and smiled. Freddie knows people outside of boxing want him to condemn it, to cry "look what it did to me," but Freddie has no regrets about boxing. It's mysterious to outsiders but not to me.

Why do we do anything? My first serious art teacher used to say, in his sad voice, "We draw because we want to be loved" (he was a dapper man, a quiet alcoholic with cold talent). Those kids from the broken place, from the howling wilderness of a childhood unloved, unvalued, they find something in fighting, they can take that love. The feeling of worth that the missing father never provided—you can force the issue, for one night, for one moment.

Training is a recurring habit, you get drawn to the savage joy again and again. I heard Rory Markham say to an interviewer, "I'm on the path, you know?" and what he meant, perhaps without fully understanding it, was the path to enlightenment, to self-understanding. Fighting is a way for the unwise, the damaged, and the angry men and women to find wisdom. It makes you a better person. When Munenori wrote that the sword could be "life giving," he meant many things, one of which was that proper study of the sword would lead a student to the Way.

Why? There are a million different reasons, and there is one reason. Yours.